THE POLICE
AND YOUNG PEOPLE
IN AUSTRALIA

THE POLICE
AND YOUNG PEOPLE
IN AUSTRALIA

Edited by

ROB WHITE and
CHRISTINE ALDER

*Department of Criminology,
University of Melbourne*

CAMBRIDGE
UNIVERSITY PRESS

Published by the Press Syndicate of the University of Cambridge
The Pitt Building, Trumpington Street, Cambridge CB2 1RP, UK
40 West 20th Street, New York, NY 10011-4211, USA
10 Stamford Road, Oakleigh, Melbourne 3166, Australia

© Cambridge University Press 1994
First published 1994

Printed in Hong Kong by Colorcraft

National Library of Australia cataloguing in publication data
The Police and young people in Australia.
Bibliography.
Includes index.
ISBN 0 521 43426 2.
ISBN 0 521 43574 9 (pbk.).
1. Juvenile justice, Administration of – Australia. 2. Police –
Australia – Attitudes. 3. Youth – Legal status, laws, etc. –
Australia. 4. Juvenile delinquency – Australia – Prevention.
I. White, R. D. (Robert Douglas), 1956-   . II. Alder, Christine.
364.360994

Library of Congress cataloguing in publication data
The Police and young people in Australia/edited by Rob White and Christine Alder.
p.   cm.
Includes bibliographical references and index.
ISBN 0 521 43426 2.
ISBN 0 521 43574 9 (pbk.).
1. Juvenile delinquency – Australia. 2. Juvenile justice,
Administration of – Australia. 3. Police services for juveniles –
Australia. I. White, R. D. (Robert Douglas), 1956-
II. Alder, Christine, 1950-
HV9230 .A5P65 1993
364.3'6'0994 – dc20   93-23286
                                              CIP

A catalogue record for this book is available from the British Library.

ISBN 0 521 43426 2 hardback
ISBN 0 521 43574 9 paperback

Contents

Tables and Figures   vii

Introduction
ROB WHITE AND CHRISTINE ALDER   1

1   Larrikins, Delinquents and Cops: Police and
Young People in Australian History
MARK FINNANE   7

2   The Legal Framework of Juvenile Justice
KATE WARNER   27

3   Cautions and Appearances: Statistics About
Youth and Police
DAVID TAIT   59

4   Young People and Their Rights
IAN O'CONNOR   76

5   Street Life: Police Practices and Youth Behaviour
ROB WHITE   102

6   Enforcing Genocide? Aboriginal Young People
and the Police
CHRIS CUNNEEN   128

7   The Policing of Young Women
CHRISTINE ALDER   159

8   Policing Youth in 'Ethnic' Communities:
Is Community Policing the Answer?
JANET CHAN   175

9   Contemporary Programs with Young People:
Beyond Traditional Law Enforcement?
STEPHEN P. JAMES   199

10   Reform and Change: An Agenda for the 1990s
STEPHEN HALL   232

Index   244

Contributors

CHRISTINE ALDER has held posts at the National Council on Crime and Delinquency, San Francisco, the University of Oregon and has been a guest lecturer in Holland, Canada and the United States. She currently teaches in the Department of Criminology at the University of Melbourne. She is the former editor of the *Australian and New Zealand Journal of Criminology*.

JANET CHAN is a Senior Lecturer in the School of Social Science and Policy at the University of New South Wales. Her research interests have been in criminal justice reforms and innovations. Her latest publication is *Doing Less Time: Penal Reform in Crisis*.

CHRIS CUNNEEN is a Senior Lecturer at the Institute of Criminology, Sydney University Law School, and a research consultant to the Human Rights and Equal Opportunity Commission. He has published widely in the area of policing, juvenile justice and the relationship between Aboriginal people and the criminal justice system.

MARK FINNANE is Associate Professor and Head of the School of Australian and Comparative Studies at Griffith University, Queensland. He specialises in criminal justice history and is currently writing a book on histories of policing in Australia.

STEPHEN HALL is the Executive Officer of the Anglican Social Responsibilities Commission in Western Australia. He has developed an active interest in youth issues after many years' work in a rural community-based youth agency.

STEPHEN P. JAMES is a Senior Research Fellow in the Criminology Department at the University of Melbourne. He has taught and published in policing and crime prevention, and is currently researching the enforcement of drug trafficking laws in Australia.

IAN O'CONNOR teaches in the Department of Social Work and Social Policy, University of Queensland. He has published widely in the areas of youth rights, juvenile justice and homelessness.

DAVID TAIT teaches in the Department of Criminology at the University of Melbourne.

KATE WARNER is an Associate Professor and Dean of Law at the University of Tasmania. She has published reports and articles on children's courts, child witnesses and sexual assault and a book on sentencing – *Sentencing in Tasmania*.

ROB WHITE has taught at various universities in Canada and Australia, and is currently teaching in the Department of Criminology at the University of Melbourne. He is the author of *No Space of their Own* and *Law, Capitalism and the Right to Work*.

Tables and Figures

Table 1   Juvenile 'offenders' recorded by police 1990–91:
selected offences, South Australia and Queensland   68

Figure 1   Juveniles apprehended by police: from
apprehension to conviction, Queensland 1990–91   63

Figure 2   Offenders by age, South Australia 1990–91   66

Figure 3   Offenders by age, Tasmania 1988   67

Figure 4   Juvenile females apprehended by police,
Victoria 1990–91   69

Figure 5   Alleged assaults by juveniles or police:
proportion (%) found 'substantiated'   72

Introduction

Rob White and Christine Alder

In recent years there has been a burgeoning interest in police–youth relations in Australia. This has been especially so in the light of repeated media stories and persistent community concerns regarding conflicts at the local and street level involving young people and the police. Reports prepared by such organisations as the Human Rights and Equal Opportunity Commission, the Royal Commission into Aboriginal Deaths in Custody, community legal centres, and various church groups have also highlighted a number of issues relating to police violence and harassment, and pointed to the existence of a generally negative relationship between young people and the police. There has been an increase in academic attention on these kinds of issues as well. Researchers from around the country have in recent times systematically documented such phenomena as the denial of legal rights, victimisation of various kinds, and the situational, organisational and structural factors which influence or shape the nature of police–youth interactions.

The growth in community and academic concern about the relationship between young people and the police prompted us to undertake this project. We thought it was important from the point of view of analysis and policy development to bring together available research and informed opinion in this area. By providing a consolidated picture of what is happening in youth–police relationships our intention is both to inform the reader of what is occurring in Australian society today, and to stimulate further discussion and debate on the questions raised by the various findings and interpretations offered in the book.

In putting the collection together we wished to draw upon the work of those people in the area who would be able to provide insights into how the young are policed, and who could identify the main sources and nature of the conflicts between police and young people. The overall objective of the book was to provide an investigation into the links between policing as a distinct form of

1

social practice, and the specific position of young people economically and socially in Australian society.

In developing the book we were initially guided by four main concerns stemming from our own previous research in this field. These were: policing in the context of the extension of different forms of social control over the activities and behaviour of young people; the relationship between 'normal' police practices and police culture, and the negative aspects of the interactions between young people and the police; the social and legal construction of 'rights' of young people and the difficulties in exercising these rights in their contact with the police; and the violence directed at young people, some groups in particular, by the police.

As the project evolved, however, it became clear that attention needed to be directed to a number of additional issues as well. For example, the introduction of new police programs, especially in the area of 'community policing', meant that a one-dimensional analysis of the topic simply would not suffice. While recognising that the police are very often divided among themselves when it comes to how they feel they should interact with young people, the time and location of these interactions also very much influence the character of the contact. To understand police–youth relationships, therefore, we felt there was a need to investigate further the character of the police as an occupational group and the policy context within which they operate.

While concerned about the current relationship between young people and the police, we were nevertheless aware of new initiatives and innovations which indicated that some police officers were trying to move beyond the 'us' and 'them' assumption which appears to be an inherent feature of the general relationship. The design of such programs, however, often leaves something to be desired in terms of youth participation. Furthermore, wider state government and police organisational policies, especially those centred around a more conservative 'law and order' agenda, can seriously undercut or erode support for more progressive policing strategies.

Currently there are considerable political pressures upon the police to keep young people under control and publicly invisible. In a period of extremely high levels of youth unemployment, poverty and homelessness, a range of tensions and conflicts may surface when the police 'do their job' and young people 'do their thing' in the same public spaces. These conflicts in turn raise major questions regarding the use of police discretion, and the manner in which the police intervene in particular communities of young people.

Underpinning many of the issues raised throughout the book is concern about the implications of contemporary police methods and practices for the exercise of basic legal rights in Australian society. If the 'rule of law' is to be meaningful, then concepts such as 'due process' and the restraints on state power must apply in the case of juveniles as well as adults. The issue of rights is increasingly pertinent since the evidence indicates that a high proportion of young people encounter police intrusion.

The ways in which some young people become victims of police misconduct or harassment, and the manner in which police respond to young people as victims of crime, are other issues of importance. Throughout the research literature there is evidence of a relatively high incidence of victimisation of young people by the police. As a consequence of the resultant negative perception by youth of the police, many young people do not seek assistance from police when they themselves are victims of crime. Since young people make up a substantial proportion of crime victims, this means that a good deal of crime in our society, often serious crime, is not being brought to the attention of the police.

In the end we have tried to construct a book of readings which provides a reasonably integrated and detailed overview of police–youth relations in Australia, while not claiming to have covered all of the perspectives on the issues outlined above. The contributions to the book are written by people who are involved with or are particularly concerned about the status and rights of young people. The book is not, therefore, about the 'police' *per se*. The organisational processes, work culture, management and policy context of policing are discussed only insofar as these impinge upon the relationship that exists between the police and young people.

In most cases, each chapter combines empirical material and theoretical analysis. Our intention was to provide the reader with a solid grounding in the social, legal and institutional aspects of the police–youth relationship. To achieve this, we wanted to ensure that, where appropriate, each chapter provided a description of broad trends, programs or legislation as well as an interpretation of what these might mean in terms of the broad dynamics of police–youth relationships.

The book begins with a discussion by Mark Finnane of the way in which police–youth interaction was constructed historically (chapter 1). Themes relating to the policing of youth culture and of 'informality' in police–youth relations are essential parts of this history. As this chapter makes clear, an interventionist strategy in governing the social lives of young people is not a new phenomenon, and the problems which this entails tend to persist over time.

The next few chapters provide important overviews of different facets of the juvenile justice system as these pertain to the issues of police work and youth activities. Kate Warner summarises the main components of the legal framework of police–youth interaction across the Australian states and territories (chapter 2). Areas such as police investigation, use of discretion, and the general processing of young offenders by the police are reviewed. Thus, the chapter establishes the statutory and regulatory framework within which the policing of young people occurs.

Chapter 3 provides a discussion of the statistical information relating to youth offending and interactions with the police. Here David Tait provides a critical perspective on the manner in which statistics on youth offending and police activity are constructed. In addition to reporting on the figures reported from various jurisdictions around the country, the chapter provides a thought-provoking analysis of the particular images and concepts of 'young people' which are conveyed via the language and data-gathering emphasis in police annual reports.

When young people and police do meet, questions can be asked regarding the nature of their contact. Ian O'Connor argues in chapter 4 that it is in the daily interactions with young people and police that rights are negotiated and given meaning. A disturbing analysis of young people and their rights, this chapter illustrates how too often there is a lack of respect for the rights of the young, and indeed a lack of knowledge of their rights by young people. The chapter discusses the implications and consequences of this for police–youth interactions.

The next series of chapters considers the impact of particular social characteristics and structural inequalities on the nature of the police–youth relationship. Issues relating to class, race, ethnicity and gender are in many ways and in different types of situations crucial to an understanding of the antagonisms and dynamics of the relations between young people and the police at a neighbourhood or community level and more generally.

The street is a major site of police–youth contact. The ways in which public spaces such as the street, shopping centres and malls are policed is one of the themes explored by Rob White in a chapter on street life (chapter 5). In general 'public spaces' are converted into more narrowly defined 'consumer' or 'commercial' spaces from the point of view of businesses and the police. One result of this is that economically and socially marginalised young people are increasingly being squeezed out of the public realm due to their status as non-consumers. This in turn creates feelings of mutual distrust and dislike on the part of police and young persons alike.

The chapter by Chris Cunneen begins by discussing the legacy of colonial rule as this has impacted upon Aboriginal people in Australia (chapter 6). From both an historical and contemporary perspective, the chapter systematically demonstrates the ongoing persecution and inequalities associated with the policing of Aboriginal young people. The chapter provides a theoretical framework for understanding the reasons for this, as well as considerable documentation of the actual nature of contact between the police and young Aboriginal people. It is argued that concepts such as self-determination are central to any positive policy development which might purport to address policing issues in this particular instance.

A significant area of concern which has by and large been neglected in the study of police–youth interaction has been that of the influence of gender. Christine Alder provides an overview of the literature which deals with the relationship between the police and young women, and identifies a number of key questions which research in this area must address (chapter 7). Fundamentally, the chapter illustrates the importance of feminist analysis in research into male and female relationships with the police. It also highlights a series of policy-related concerns, such as the dilemmas faced by young women who as victims of crime may have to turn to the police for assistance.

In a diverse polyethnic society, where for many years there has been bipartisan political support for the concept of 'multi-culturalism' at an official policy level, it is surprising that so little has been written about the relationship between the police and different 'ethnic' groups in Australia. This is particularly so with respect to non-English-speaking migrants and members of so-called visible ethnic minority groups. Chapter 8 by Janet Chan pro-vides a survey of policing in the context of identifiable 'ethnic' communities. In doing so, the chapter raises a number of questions regarding the efficacy of 'community policing' models as these pertain to young people from particular ethnic and cultural backgrounds.

The main concern of the next two chapters is to outline the sorts of responses which have been, and which could be adopted, at policy and institutional levels to address the issues previously explored in the book. The chapter by Stephen James provides an overview of the diverse programs organised by or involving the police which are of a 'preventive' nature (chapter 9). Police contact with young people does not always involve formal processing: police also participate in services designed to prevent young people from getting into trouble or to assist them out of trouble. In essence, this chapter is about the dimensions of 'community policing', which involve a wide variety of programs and activities beyond traditional law enforcement. The chapter reviews the developments in this area of policing, and raises a number of crucial questions regarding how such developments could or should be evaluated.

The final chapter by Stephen Hall provides a practitioner's view of the issues, problems and potential directions for policy in the area of police–youth relations (chapter 10). This chapter provides a brief overview of many of the issues covered in the book. It also suggests several practical areas where reform could be carried out or extended. Basically it calls for the development of a more democratic, responsive, equitable and constructive form of policing of young people in Australia. For this to occur, change and reform will have to take place at a number of levels, including those of institutional practices, policy development and general public and police attitudes.

The aim of this book is to reveal the many facets and complexities of the relationship between young people and the police in Australia. In exposing the nature of these relationships, from a variety of theoretical perspectives and empirical viewpoints, we hope that the reader will gain a sense of the main issues at the core of the policing of young people today. As well, we hope that the analysis provided in the book will add weight to calls for the adoption of different measures and strategies in this area – those which will ensure that the rights of children are protected and which will lead to a genuine improvement in the relationships between the police and young people.

CHAPTER 1

Larrikins, Delinquents and Cops: Police and Young People in Australian History

Mark Finnane

Modern studies of policing have emphasised the importance in police work of duties unrelated to crime detection and the arrest of offenders. The policing of young people exemplifies this aspect of police work. A large number of police interventions with young people are of an informal kind, whether pro-active in the course of patrol or reactive in responding to complaints about behaviour which may lie below the criminal offence threshold. The very informality of such police contacts makes it difficult to document these interactions authoritatively. When we turn to historical conditions and experience in this field, the problems of documenting such interactions are compounded.

A central figure in Australian cultural history is that of the larrikin, a mythical type born in the last third of the nineteenth century and pitted against the policeman in the drama of urban social conflict of that time (Murray, 1973; Walker, 1986; Pearson, 1983; Grabosky, 1977; McLachlan, 1950). A couple of generations later the juvenile delinquent, another important cultural type, was similarly regarded as a threat to the social order which needed to be combated by police (Stratton, 1984; Finnane, 1989; White and Wilson, 1991). However, these two central figures in Australian history must be approached with caution as emblems of the history of the policing of young people. Focusing attention on these constructions in moments of crisis or transition in cultural and social history may obscure the larger continuities in the policing of young people which they briefly disrupt. It is these continuities which are the subject of this chapter

I argue in this chapter that historically police were given responsibilities for surveilling the lives of children and young people in ways that extended well beyond the notion of criminal offence or its prevention. Police policies and concerns, which were much more interventionist than those considered acceptable for adults, were developed in the context of monitoring and controlling the social life of young people. While historical documentation of police behaviour in relation to young people, when judged by the volume of formal prosecutions, suggests a continued preoccupation with the control of petty crime and public order offences, there was a less visible side of police work in the role of welfare agents, truant officers and morals guardians. The history of the state's relation to young people in Australia requires historical understanding of the shifting relations between these two kinds of police work.

How and with what effects have police powers been exercised in relation to young people? This paper explores this central question along a number of lines. I am not concerned here with explaining the forms of or changes in young people's lives and behaviour which may have affected their exposure to police intervention (see, for example, Stratton, 1984; Davey, 1986; Hetherington, 1986; Walker, 1988; White, 1990). Rather, we look first at some of the mundane responses of police to complaints about youth behaviour during the era of larrikinism; second, at the genesis of some specific categories of legal regulation of the child, entailing police powers of intervention; last at some statistical indicators of the patterns of policing of children and young people during the earlier part of the twentieth century. The object is to highlight issues which warrant further study as well as to provide an overview of the legal and policing framework which resulted in young people being detained or prosecuted.

PUBLIC COMPLAINTS AND POLICE RESPONSE

Under what conditions do police come into contact with young people and what do they do in those contacts? These important questions, underlying the preoccupations of this book, can be addressed historically through a review of official statistics and through detailed scrutiny of archival records and media reports. In both approaches we are faced with the dilemma that, if crime has its dark figure, so too does policing (see chapter 3). This section summarises material from archival sources relating to the policing of 'larrikins', identifying some of the conditions under which such youth behaviour came to police notice. From such data we can do no more than speculate on the nature and volume of those interactions which were never recorded in police reports or which never resulted in formal court proceedings. Nevertheless, examination of these archival sources enables some judgements to be made about the conditions under which police decided to intervene in a particular situation or to take no further action.

Drawing on research for studies of the history of the NSW and Queensland criminal justice systems (e.g. Finnane, 1987; Finnane and Garton, 1992), we can indicate the basic form of police interaction with a child or young person from the 1890s. Knowledge of an offence or behaviour would originate in a complaint from a family member, a neighbour or other member of the public. Some offences would also be noted by police on patrol which, until the 1950s, was most often on foot or bicycle. Police response to a complaint, whether observed by them or not, was highly varied. Informal policing, involving identification of the child and direct chastisement or warning, was undoubtedly frequent: on occasions this might involve police acting with or on behalf of a parent or overseeing a parent's punishment of the child. Formal investigation of the event, followed by denial of the incident or of the seriousness of the complaint, was another possible result.

More formal responses constituted a lower proportion of cases. Exemplary prosecutions by way of summons might deal with local outbreaks of trouble. Arrest of the child or young person was of course the most serious formal outcome. Arrests of those aged under 21, accounting for nearly one in fifty of all arrests in Queensland around 1890, covered a range of offences, including larceny and that of child neglected or uncontrollable (Queensland Police Department, 1890).

Qualitative evidence filling out this picture is acquired through detailed investigation of local areas. For Brisbane, for example, there is an illuminating series of police files from the 1890s to 1930s, classified originally by police under the head of 'larrikinism' or sometimes 'larrikinism and pushes' (see Police Dept files, POL/J4-8, Queensland State Archives, hereafter QSA). The larrikinism files disclose principally one level of policing, that of peace-keeping on the streets and in public spaces. Files were typically initiated by the receipt of letters of complaint from the public. In some periods, a wave of media reports about the larrikin 'menace' would also precipitate police inquiries. Complaints came to police about a relatively narrow range of behaviours: stone throwing, obscene language, insulting women and girls, fighting, playing cricket, throwing hats in the air and so on.

The overwhelming impression gained from these files is of the high volume of complaints rejected by police. The meaning of these denials is a matter for speculation. Police then and now, and like other workers, dislike being told how to do their job. They are defensive of their reputation for effectiveness. When complaints shifted from a litany of instances of misbehaviour of young people to accusations of police neglect or indifference, the constables concerned were hardly likely to offer concessions of truth or contrite apologies.

On the other hand, the nature of the complaints themselves frequently appears trivial and contemporary constables responded accordingly. For example, a resident's complaint about cricket playing in a neighbouring vacant allotment in inner-city Paddington in the early 1900s was prompted by the bad language of the fifty or so males aged between 6 and 30 who were regular participants: the police could find little reason to justify a summons in such cases (POL/J4, complaint of J. Wilkinson, March 1908, QSA).

Police rejection of public complaints, however, might be based on grounds other than the evident triviality of the complaint. More accurately we might consider that public complaints flowed from social differences in attitudes about the proper modes of behaving on the street. These differences could be inter-generational, inter-class or inter-sex. Police might or might not sympathise with the aggravation caused by the behaviour of young people which breached the social norms variously constructed around these social divisions. While criminology, particularly critical criminology, has tended to appraise the evolution of public order policing in terms of its class- or race-based functions and effects, there has been less consideration *historically* of the sex-skewed and age-skewed functions and effects of street policing (see, e.g. Cunneen, 1988; Cohen, 1979; Brogden, Jefferson and Walklate, 1988; White, 1990).

To understand the basis of police rejection of public complaints about youth behaviour, such as is evident in the larrikinism files examined here, we need to consider the possible contribution of the masculine character of policing. A sex-based dimension to conflict over the appropriate response of police to the misdemeanours of young men is evident, for example, in a 1920 complaint by a woman about larrikinism in Brisbane's suburban Albion. The police followed up with what they said were detailed inquiries. The local Salvation Army officer reported that Albion was one of the 'most orderly centres' he had ever been in. Yet claims that the area was free of aggravation continued to be disputed by women. One of them, writing to the press, identified the polarities of street order – insulting remarks to ladies at the tram station did not arise when women were walking with husbands or brothers, but they did when two women were walking together (POL/J6, complaint in Albion, 1920, QSA).

This incident suggests that police actions in regard to male youth in such circumstances may be explained from a number of perspectives: evidence requirements inhibit prosecution of insulting remarks which police do not hear; what appears to women as insulting may appear to police as lying below the threshold of justifiable or desirable intervention; or what appears to female complainants as insulting may be regarded by police, male and working class in origin themselves, as frivolous. Whatever the case, this aspect of public order policing suggests that race and class effects are not the only important dimensions of the history of the occasions of police intervention against young people (see chapter 7).

While the comments above help to re-focus attention on the dimensions of police *inaction*, we cannot neglect the important history of police targeting of particular populations. Thus youths who were members of the popularly named 'pushes', the territorial gangs which characterised Australian inner cities from the mid-colonial period to the inter-war years, were the objects of more concerted police attention (Murray, 1973; Walker, 1986; Pearson, 1983; Grabosky, 1977; McLachlan, 1950). Here the task was to keep the 'lads' in check. The occasional exemplary summons could be useful, but police reports in the Queensland files suggest the highly calculated use of such a means of control. Typically the police reports note summons actions against those they deem 'leaders' of such gangs and claim that such actions were enough to bring them in tow again.

Predictably police calculations about the seriousness of complaints were closely related to the social distinctions they drew historically between the rough and the respectable. These terms, derived from the English urban policing culture which was so influential in nineteenth-century policing, were readily invoked by police themselves to justify intervention or inaction in response to public complaints (cf. Cohen, 1979; Conley, 1991). They are evident for example in the police defence of the conditions of public order at Kangaroo Point in inner Brisbane in 1905 and again in 1913. E. J. Stevens, MLC, and of the Brisbane Newspaper Company Ltd, had complained that the youths gathering in Main Street needed, as he said, a 'lift under the ear'. Acting Sergeant Robert Clark riposted that such an action would constitute an assault: 'the Police would not be justified in doing so, as they were respectable youths, and some were sons of Justices of the Peace'. He had moved them on, yet they 'are not of the larrikin class, but are young men who are learning their trades at the foundries' (compare O'Brien, 1988:165, for comparable police observations on the social origins of larrikins in Sydney involved in skirmishes with the military in 1902). Later he conceded that they undoubtedly insulted ladies, but remarked that it was difficult to catch them (POL/J4 (complaint of E. J. Stevens, MLC), QSA).

Eight years later these social distinctions are substantially repeated by Constable Kearney when countering the *Daily Mail's* reports of hoodlums gathering under the old fig tree near the hotel. The fig tree, reports the constable,

> throws a beautiful shade, which is taken advantage of by a great number of persons of this locality, both by day, and in the evenings and I have continually seen hard working class of men at their meal hours enjoying this shade and some of them after finishing their meal would lay down on the grass, and sleep a short time.

He has had to shift some local fellows, aged 13 to 18, from the 'curbstones' at the hotel and fruit shop, but they now take advantage of the fig tree ground where they have a game of 'scrum up as known to be in the game of Rugby football'. All of them are employed and do not visit the ground till late. Finally, denying allegations about larrikins insulting women, Constable Kearney replies that 'the female class of people use Main Street & Holman Street after dusk where there is plenty of light' (POL/J4, re report in *Daily Mail*, 6 March 1913, QSA), the implication being that verbal banter should not be taken as a threat to the safety of women.

In Kearney's view, hard-working and well-employed males, young and old, have a right to the use of public space. The ambivalent concession that the 'female class' also uses the streets suggests something that had come up before in 1905 and occurs elsewhere in the files: 'insulting ladies', as it is put, occurs, but is either difficult to observe or not a matter deserving police attention. Whatever the case, the policing of youth, i.e. of young males, in this context is evidently benign. In such contexts, these police are not inclined to counter street-wise behaviour which has the stamp of popular, masculine acceptance about it.

It may be otherwise with the 'rough' end of town. Police in northern Brisbane in the 1920s rejected allegations of larrikinism (this time including claims of indecent exposure of youths at a swimming waterhole, thereby forcing women to take a different route home from Sunday church) in the respectable estates of Virginia and Northgate. Here 'there are no places where rough and low class people inhabit & there are no professional larrikins'. By contrast the adjacent suburb of Hendra ('where many training stables are situated & jockeys reside') has to be patrolled at night time. It was similarly noted that

> a rough class of people reside at Clayfield & Eagle Junction which is an old settled place and where cheaper rents are paid, and where a push known as the Porky push have existed for a long time, but have given no trouble now for some time past.

The local police claimed that bicycle and foot patrols had eliminated the threat (POL/J6, complaints, 1919–27, Northgate-Virginia, QSA).

Such evidence shows how police perceptions of male youth were articulated to social images of class and sex. Such perceptions did not necessarily mean that police would deferentially side with the wishes of social élites against the alleged depredations of working-class youth. But they did work with social distinctions which pitted the respectable against the rough, the latter being those the police had to watch, the former those whose chief attribute was perhaps the fact that they gave no trouble. On this social spectrum, the complainants, those who wrote alleging larrikin behaviour, may have been from the respectable classes. Yet this in itself gave their complaints little privilege, since they were a source of irritation, the origin of all those lengthy police memoranda defending the integrity of police actions and the appropriateness of judgements about priorities. In any case, chasing stone throwers or arresting larrikins shouting obscenities was not a high priority for police. And complaints to the press, or to the police commissioner, scarcely endeared complainants to local police, particularly when, like that of one resident in Wooloowin, they were accompanied by the sarcastic charge that the local constable was too stout to catch the larrikins (POL/J5, complaints of Windsor Progress Association, 1912, QSA).

This is not to say that public complaints were inevitably met with a stone wall of police obfuscation. Complaints of inter-personal violence involving more serious criminal offences were likely to bring a police response. Henry Levy of Spring Hill complained in 1908 about members of a local gang who had abused him with anti-Semitic slogans ('Who killed Christ?' they had called) and assaulted him on occasion: the police prosecuted and claimed that the gang had dispersed (POL/J5, complaint of Henry Levy, 1908, QSA).

Such an ugly side of larrikinism lurked not far from the surface of the various gangs and pushes which were part of male youth culture in turn-of-the-century cities. Large-scale fights between mobs of youths and men, such as that between the combined City and Boggo Road pushes and the Kangaroo Point push in 1902 involving over 200 people, were occasions for police intervention, resulting in arrest of some of the combatants (POL/J4, re report *Evening Observer*, 7 April, 1902, QSA and cf. Johnston, 1992:169–70). But these were evidently rare, perhaps in part because such large groups inevitably attracted police attention. As one police report put it in 1907, there was a distinction between those Brisbane pushes, some of them centred on inner-city hotels, which had required prosecution of leaders, and others which were not dangerous, but required 'a lot of looking after to keep them in order'. We know from court figures the consequences of the former type of policing. But the latter, perhaps the more important in terms of understanding police–youth relations, is of course largely undocumented.

We are left therefore to speculate on the mechanisms available in the 'looking after' strategy. Central to this tactic must have been the police caution, the taking of names, the approach to parents of children found on the streets. In 1911 anxieties about the effect of picture shows on children brought police attention to youths who were cautioned in Red Hill for imitating cowboys (Home Office, *Vagrants Act*, 1908–32, A/6670, QSA). Complaints about bad language or stone throwing often met with the taking of names, accompanied by a caution. The approaches of police to parents in this context in Brisbane are rarely documented in these files, though we can presume that frequently they involved the taking of names or the issuing of cautions.

In a different context, however, the scope for police collaboration with parents is well documented in a case involving punishment for a non-prosecuted offence. In 1907 police in New South Wales reported that they did not want to prosecute a case of indecent assault of a 10-year-old on a 6-year-old boy. The Attorney-General agreed that prosecution would be inappropriate, adding that 'a flogging by his mother would be more effective'. Police conveyed the decision to the boy's mother, who was reportedly grateful for the leniency and (so the police report says) 'administered a severe thrashing to the boy in the Constable's presence' (Correspondence, NSW Attorney-General and Justice, 07/19402, 7/5410, NSW State Archives). Such an incident stands on the boundary of public and private domains which the policing of children constantly straddles during this period (cf. Emsley, 1991:75, for comparable English evidence).

In other cases, police took their own initiative, what might be called the 'lift under the ear' approach. The most famous journalistic expose of larrikinism originated in the witnessing by Ambrose Pratt of a police bashing of an alleged king of the push (see Murray, 1973: 146). Less severe assaults were perhaps culturally condoned in the nineteenth and early twentieth century or even later, when corporal punishment of the young in institutional settings was legitimate.

An undiscoverable proportion of interventions by police ended of course in more formal proceedings, by way of arrest and prosecution, or else by summons. Before assessing some evidence about the more formal outcomes we need to consider some of the changing forms of governmental intervention which brought additional police attention to children and youth from the later part of the nineteenth century.

WELFARE POLICING AND POLICE POWERS

An important part of policing of youth was related to the expectation that police would keep order in localities and especially on the streets, through the discretionary use of powers available under street offences, towns police and vagrancy acts (Finnane, 1987). But there were other powers increasingly available to police which were specific to the child's status. Offences constituted by the truancy clauses of the education acts, by neglected children statutes and by Aboriginal legislation required police intervention. All indicated the important development in the nineteenth and twentieth centuries of a new relation of the state to family life and the perceived responsibilities of parents.

In origin, these growing police powers were often interrelated with the public order problem of larrikinism, or else with the question of prostitution of young girls. The nineteenth-century development of compulsory education was linked, among other things, to the hopes of social reformers that schools would prevent the generation of criminal tendencies in the cities (see, e.g., Smith, 1991; Wimshurst, 1981; van Krieken, 1992; Carrington, 1990). The mid-century 'invention' of the concept of juvenile delinquency resulted in an array of institutional reforms which provided for the retraining of 'street arabs' and uncontrollable girls who were considered at risk of being recruited to prostitution. These solutions were directed at those seen as requiring exceptional measures of intervention. The more universal innovation of compulsory education brought with it new norms of institutional conformity which were inevitably at odds with the expectations of working-class or poor rural family economies (Wimshurst, 1981; Phillips, 1985).

The police became the regulatory instrument rendering compulsory education effective since the truancy clauses required police assistance. In NSW, for example, police took on the responsibility for monitoring truants in the early 1890s, following unsatisfactory results from school attendance officers. Some police authorities complained about the duty as extraneous to their real responsibilities (van Krieken, 1992:90). But the education authorities considered the police to be better able to track down the errant youngsters: 'The class of children which the [Education] Department has hitherto been unable to reach ... come more readily under the notice of the Police, and are more amenable to their authority than to that of ordinary attendance officers.' Further, police saw the truancy clauses as linked to their own mandate of crime prevention, a benefit also acknowledged by the education ministry:

> It may be mentioned that much of the work done by the Police is not represented by any action taken by this [Education] Department, for it would appear that, outside the warnings issued from this office, a considerable amount of default is prevented by the activity of the Police. (NSW Police Department, 1896:2–3)

That is, far from the school authorities initiating requests for police assistance, it is evident that police had added the truancy clauses to their everyday reasons for intervention.

The truancy clauses are perhaps the archetypal example of the multivalent forces marking out the field of policing of young people during this period. Truancy was seen as a symptom of parental neglect or indifference and it nurtured crime: on both counts it warranted police intervention, which was provided.

The companion of truancy legislation, in a social policy context, was legislation governing neglected children. The neglected children legislation, which dated from the 1860s, drew upon the articulation in Britain, transmitted to the colonies, of the problem of juvenile delinquency (Ramsland, 1986; O'Brien, 1988; van Krieken, 1992). The statutes provided for the establishment of industrial and reformatory schools to which child offenders and deserted or neglected children were directed by the courts. Again police were central to its early administration. Further legislation in the 1900s refined the range of options available to courts, and provided especially for the establishment of Children's Courts (Cashen, 1985; Garton, 1986; van Krieken, 1992).

In all these reforms, the state was indicating the separate and special status of the child or young person, providing the police with an often ambiguous mandate for intervention. Were the police to increase their attention to the conditions of life of the child? Some had little doubt that they should. For one of the architects of child welfare policy in New South Wales in this period, C. K. Mackellar, the effect of such innovations as neglected children legislation and special courts for children was to increase the likelihood of police taking action over juvenile offences. Before the *Neglected Children's and Juvenile Offenders Act* of 1908, reflected Mackellar in 1916, very many (allegedly criminal) offences by children had been passed over by police and others. Now police had no hesitation in taking them to the Children's Court, to be dealt with in 'a rational and humane manner ... there is no fear that they will be contaminated by the ordinary blackguardism of the people who assemble at the police court' (Select Committee, 1916: Evidence, para. 651).

Refinement of court dispositional options increased the potential for greater police intervention in children's affairs. Such police powers mandated an oversight of the conditions of family life in ways which were otherwise limited by notions of the privacy of the family. The use of such powers, however, should not be regarded as depending on police initiative alone. In surveying the evidence of police involvement in child welfare cases in NSW early this century, van Krieken concludes that the initiative was more likely to be that of parents and families (van Krieken, 1992:91–109). We should also note, however, the potential of such child welfare legislation to be used in ways which protected children from abuse by those in power over them: hence the evidence of C. K. Mackellar on police prosecutions of a schoolteacher and a clergyman who had each flogged a state ward (Select Committee, 1916: Evidence, para. 677).

In regard to another arena of police powers over young people, the historical judgement can find little cause for satisfaction of any kind. The history of the twentieth-century removal of Aboriginal children from their parents' control has now been widely documented in histories of policy and in Aboriginal oral history (Read, 1981; Goodall, 1990; Johnston, 1991; see also chapter 6). Police had a key role in such removals, one which was mandated by the extensive social engineering powers embodied in the various state Aboriginal statutes. The long-term consequence of such police interventionism was felt beyond the ending of the protection regimes under which removals had been instituted. During the transition towards citizenship in the 1960s and 1970s and the increasing urbanisation of many Aborigines, the traditions of a special police involvement with Aboriginal children have intensified (see Cowlishaw, 1988; Gale et al., 1990).

The increasing powers invested in police by legislation governing truancy, neglected children and removal of Aboriginal children from their parents and communities show the important role which police were expected to play in the government of young people from the later nineteenth century. To a greater extent than for other police duties, these powers were articulated to the functions of non-criminal justice institutions: the truancy clauses to universal public education as a means of addressing urban crime and disorder as well as preparation for working life; the neglected children statutes to the replacement of 'failed' family life through boarding out or reformatory placement; the removal of Aboriginal children as a means of dealing with the 'half-caste' population in an era emphasising racial purification. Welfare policing of this kind, however, did not wholly displace other mechanisms of the criminal justice system for dealing with street offences and minor crime. These continued as important outcomes of policing as discussed in the next section.

CRIMES AND OFFENCES

The sources for measuring the incidence of police interactions with young people in Australia over time are very unsatisfactory. Before the 1920s the low visibility of young people as a category in police annual reports is inconsistent with the frequent comments of police in public inquiries in relation to the problems of urban larrikinism from the 1870s.

From earlier this century, however, a number of jurisdictions provided some measure of the policing of juveniles. Before this time, the statistical evidence relating age with arrest and prosecution data is thin. Some such data are available in Queensland police arrest statistics in the later nineteenth century (Queensland Police Department, 1877–1893). Analysis of age breakdowns of arrest in the 1880s suggests that stealing offences did not play the dominant part they evidently came to play in policing of juveniles after the 1920s. Public order offences were considerably more important, for those aged between 15 and 20, while for those below this age the most common reason for police prosecution was the status offence of neglected child.

Twentieth-century indices suggest that the bulk of police actions involving prosecutions of young people were for petty criminal offences and public order infractions down to mid-century. Overwhelmingly, these involved male defendants. Indeed the sex disproportions are much greater for youth than for adults, though this difference eases somewhat by the 1950s.

Western Australian police statistics allow us to judge the age distribution of those whom police prosecuted at various periods. In the 1920s, as in the 1950s, police prosecutions for criminal offences involved children as young as 7 years, with a not inconsiderable number being below the age of 13. In the 1920s the principal occasions of police intervention were three in that state: stealing, traffic act offences, and Defence Act offences (the last relating to military service, applying mainly to youths of 16 and 17 years). By the 1950s, the balance had changed somewhat, with traffic act offences (presumably mainly unlicensed driving) and stealing being the dominant offences. And whereas police formal actions had scarcely touched young females in the 1920s, by the 1950s their appearance was somewhat more frequent, for much the same offences as those of males. In familiar patterns, the sex balance was reversed in the case of neglected child actions, dominated in the 1950s by female cases (see also Hancock and Chesney-Lind, 1985; van Krieken, 1992:93).

For South Australia the picture is much the same. In the 1920s the main charges against juveniles were for stealing and traffic act

offences. By the 1950s, the picture is complicated by the new focus
on delinquency. On the assumption that the South Australian
reports (like those in Western Australia and unlike those in NSW)
define juvenile as under 17 years, we need to take account by the
1950s of a range of offences involving the policing of youth culture
which were explicitly targeted by police. Indeed, in 1955 the Police
Department claimed responsibility for the large increase in charges
in the 'offences against morality' category, the highest recorded to
that date. These high returns were 'due to police activity generally
but particularly the efforts against the social menace known as the
"bodgie" and "widgie" cult' (South Australia Police Department,
1955:6).

Ages of those prosecuted under the heading of offences against
morality (offences which these comments indicate were regarded as
falling within the domain of juvenile delinquency) are not known,
but the offences themselves were all sexual offences, including
indecent assault and carnal knowledge. As the report notes:

> Many homes were visited and parents acquainted with the movements
> of their children found to be members of bodgie and widgie groups.
> Some parents openly admitted that they did not know what their
> children were doing and, when told, appeared deeply shocked. (South
> Australia Police Department, 1955:6; see also White and Wilson, 1991)

Outside this area of special interest in the 1950s, the major occasions
for police interventions in South Australia at this time were those
of stealing and traffic act offences. The sex differentials noted earlier
for Western Australia generally applied: again the social norms
drawing police attention to girls came not from their offending but
from their perceived vulnerability or bad behaviour. Hence, while
female juveniles made up only 6.5 percent of total juveniles dealt
with in 1955, they constituted 92 percent of the uncontrolled child
cases, and 46 percent of the neglected children cases. The extraordinary growth in intensity of policing of juveniles in the 1960s
amplified these patterns: a decade after the mid-1950s, girls were the
target of the great majority of child welfare actions. By the 1970s,
yet another change in sex differentials is notable: females had
doubled proportionally their appearance in juvenile crime statistics
in South Australia. This change appears almost entirely attributable
to the newly reported offence of shop stealing, the only category in
which female juveniles exceed males in the mid-1970s reports.

More detailed investigation of the official statistics in particular jurisdictions would undoubtedly be repaid by a refinement of these generalisations. A comparison of police returns in NSW in the 1930s and 1940s substantially confirms the picture outlined for the jurisdictions discussed above. Notable is the very substantial increase in policing of female juveniles during the war. While females (under 21) constituted just over 5 percent of the total offenders reported in the NSW reports in the mid-1930s, by the end of the war they accounted for over 18 percent of the total. There were a great number of charges of neglected or uncontrollable child, these cases constituting the largest single part of this increase, with a further substantial increase in unspecified offences, which may include vagrancy and wartime National Security Act charges. In this respect, the pattern of policing of female juveniles in New South Wales was substantially different from that of males, whose offending was dominated by stealing throughout this period.

The patchwork of impressions we can stitch from these different sources suggests a number of things about the historical development of the policing of juveniles. In the first place, judged by the formal evidence of police detentions and prosecutions and in spite of the multiplication of different legal enactments affecting the status of the child, with attendant police powers, the policing of youth from the late nineteenth century was concerned primarily with petty crime and public order.

Nevertheless, there was also a significant policing impact derived from the accretion of police powers in what we broadly think of as the welfare complex, centred on education, health and social reform (see also van Krieken, 1992; White, 1990). The surveillance of truants and the detention and processing of neglected or uncontrollable children constituted important occasions of police involvement with young people.

These two arenas of concern were qualified by their sex-specific impacts. That is, petty crime and public disorder offences accounted for the bulk of police attention to young males, as did truancy, an offence which was defined ideologically in the later nineteenth century by its links to the problem of street larrikinism. The very low levels of policing of young females in these areas contrasted with the increasing visibility of girls as uncontrollable children in the police statistics.

By the mid-twentieth century and later, these patterns were shifting somewhat. Changes in the organisation of consumption, and in the organisation of the family are likely to have contributed very significantly to the increasing numbers of female juveniles involved in stealing, while the dramatic growth of young males involved in car and driving offences has its own predictable but yet to be written history (cf. White, 1990).

Finally, lying outside the official police statistics but constituting a major function of police in some regions was the special police power of removal of Aboriginal children. This constituted the most substantial impact of policing on any particular juvenile population, with what we know now have been the most severe long-term consequences (Johnston, 1991).

OVERVIEW

A modest conclusion of any long-term consideration of the relations of police and young people in Australian history must caution against too great an emphasis on particular periods of cultural crisis over the status of youth, such as the larrikin scares of the 1880s and 1890s, or the juvenile delinquency alarm in the 1950s.

The beginnings of modern police forces in the Australian colonies in the 1860s were contemporaneous with important changes in the organisation of the state's relation to young people. The postulation of the problem of juvenile delinquency, the development of compulsory education and its associated truancy regimes, the administration of neglected children were all developments of the later nineteenth century which profoundly depended on police for their operation. In the late nineteenth century, these modes of regulation were closely linked with the maintenance of a variety of institutional remedies for the problems they addressed.

Over time, however, the institutional (i.e. carceral) resolution of a young person's conflict with social norms became only one possible result of any police interaction. It was a destination, that is, reached by only a few of all those with whom police came in contact. Fines and probation came to play the dominant role in criminal justice processing of young people. Probation was increasingly articulated to the welfare networks that grew in importance in the twentieth century. Counselling and psychological interventions began to exert their influence in the management of the problem child.

Whatever the eventual destination of those policed, however, in practice the reasons for police intervention derived from the police mandate of crime prevention and peace-keeping. Juvenile property offences, whether petty stealing or later car stealing and unlawful use of vehicles, occasioned most police action against young males. Females, however, were more likely to fall foul of status offences legislation, the product of the child-saving movement and its successors.

Police were slow to develop new strategies in response to the social concerns expressed about juvenile offending and the status of juveniles considered at risk. Where their role was refined, it was usually as a result of statutory direction, their powers in relation to the removal of Aboriginal children being a good example. But in the post-war period the genesis of strategies of diversion and prevention is evident. The Police–Citizens Boys (later Youth) Clubs, the Juvenile Aid Bureaux, the cautioning programs in Victoria and later Queensland, illustrate the dispersal of police attention away from court prosecution. (see e.g. van Krieken, 1992:131; Challinger, 1985:290–302; and chapter 9).

Yet other policing evidence, the Queensland larrikinism files for example, draws attention to the number of instances of surveillance and interaction which stopped well short of arrest or charge. This evidence suggests a domain of interaction which can only be hazily sketched historically.

Further, such evidence raises the question of the importance of police as a cultural phenomenon, an agency in the formation of new patterns of behaviour. What the statistics and the official police reports can never tell us very well is what impact the very presence of police had on the dispositions and behaviour of youth historically (cf. Cunneen et al., 1989, and White, 1990 for more recent evidence). A closer examination of such an issue might choose, for example, to assess the possible impact of the changing modes of police patrol and surveillance since the late nineteenth century. The move from foot to bicycle in beat patrols may not have disturbed the patterns of police interaction with the populace greatly. But the transition to mobile car patrols is unlikely to have contributed much positive to the capacity of police to undertake their duties in ways which were oriented to preventive and diversionary ends rather than to detention and prosecution. Such a speculation takes us into a new region of debate about the styles and objects of policing which lies beyond the ambit of this chapter.

REFERENCES

Brogden, M., Jefferson T. and Walklate, S. (1988) *Introducing Police Work.* London: Unwin Hyman.

Carrington, K. (1990) 'Truancy, Schooling and Juvenile Justice: "She says she hates school" ', *ANZ Journal of Criminology*, 23 (Dec.): 259–268.

Cashen, P. (1985) 'The Truant or Delinquent: The psychological perspective in South Australia, 1920–1940', *Journal of Australian Studies*, 16: 71–83.

Challinger, D. (1985) 'Police Action and the Prevention of Juvenile Delinquency', in A. Borowski and J. Murray (eds), *Juvenile Delinquency in Australia.* North Ryde, NSW: Methuen.

Cohen, P. (1979) 'Policing the Working-class City', in National Deviancy Conference/Conference of Socialist Economists, *Capitalism and the Rule of Law.* London: Hutchinson.

Conley, C. (1991) *The Unwritten Law: Criminal justice in Victorian Kent.* Oxford: Oxford University Press.

Cowlishaw, G. (1988) *Black, White and Brindle: Race in rural Australia.* Cambridge: Cambridge University Press.

Cunneen, C. (1988) 'The Politics of Public Order: Some thoughts on culture, space and political economy', in M. Findlay and R. Hogg (eds), *Understanding Crime and Criminal Justice.* North Ryde, NSW: Law Book Co.

Cunneen, C., Finlay, M., Lynch, R. and Tupper, V. (1989) *Dynamics of Collective Conflict: Riots at the Bathurst Bike Races.* North Ryde, NSW: Law Book Co.

Davey, I. (1986) 'Growing Up in South Australia', in E. Richards (ed.), *The Flinders History of South Australian Social History.* Netley, SA: Wakefield Press.

Emsley, C. (1991) *The English Police.* Brighton: Harvester Wheatsheaf.

Finnane, M. (1987) 'The Politics of Police Powers', in M. Finnane (ed.), *Policing in Australia: Historical perspectives.* Kensington, NSW: NSW University Press.

Finnane, M. (1989) 'Censorship and the Child: Explaining the comics campaign', *Australian Historical Studies*, 92: 220–40.

Finnane, M. and Garton, S (1992) 'The Work of Policing: Social relations and the state in Queensland, 1880–1914', *Labour History*, Part I, no. 62: 52–70; Part II, no. 63: 43–64.

Gale, F., Bailey-Harris, R. and Wundersitz, J. (1990) *Aboriginal Youth and the Criminal Justice System.* Cambridge: Cambridge University Press.

Garton, S. (1986) 'Sir Charles Mackellar: Psychiatry, eugenics and child welfare in New South Wales, 1900–1914', *Historical Studies*, 22 (86): 21–34.

Goodall, H. (1990) ' "Saving the children": Gender and the colonization of Aboriginal children in NSW, 1788–1990', *Aboriginal Law Bulletin*, 2 (44) (June): 6–9.

Grabosky, P. (1977) *Sydney in Ferment. Crime, dissent and official reaction, 1788–1973.* Canberra: ANU Press.

Hancock, L. and Chesney-Lind, M. (1985) 'Juvenile Justice Legislation and Gender Discrimination', in A. Borowski and J. Murray (eds), *Juvenile Delinquency in Australia*. North Ryde, NSW: Methuen.

Hetherington, P. (1986) 'Childhood and Youth in Australia', *Journal of Australian Studies*, 18: 3–18.

Johnston, E. (1991) *Final Report*. Royal Commission into Aboriginal Deaths in Custody. Canberra: AGPS.

Johnston, W.R. (1992) *The Long Blue Line: A history of the Queensland Police*. Brisbane: Boolarong Press.

McLachlan, N. (1950) Larrikinism: An interpretation. MA thesis, University of Melbourne, 1950.

Murray, J. (1973) *Larrikins: 19th century outrage*. Melbourne: Lansdowne Press.

NSW Police Department (1896) *Annual Report*.

O'Brien, A. (1988) *Poverty's Prison: The poor in New South Wales 1880–1918*. Melbourne: Melbourne University Press.

Pearson, G. (1983) *Hooligan: A history of respectable fears*. London: Macmillan.

Phillips, D. (1985) *Making More Adequate Provision: State education in Tasmania, 1839–1985*. Hobart: Government Printer.

Queensland Police Department, *Annual Reports, 1877–93*.

Ramsland, J. (1986) *Children of the Back Lanes: Destitute and neglected children in colonial New South Wales*. Kensington, NSW: NSW University Press.

Read, P. (1981) *The Stolen Generations: The removal of Aboriginal children in NSW*. Sydney: Ministry of Aboriginal Affairs.

Select Committee on the Whole Administration of the State Children Relief Act, 1901 (1916) 'Further Progress Report', *NSW Parliamentary Papers*, 1916, v. 2: 1011.

Smith, B. (1991) 'Crime and the Classics: The humanities and government in the nineteenth century Australian university', in I. Hunter et al., *Accounting for the Humanities; the Language of Culture and the Logic of Government*. Brisbane: Institute for Cultural Policy Studies.

South Australia Police Department (1955) *Annual Report*.

Stratton, J. (1984) 'Bodgies and Widgies: Youth culture in the 1950s', *Journal of Australian Studies*, 15: 10–24.

van Krieken, R. (1992) *Children and the State: Social control and the formation of Australian child welfare*. Sydney: Allen and Unwin.

Walker, D. (1986) 'Youth on Trial: The Mt Rennie case', *Labour History*, 50: 28–41.

Walker, D. (1988) 'Youth', in G. Davison (ed.), *Australians 1888*. Sydney: Fairfax, Syme and Weldon.

White, R. (1990) *No Space of Their Own: Young people and social control in Australia*. Cambridge: Cambridge University Press.

White, R. and Wilson, B. (eds) (1991) *For Your Own Good: Young people and state intervention in Australia.* Melbourne: La Trobe University Press.

Wimshurst, K. (1981) 'Child Labour and School Attendance in South Australia 1890–1915', *Historical Studies,* 19 (76) (April): 388–411.

CHAPTER 2

The Legal Framework of Juvenile Justice

Kate Warner

INTRODUCTION

The official response to juvenile crime can be divided into three stages. The investigatory stage, the adjudicatory stage (the decision as to guilt) and the dispositional stage (the sentence). The focus of this chapter is the legal framework of the investigatory stage, i.e. the policing of juvenile suspects and offenders. The powers of the police in child welfare and child protection matters are not addressed in detail. The components of the legal framework of policing of juvenile suspects and offenders are statutory law, common law and internal police instructions. The generally accepted view of the legal status of internal police instructions, variously described as instructions, standing or general orders, is that they are not absolute rules, but guidelines (*R. v Anunga* (1976) 11 ALR 41 at 45; *M. v J.* [1989] TasR 212; but see Wallace-Bruce (1989)). In a recent case, *M. v J.* ([1989] TasR 212 at 219) Neasey J said: '. . . the police standing order has no particular status in this court, but its content is symptomatic of the standard of fairness which ought to be observed during questioning by a police officer of a child'. As courts may refuse to admit evidence obtained in breach of such guidelines, it is submitted they can properly be regarded as part of the legal framework.

In order to understand fully the legal framework of the juvenile justice system in Australia and thereby the place of police in juvenile justice, it is necessary to be aware of both the source of legislative and administrative authority for juvenile justice and the history of its emergence as a distinct part of the criminal justice system.

Under the Australian Constitution, criminal law and its administration including juvenile justice is primarily the responsibility of state governments and territories. The legal framework of juvenile

27

justice is therefore found in state or territory laws which are administered by state (or territory) departments and institutions. Child welfare, issues of neglect and child protection are also primarily state, rather than federal, matters.

The Commonwealth has no express power to legislate in relation to criminal justice, juvenile justice or child welfare. It only has legislative power relating to subjects of its express Constitutional powers, for example in relation to Commonwealth property, social security, marriage and divorce. No specialist federal legislation dealing with the processing of juvenile offenders for federal offences has been enacted. When a young person is suspected of committing a federal offence, by virtue of the *Judiciary Act* 1903, ss.68(1) and 79, the state laws relating to arrest, custody, summary conviction, trial on indictment, procedure and evidence that would apply to a young person charged with an offence under state law apply. Section 20C of the *Crimes Act* 1914 (Cwlth) has the effect of making the local sentencing options available for young federal offenders. Theoretically the Commonwealth could, by entering into treaty obligations, rely upon the external affairs power to support federal legislation dealing with juvenile justice under state law (Freiberg, Fox and Hogan, 1988, para. 37; Youth Justice Coalition, 1990:80). Although Australia is a signatory to the *United Nations Convention on the Rights of the Child* (1990) and participated in the development of the *United Nations Minimum Rules for the Administration of Juvenile Justice* (1986) (the 'Beijing Rules'), the Commonwealth has not attempted to legislate on the subject.

The consequence of the federal system is that in Australia there are eight different systems of juvenile justice. In most jurisdictions there are a number of statutes dealing with its main aspects. As well there are many statutes that deal with both adults and juveniles, such as acts defining offences and those dealing with police powers such as search and bail. In general, three different government departments are involved in administering the system of juvenile justice: the police, Community Service and the Attorney-General's Department or their equivalents. Inter-jurisdictional differences can make a detailed discussion of the legal framework of juvenile justice in this country very long, if not tedious. In the context of a book on police and young people it is appropriate to concentrate on the laws relating to the investigation and prosecution of young suspects by the police. To put the police decision to prosecute or caution in context, a brief discussion of diversionary mechanisms such as panels is useful.

THE DEVELOPMENT OF THE JUVENILE JUSTICE SYSTEM

When Australia was settled in 1788, there was no distinctive or separate juvenile justice system. The applicable law was taken to be the English common law including the English criminal law. This made few concessions to young people. The first Australian statutes dealing specifically with young offenders were enacted in the middle of the nineteenth century. The most significant of them provided the foundation for the children's courts by allowing certain indictable matters to be dealt with summarily, by providing less severe sanctions and a power to order dismissal. Seymour regards the first major step towards the creation of a separate and distinctive system for young offenders as the establishment between 1863 and 1874 of reformatory and industrial schools – 'to save children, to reclaim them, to rescue them from their harmful surroundings' (Seymour, 1988:39). The next step was the creation of children's courts, first in South Australia in 1890 and early in the twentieth century in the other states. The idea of separate courts for children came from the United States of America where such courts were established in response to the child saving movement with its emphasis on needs rather than deeds, promotion of rehabilitation rather than punishment and informality rather than formality. The jurisdiction of the American courts was based on the equitable concept of wardship or *parens patriae*. The issue was not whether a child had committed an offence, but whether he or she was in a condition of delinquency or dependency. The child was not arrested, prosecuted, convicted or sentenced, but rather brought to court where a probation officer represented his or her interests. Then, if found to be delinquent or dependent, the child was admitted to the care of a probation officer or an institution (Freiberg, Fox and Hogan, 1988, para. 9).

It was the North American *idea* of children's courts rather than the model that influenced their creation in Australia. Children's courts here did not embody the radical shift in philosophy that the North American counterparts did and therefore did not move as far away from the criminal justice system. In Australian children's courts, young suspects were still prosecuted for specific offences, and the laws of evidence and the criminal standard of proof still applied. Modifications were made to procedure and sanctions, and by the 1960s there were a number of features that distinguished children's courts from adult magistrates' courts: the use of separate premises and remand facilities (at least in the big cities); the development of a paternalistic approach, sometimes with statutory exhortations to have regard to the welfare of the child or to treat young offenders not as criminals but as misguided children; the frequent use of probation officers to supply presentence information; indeterminate sanctions and closed courts.

A significant difference between adult magistrates' courts and children's courts was the difference in jurisdiction. Not only did children's courts have jurisdiction over a wider range of indictable offences, but as well they had concurrent jurisdiction over children in need of care. Just as the children's courts had jurisdiction over both young offenders and children in need of care, the police too had a prominent role in relation to criminal offence and neglect procedures, apprehending and charging children with being neglected or uncontrolled (Australian Law Reform Commission, 1981:190), and in some jurisdictions handling the majority of court applications in relation to neglect procedures (McNiff, 1979:25, Australian Law Reform Commission, 1981:190).

Until the 1960s the criminal justice system only had special provisions for young people at the adjudicatory and dispositional stage. In relation to investigation, arrest, bail and prosecutorial discretion, there was little in the way of special legislative provisions for children. Unofficial cautioning of young people by police has probably always been a feature of police handling of young people. The extent of this 'informal' processing is difficult to determine. The 1960s and 1970s saw the emergence of policies for formalising alternative methods to arrest for young offenders. These took the form of the creation of cautioning schemes and panels, either supported by a statutory framework, or administrative guidelines. The 1980s and 1990s have been a period of further reassessment and change. Many states have rewritten their legislation dealing with young offenders and child welfare. This has affected the role of the police in a number of ways. In line with the trend to split the welfare and criminal jurisdiction of the children's courts, the responsibility for the apprehension of children in need of care and for initiating court proceedings in such cases has shifted away from the police.

The increased emphasis on procedural rights has focused attention on the rights of young offenders during police investigation. A continued emphasis on diversion and attempts to adopt the least intrusive solution to juvenile offending have led to support for a greater use of police cautioning.

The police with their powers to interrogate, arrest, search, fingerprint, and bail or detain young offenders are the door to the juvenile justice system. However, while in recent years there have been changes to court systems and sentencing options for young people in most states, modifications to police powers have been less extensive. This reflects a relative lack of legal regulation of police powers and statutory rights of suspects in the face of police investigation in the criminal justice system as a whole.

INTERROGATION

In determining whether an offence has been committed, the police may put questions to any person, whether suspected or not, from whom they consider useful information may be obtained. At the same time the person questioned has a right to silence. Subject to a number of statutory exceptions, there is no requirement to give any information. The law and police standing orders provide a number of protections of this right: rules in relation to cautioning and admissibility of confessions, as to length of time in custody before being taken to a court and as to the presence of witnesses. Some of these rules are stronger where the suspect is a 'child'. They will be considered in some detail.

Voluntariness of confessions

A confession is only admissible in evidence in court if it is voluntary: 'made in the exercise of a free choice to speak or be silent' (*R. v Lee* (1950) 82 CLR 133 at 149). Doubts as to voluntariness are raised if there is evidence of pressure or inducement which might have overborne a suspect's will. The onus of proving a confession is voluntary rests with the Crown (Byrne and Heydon, 1991, para. 33675). In addition to the voluntariness rule, courts have a discretion to exclude evidence which is voluntary, but improperly or unfairly obtained. These common law rules as to admissibility of evidence (the voluntariness rule and the discretion rule) apply equally to adults and children. But as Seymour has pointed out, when the suspect is a juvenile particular care must be taken in the application of these rules:

> If a juvenile has made an admission it might sometimes be more difficult for a court to feel satisfied that 'a free choice to speak or be silent' has been made. Similarly, police practices which may seem fair when the suspect is an adult may raise doubts in the mind of a judicial officer if the defendant is a child. (Seymour, 1988:193)

Confessions of children have been held to be inadmissible on grounds of involuntariness where Aboriginal children aged 13 and 14 who made written statements witnessed their 11-year-old friend assaulted by the police (*Dixon v McCarthy* [1975] 1 NSWLR 617) and where it was suggested to a 14-year-old girl that it would be better for her to tell the truth (*Pascoe v Little* (1978) 24 ACTR 21). The absence of a caution has been considered by some courts to be relevant to voluntariness because of the possibility of the child assuming he or she must answer questions (*R. v R. (No. 1)* (1972) 9 CCC (2d) 274 cited with approval in *Dixon v McCarthy (supra)* and *M. v J.* [1989] TasR 212 at 219).

Presence of parents or independent adults

All Australian jurisdictions require the presence of adult witnesses when juvenile suspects are interviewed. This may be required by internal police regulations or in five jurisdictions (New South Wales, Australian Capital Territory, South Australia, Victoria and the Northern Territory) by legislation. These provisions are by no means uniform. There are differences with respect to the categories of adult required to be present, with regard to the offences to which the provisions apply, the scope of the protection, and the investigative activities covered by the provisions.

In Victoria, the *Crimes Act* 1958, s.464(E) requires that questioning of a young person under the age of 17 who has been arrested or in respect of whom there is sufficient information to justify an arrest must not occur without the presence of a parent, guardian or independent adult, unless the questioning is so urgent having regard to the safety of other people that it should not be delayed. In New South Wales, the *Children's (Criminal Proceedings) Act* 1987, s.13 provides that any statement made or given by a child to a police officer shall not be admissible in proceedings in which the child is a party unless there was present throughout a person responsible for the child or, in the case of a child of or above the age of 16, an adult (other than a police officer) present with the consent of a child. There is a proviso that if there is proper and sufficient reason for the absence of a required adult, the evidence may be admitted. Legislation in the Northern Territory provides for the presence of a third party if the juvenile is being interviewed in relation to an offence punishable by twelve months or more and for exclusion of evidence (*Juvenile Justice Act* 1983 (NT) ss.25, 34). In the Australian Capital Territory's *Children's Service Ordinance* 1986, ss.30 and 40 contain similar provisions for children suspected of committing a serious offence or an offence against person or property. South Australian legislation, the *Summary Offences Act* 1953 s.79a, provides that all minors, apprehended on suspicion of having committed an offence, must not be subjected to an interrogation or investigation until a solicitor, relative or friend or other designated person is present. There is a proviso if the offence is not punishable by imprisonment for two years or more and it is not reasonably practicable to secure the attendance of a suitable representative of the child's interests.

In the other states parental presence is dealt with in internal police regulations. In Queensland for example, General Instruction 4.54A(b) states that a child must be questioned in the presence of a parent, guardian or adult nominated by the child or parent. The instruction goes on to state that, if no adult is nominated, an independent person, preferably of the same sex, should be present with whom the child would not be 'overborne or oppressed'. The relevant Western Australian provision is Routine Order 3-2.20 and 3-2.21, and in Tasmania it is Standing Order 109.14. In Tasmania new legislation is currently being prepared dealing with this issue and in Queensland the yet to be proclaimed *Juvenile Justice Act* 1992 contains in s.36 a provision similar to that operating in New South Wales.

Effect of non-compliance

There are three common law rules which are relevant in considering the exclusion of confessions obtained in the absence of parents. First, the fact that no parent or independent person was present when an admission was made, may be, at least in part, reason for doubting the voluntariness of the confession (*Dixon v McCarthy* [1975] 1 NSWLR 617; *Collins v R.* (1980) 31 ALR 257 at 321 and see

Seymour, 1988: 204). As discussed above, voluntariness is a prerequisite for admission. Second, for reasons of public policy, courts have a discretion to exclude evidence which is unlawfully or improperly obtained (*Bunning v Cross* (1978) 141 CLR 54; *Cleland v R.* (1982) 151 CLR 1). And third, evidence may be rejected if in all the circumstances it would be unfair to use it against the accused (*McDermott v R.* (1948) 76 CLR 501; *R. v Lee* (1950) 82 CLR 133). The onus is on the defendant to show a case for the exercise of the judge's discretion to reject a voluntary confession.

In Western Australia, Queensland and Tasmania the requirement for parental presence is contained in police instructions. In most jurisdictions the legal status of internal police instructions, variously described as instructions, standing or general orders, is that they are not absolute rules, but guidelines. So while it may not be unlawful, departure from the requirement in standing orders of parental presence may lead to an exercise of discretion according to the principles in *Bunning v Cross* and *R. v Lee* excluding the evidence on the grounds it was obtained by improper or unfair means. Reported decisions indicate that although evidence of admissions or confessions may be rejected where police instructions requiring presence of parents were not complied with (see *T. v Waye* (1983) 35 SASR 247; *M. v J.* [1989] TasR 212; *Jones* (1978) 2 CrimLJ 169), in other cases the evidence has been admitted (*Frijaf v The Queen* [1982] WAR 128; *R. v Crawford* [1985] 2 QdR 22; *Peters v The Queen* (1987) 23 ACrimR 451). In Victoria there is a statutory requirement for parental presence during interviewing. Failure to comply with this may lead to the exclusion of evidence obtained in accordance with the above common law rules, but just as with breach of police instructions, it will not necessarily do so. Confessions and admissions that are voluntary can be admitted although illegally obtained. In New South Wales the relevant statutory provision, the *Children (Criminal Proceedings) Act* 1987, s.13 is stronger in that it makes a confession obtained in the absence of one of the specified persons inadmissible, unless there is sufficient reason for the absence. If there is no such reason, there is no discretion to admit the evidence.

Scope of presence requirements

Do presence requirements apply to all stages of questioning? Clearly the Victorian legislative provision does not apply to preliminary questioning, but in other states the relevant provisions are not so explicit. The courts have not been consistent in their interpretation of them. There are some cases which indicate that the courts do not treat the holding of a preliminary interview as objectionable in itself, and which largely condone the police practice of obtaining an initial confession without a parent or substitute present and then requiring it to be repeated in the presence of a witness (Seymour, 1988:196–198). Other cases have explicitly condemned such practices (*T. v Waye* (1983) 35 SASR 247 at 250; Seymour, 1988:197–8). More recently, in *M. v J.* ([1989] TasR 212), Neasey J rejected the argument that there was no failure to comply with the standing order because the admission was made in the course of a general inquiry before an 'interview' had commenced. He stated:

> I do not accept the distinction that an 'interview' had not yet commenced. If that distinction were to be made, it would be a simple matter to by-pass the protections of the standing order. The rule should be, in my view, that if a police officer intends to ask any investigatory questions of a child, he should first ensure that the accompanying presence of the parent or substitute adult is obtained.

Are the rules observed?

The practice of obtaining preliminary statements in the absence of adult witnesses appears to be widespread (Seymour, 1988:196–7). But for some time there has also been evidence that many investigations are completed without parents or other adult witnesses being present at any stage. In Western Australia the Report of the Legislative Review Committee noted that police rarely adhere to the guidelines, citing a survey in 1988 of young people at Longmore Remand Centre and the Perth Children's Court where it was found that in 86 percent of interviews no independent adult was present (Legislative Review Committee, 1991:73). Earlier Western Australian studies reported similarly small percentages of parents or other adults being present (McDonald, 1981:108). In New South Wales a study of 50 remandees reported that nearly half had not had an independent adult present at any stage, and half of those who had had an independent adult present at some time had already been interviewed (Staden, 1986). Contrasting figures were produced in a Victorian study where only 5 percent of a sample of young offenders were interviewed alone (Higgins, 1982). The most recent study showed that in a sample of young people from Victoria, Queensland,

Western Australia and Tasmania, only one-third of those taken to a police station for questioning reported having had an independent adult present during questioning (Alder, 1992:24). Lawyers interviewed in this study reported a significant minority of their young clients were interviewed in the absence of a parent or guardian (O'Connor, 1992:39).

Presence of a solicitor

In most Australian jurisdictions neither an adult nor a child has a statutory or common law right to the presence of a lawyer during interrogation. The exceptions are South Australia and Victoria where there are statutory provisions for access to a friend or solicitor during interrogation or investigation (*Summary Offences Act* (SA) s.79a; *Crimes Act* 1958 (Vic.) s.464C). In New South Wales, the Australian Capital Territory and the Northern Territory, a legal practitioner may be present during interrogation instead of a parent or guardian or person responsible for the child (*Children (Criminal Proceedings) Act* (NSW) s.13(1)(a)(iv); *Children's Services Ordinance* 1986 (ACT) s.30(1)(d)(iii); *Juvenile Justice Act* 1983 (NT) s.21(c)(iv)). In the absence of statutory provisions, police instructions typically provide that if legal advice is requested, reasonable facilities should be granted to obtain that advice. But as explained above, these are merely administrative guidelines and breach of them may or may not be used by the courts to exclude confessional evidence. In a number of reported cases, refusal of requests for the presence of a solicitor have led to exclusion of evidence (*Borsellino* [1978] QdR 507; *Hart* [1979] QdR 8 and Faine, 1988:168). In *Spaulding* (Unreported Serial No. 48/1981), Everett J of the Supreme Court of Tasmania refused to admit the record of interview of a 17-year-old girl charged with burglary and stealing where her solicitor had telephoned the CIB and was not allowed in until the record of interview had been conducted. Police instructions appear to make no special mention of the presence of solicitors in the case of child suspects. It has been claimed that in Victoria lawyers have been frequently refused access to their clients and clients have not been allowed to telephone for legal advice (Faine, 1988:168).

Evaluation of presence requirements

There are judicial statements to the effect that presence of an independent adult during questioning and investigation is important to ensure that statements made are free and voluntary and not obtained by improper means (*Dixon v McCarthy* [1975] NSWLR 617 at 640). Courts, it has been said, should be reluctant to receive in evidence an admissional statement made in the absence of a parent or responsible adult: first, because questioning in the absence of a parent or responsible adult is always likely to be intimidatory and unsettling; second, if a child's version of the interview differs from that of the police officer, the chances of the child's version being accepted are slight; and finally, the police knowing this may be tempted to invent an admissional statement if one is not made (*M. v J.* [1989] TasR 212 at 220).

The available evidence suggests that the existing legal position is inadequate to ensure that police instructions and legislative requirements for parental presence are complied with. Statutory provisions, such as the Victorian provision requiring parental presence during interview, are stronger than police instructions, but are nevertheless open to the criticism that they do not apply to a preliminary interview and so can be easily circumvented by the police. And statements made in contravention of statutory provisions may be admitted although illegally obtained. Courts are presented with a difficult choice when confronted with apparently convincing confessional evidence that points to guilt of a serious crime. The New South Wales position of providing that such statements are generally inadmissible is preferable, but is deficient in that it only provides a retrospective control on police questioning. It will only be in a minority of cases that the issue will be litigated and the court will have the opportunity to exclude evidence obtained in breach of the requirements. As well as a provision for inadmissibility, prospective statutory requirements for presence are needed, with exceptions for occasions when urgency and impracticability demand that ordinary practice is inappropriate. The provisions should be so drafted as to make it clear that they apply to all stages of the investigative process, and cannot be circumvented either by not applying to initial questioning, or by the courts accepting evidence of a repeated admission in the presence of a parent or responsible adult which is first obtained without such a witness.

As in South Australia, all suspects, whether adults or children, should have a statutory right to a phone call to a relative or friend and to the presence of a solicitor during interrogation or investigation. Police should be required to go further and inform the suspect of this right.

The issue of the role of parent, responsible adult or solicitor during investigation also needs to be addressed. The presence of a parent or responsible adult can provide protection to the child ensuring that statements are voluntary and not improperly obtained or manufactured. As well, parental presence can reassure the child. But a child needs advice. Parents or other civilian witnesses may only be suited to the role of supportive observer rather than adviser to a child of his or her rights. As one report put it:

> Most do not know what kinds of questioning are permissible, so that they do not intervene. They are usually unable to give the basic legal advice which a suspect who is being questioned requires; this includes appropriate responses to leading or unfair questions, indication of the significance of questions about intent, and when appropriate, refusal to answer questions. (Youth Justice Coalition, 1990:251)

Some parents may see their role as being to assist the police to put pressure on the child to confess. Parental presence is not enough to protect a young suspect's interests. Access to legal advice is also required. A lawyer is clearly appropriate for a more active role. Calls for a statutory right for suspects to legal advice have been many. In addition, substance should be given to this right by a requirement to inform suspects of this right and the establishment of publicly funded duty solicitors to ensure availability of legal advice. Legislation should also clarify the role of a lawyer during interrogation (Seymour, 1988:201; Youth Justice Coalition, 1990:250; Legislative Review Committee, 1991:73).

ARREST

Early in the investigative process a decision is made as to whether a suspect should be arrested. In theory, the arrest of a young suspect should not preclude release without prosecution. The decision to prosecute or to caution or refer to a panel will be discussed below. Common law powers of arrest have been considerably enlarged by statute. In all jurisdictions it may be open to the police to proceed by way of summons and the policy trend is to encourage alternatives to arrest wherever appropriate. This trend is accentuated in the case of young offenders and restrictions are placed on the power of arrest of children by police instructions or by statute in all jurisdictions.

In New South Wales and Western Australia, the alternative procedures include an attendance notice, a simple oral or written direction requiring a young offender to appear in court at a specified time. In New South Wales, proceedings against children must be by way of summons or attendance notice rather than arrest. Ordinary charge is deemed appropriate only if a serious offence is involved or if the violent behaviour of the child or the violent nature of the offence indicates that the child should not be allowed to remain at liberty (*Children's (Criminal Proceedings) Act* 1987 s.8). This is in addition to the guidance in *Police Regulation Act* 1899 rule 56b that arrest powers should only be used for minor offenders when it is clear that a summons will be insufficient to ensure the suspect's attendance at court. The practice in Western Australia was in the past heavily weighted in favour of arrest. In 1989 it was reported that some 74 percent of young people brought before children's courts in Western Australia were subjected to arrest (Lipscombe, 1989:35), largely because of the time and resource-consuming nature of issuing and serving summonses (Legislative Review Committee, 1991:75). The solution proposed and ultimately adopted in the *Child Welfare Act* 1947, s.33(1) was the introduction of court attendance notices, which can be issued on the spot as an attractive alternative to arrest or summons. It is police policy to promote the arrest option as one of final resort among a number of alternative strategies of oral warnings, written cautions, panel procedures and if prosecution is necessary, notices to attend court or summons. Departmental policy reserves arrest for serious offences where loss or destruction of evidence is likely if the child is not arrested; to prevent a continuation or repetition of the offence; where it is necessary to ensure appearance in court and his or her identity is in doubt; or for offences in the Fourth Schedule which lists serious crimes.

In Victoria the power to arrest children is governed by police standing orders and legislative restraints. By Standing Order 4.12, permission of a commissioned officer is required before arresting an offender under 17 if practicable; if not, authorisation must be obtained before a juvenile is lodged in custody. Permission should be given only in extreme cases where it is thought that a summons would not meet the case. The *Children and Young Persons Act* 1989 s.128(1) provides that a registrar must not issue in the first instance a warrant to arrest a child unless satisfied by evidence on oath or affidavit that the circumstances are exceptional. In the territories, there are also legislative restraints on the arrest of children, exhorting police not to charge unless summons procedures would not be effective. And in the Australian Capital Territory, a list of factors justifying arrest is included in the *Children's Services Ordinance* 1986 (ACT) s.31.

Queensland, South Australia and Tasmania have no legislative provisions discouraging arrest, although they are contained in Queensland's unproclaimed *Juvenile Justice Act* and Tasmania's Draft Judicial Proceedings Bill. Currently police instructions exhort police to refrain from arrest where procedure by way of complaint and summons would be effective (General Instruction 1.23 (Qld); Standing Order 109.4 (Tas)). In South Australia, there is also a list of factors justifying arrest and requiring that a commissioned officer's permission should be obtained before arrest (General Orders, 3065/1 and 3065/8). Policy instructions issued by Queensland's Juvenile Aid Bureau stress that summons should be used where possible and particularly for public order offences (Juvenile Aid Bureau, Information Bulletin, 4/88).

Arrest rates of children

The arguments that favour procedures which avoid arrest of children are persuasive. Arrest and custody are inconsistent with the currently accepted aim of minimising stigma and reducing children's penetration into the juvenile justice system (Seymour, 1988:215). In some jurisdictions, arrest can even result in circumvention of screening processes. How effective are internal police instructions and legislative measures in achieving the objective of encouraging reliance on procedures other than arrest? Evidence summarised by Seymour indicates that Australian police forces have 'varied greatly' in their use of alternatives to arrest. In Victoria and South Australia, most children's court cases were initiated by summons rather than arrest, but in Queensland and Western Australia the reverse was the case (Seymour, 1988:216). Recent statistics from Queensland show the position has not altered much in that state, for in 1990–91, 90 percent of children prosecuted were the result of arrests (Queensland Police Service, Information Bureau, Breakdown of Juvenile Involvement in Offences, 1990–1991). National comparative data show that Western Australia has the second highest juvenile arrest rate of all Australian states and territories and is exceeded only by the Northern Territory (Freiberg et al., 1988). In New South Wales there is some evidence of disparity in the use of court attendance notices between different areas (Youth Justice Coalition, 1990:246).

There appears to be some substance in the suggestion that it is entrenched police behaviour rather than policy directives which determines juvenile arrest rates. Arrest is seen by the police as an important way of dealing with the situation, with establishing authority of the police and providing a deterrent (Seymour, 1988:217; Youth Justice Coalition, 1990:246). If this is so, it will be no easy matter to reverse the situation in such states as Queensland and Western Australia. It remains to be seen if the Western Australian initiatives will achieve their aim.

Parental notification of arrest, proceedings, etc.

The importance of parental presence during police questioning and the right of suspects to a phone call have been discussed above. There is also the issue of notification of parents of apprehension and possible proceedings. The *United Nations Standard Minimum Rules for the Administration of Juvenile Justice* (1986) (the 'Beijing Rules') require the notification as soon as possible of parents or guardians of the apprehension of a juvenile. Is this required by law in Australia?

The most detailed provisions are to be found in the Australian Capital Territory, where the *Children's Services Ordinance* 1986, s.32 provides that a police officer who places a child under restraint shall take all reasonable steps to cause a parent of the child to be notified whether the parent resides in the territory or not, and to notify an 'authorised officer'. Section 35 requires parents to be informed of charges laid at a police station. In the Northern Territory there are similar provisions in the *Juvenile Justice Act* 1983 s.30. In the states, internal police regulations govern the situation. Western Australian and Tasmanian parents must be informed of charges (Routine Order 3-2.51 (WA), Standing Order 109.5 (Tas.)); Queensland requires them to be notified when a child is taken into custody (General Instruction 9.167(a)) and New South Wales 'immediately when taken to a police station' (Police Instructions 31.18). The *Juvenile Justice Act* 1992 (Qld) will, when proclaimed, require parents to be notified of arrest (s.22), service of attendance notice (s.28) and of a complaint and summons (s.32).

Fingerprints

In all jurisdictions, statutory provisions authorise the taking of a person's fingerprints after arrest. The provisions differ in detail and as to the time fingerprints may be taken. Restrictions on the fingerprinting of juvenile offenders may be imposed by legislation or by police instructions. They are statutory in Victoria, Tasmania, New South Wales and the Territories. In Tasmania there is no power to·fingerprint prior to conviction (*Criminal Process (Identification and Search) Act* 1976 (Tas.), s.3(1)), while Victoria and the Australian Capital Territory require a court order (*Crimes Act* 1958 (Vic.) s.464N; *Children's Services Ordinance* 1986 (ACT) s.36). Court orders are required in New South Wales and the Northern Territory only if the offender is under 14 (*Crimes Act* 1900 (NSW) s.353AA; *Juvenile Justice Act* 1983 (NT) s.31). In South Australia, Queensland and Western Australia, there are minor restrictions imposed by police instructions. In South Australia, the permission of a commissioned officer is required if the child is under 16 (Police General Order 3360/ 7). In Western Australia, the offence must be 'serious' and in Queensland, a child from 14 to 16 must be in custody on a charge of an indictable offence, and if under 14 approval from a commissioned officer is necessary and he or she must be likely to 'lapse into a career of vice and crime' (General Instruction 4.80)!

Seymour stated that fingerprinting of arrested children was common in Queensland, the Australian Capital Territory and Western Australia (Seymour, 1988:217). The recent NYARS survey found that half of those young people who reported that they had been taken to the police station said they had been fingerprinted, many claiming this had been done although they were not under arrest (Alder, 1992:23). The fact that this was reported in Victoria and Tasmania casts doubts on the efficacy of the legislative restrictions.

CUSTODY

Custody or release after arrest

The *UN Convention on the Rights of the Child* (1990) article 37 provides children are to be detained separately from adults and for the shortest possible period. In most states and territories, there is legislation relating to the release or detention of children who are arrested. Normally detention should be in institutions administered by welfare departments. The position in four states will be examined in some detail.

In Victoria, the *Crimes Act* 1958 (Vic.), s.464A requires that every person taken into custody for an offence must be released, granted bail or taken before a justice or magistrate's court. The *Bail Act* 1977 applies to an application for bail by a child. If a member of the police force inquires into a case under s.10 of the *Bail Act* 1977, a parent or guardian of the child in custody or an independent person is required by the *Children and Young Persons Act* 1989 s.129(6) to be present. Section 129(7) provides that bail must not be refused on the sole ground that a child does not have any or any adequate accommodation. If the child does not have the capacity or understanding to enter into a bail undertaking, the child may be released on bail if the child's parent enters into an undertaking to produce the child (s.129(8)). If a child is remanded in custody by a court or bail justice, the child must be placed in a remand centre (s.130).

The custody, release and detention of children in Queensland prior to first court appearance is currently dealt with in the *Children's Services Act* 1965–1980. Section 26(1) provides that until dealt with by a court or justice, a child may be released on police bail, and if not so released, the person having charge of the case shall arrange for his or her care. Grounds on which police may refuse bail to adults also apply to young people, but in addition bail may be refused to a person under 17 when satisfied that the young person should remain in custody for his or her protection or welfare (s.18(1)(b)). Pending initial appearance before a court or justice the Director of Family Services may detain the child who is not released on bail and may nominate a place where the child shall be kept until the child is dealt with, but unless safe custody cannot otherwise be provided for, the child shall not be detained in a prison or police lock-up (s.26(1)(a)(iii)). In practice, and in the metropolitan area at least, the arresting officer seeks authorisation from the Department of Family Services or Crisis Care to have the child detained at a centre such as John Oxley or Wilson pending court appearance. Considerable concern has been expressed that young people are being detained in police watch-houses or lock-ups. For many police, the demands of the job do not allow time to transport young persons to custodial centres for young people, particularly if they are arrested outside the metropolitan area of Brisbane. In such cases refusal of bail on the grounds of their protection or welfare is self-defeating. Prohibition of detention in police facilities and abolition of the exclusion of a young person from bail on welfare grounds have been recommended, as have bail conditions that respond to the circumstances of the young (Queensland Law Reform Commission, 1991:19–21). Part 3 of the *Juvenile Justice Act* 1992 contains new provisions relating to bail and custody of children.

The position in Western Australia is governed by the *Bail Act* 1982, and under clause 2 of Part B of the Schedule, a 'child' has a qualified right to release on bail which includes the right to be released by a police officer. If a child is arrested for an offence and the child is eligible to be dealt with by a children's panel, the child shall be released as soon as practicable or may be bailed until it is ascertained if the child is eligible (*Child Welfare Act* 1947 s.73(5),(6)). If a child who is in custody is refused bail under the *Bail Act* 1982, or is not released on bail, then subject to a right to remand for observation, the child must be placed in a detention centre (*Child Welfare Act* 1947 s.33(3)).

Special rules are provided for the release of young people in Tasmania. In addition to the general power of the police to release suspects arrested for a simple offence under the *Justices Act* 1959 s.34(1), the *Child Welfare Act* 1960 (Tas.) s.19(2) provides that if a child is not released or brought before a court or justice within twenty-four hours and it is not practicable to do so, a police officer may release a child on a recognisance. Section 19(5) states that relevant criteria to be considered by a police officer or justice include not only the securing of safe custody of the child but also the child's interests in being removed from bad associations. Police Standing Order 109.8(4) also provides that, in releasing a child on bail, arrangements shall be made for a parent or guardian to be present to take charge of the child on release, that the child shall be bailed and released into the custody of the parent or guardian concerned and that the parent or guardian shall endorse an acknowledgment on the bail form and sign such an acknowledgment. Detention before first court appearance is governed by the *Child Welfare Act* 1960 s.19(7). A child arrested and not released by a police officer or justice may be placed in custody in such institution as the director may appoint or in the charge of a person willing to receive him or her unless it is certified that it is impracticable to do so or that, having regard to the serious nature of the charge or to other circumstances of the case, securing of custody is of first importance. Section 19(9) provides that a certificate under s.19(7) must be produced to the court before which the child is brought.

Duration of custody before first court appearance

The High Court in *Williams v The Queen* ((1986) 161 CLR 278) has made it clear that at common law the police have no authority to detain suspects for questioning. Once arrested, a person must be taken before a justice as soon as practicable unless police bail is granted or there is a statutory right to detain for questioning. In most states and territories, children's court legislation specifically requires the police to bring a child who has been arrested promptly before a justice or children's court. In some places, time limits are set by legislation.

In Victoria, police have authority under the *Crimes Act* 1958 (Vic.) s.464A(2) to question a person in custody or carry out investigations to determine their involvement within a 'reasonable time' before taking the suspect before a justice. In the case of a child, a reasonable time cannot exceed twenty-four hours. The *Children and Young Persons Act* 1989, s.129 provides that a child taken into custody must be released, brought before the court or a bail justice within a reasonable time but not later than twenty-four hours after being taken into custody. In Tasmania there is no statutory power to detain a suspect for questioning, nor is there any absolute limit on the duration of custody of an adult before the first court appearance. A child must be brought before a court 'as soon as practicable' and if it is not practicable to do so within twenty-four hours, the child must be brought before a justice. If this is not practicable within twenty-four hours, certain police officers have the power to release the child on a recognisance (*Child Welfare Act* 1960 s.19). Neither Queensland nor Western Australia has a power to detain for questioning. In Queensland a child taken into custody must be brought as soon as practicable before a children's court or justice (*Children's Services Act* 1965–1980 (Qld) s.26(1); see also *Juvenile Justice Act* 1992, s.38). New South Wales has a similar provision in the *Children (Criminal Proceedings) Act* 1987 (NSW) s.9 and in South Australia, the duty is to bring a child before a court no longer than the next working day following his or her arrest.

Information on how the power to release or detain children prior to their first court appearance is exercised is sparse. In Western Australia, studies have reported that significant numbers of arrested young people are held in custody (Department of Community Services, Western Australia, 1986:22; McDonald, 1981). This was confirmed by the NYARS study which showed young people reported having been held in police cells in all of the four states of the survey – over half of those who had been taken to a police station had been so held. Many said they were held for more than eight hours (Alder, 1992:21).

POLICE CAUTIONS AND PANELS

Informal cautions

On-the-spot cautions are a regular feature of police activity. In most Australian jurisdictions they do not appear to be regulated in any way by police instructions or legislation. Nor do they find their way into official statistics. In New South Wales, police instructions state that an informal caution can be given in the case of trivial offences, either 'on the run', or at a station. Informal cautions are strictly limited by the specific exclusion of violent offences (including minor assaults), dishonesty and vandalism (Youth Justice Coalition, 1990:242). Only in Western Australia are informal warnings sanctioned by legislation. The *Child Welfare Act* 1947 s.33(1)(a) allows a police officer to orally warn a child who is reasonably believed to have committed any offence other than a Fourth Schedule offence. The police policy statement indicates that informal verbal warnings may be administered on the street, on patrol or at the station. Informal cautioning is intended for minor offences, parents need not be informed and there is no formal recording mechanism. In contrast, in Tasmania, informal cautioning appears to be outlawed by a provision in standing orders that a child shall not be cautioned for an offence unless such caution is first authorised by the division inspector (Standing Orders, 109.6).

Formal cautions and panels

Formal cautions are typically administered at a police station and authorised by a senior police officer. They normally result in a centralised record. They are regulated by standing orders or police instructions. In the territories, cautioning is the subject of limited legislative controls (*Children's Service Ordinance* 1986 (ACT) s.33; *Juvenile Justice Act* 1983 (NT) s.28(1)). Victoria and Queensland make the greatest use of cautions. In Victoria, whether or not a young person is arrested for an offence, a formal caution may be administered. A revised system of cautioning came into effect in 1991 replacing the Child Cautioning Program and the Shop Stealing Program. The new program is regulated by Force Circular Memo No. 90–11 cancelling Standing Order 5.3. Unless there are exceptional circumstances, the criteria to be satisfied are:

- sufficient admissible evidence to establish the offence;
- an admission of the offence;
- generally, no prior criminal history;
- the offender and the parent or guardian must consent;
- full circumstances of the offence must be known and any co-offender interviewed;
- no more than five victims or five separate incidents against one victim;
- no more than one prior caution.

Second cautions can only be given in exceptional circumstances, and the length of time since the first caution must be considered. Only a station commander or an officer of or above the rank of sergeant can authorise or give a caution. A caution is to be administered on the day of the interview if possible and at a police station if practicable. A parent or guardian must be present and should be contacted to attend the station. The circumstances of the offence should be explained to the parent or guardian, the reasons for the offence discussed and the formal caution read. A referral to a local Community Policing Squad or other agency may be made. If the parent or guardian cannot attend or be contacted, a notice to the parent must be handed to the child advising the parent to con-tact the station within twenty-four hours to make an appointment to discuss the matter. If no contact is made, efforts should be made to arrange an appointment for a caution. Computer records of particulars of cautions are required to be made.

In Queensland there is a cautioning program and, particularly in Brisbane, a dominant role is played by a specialist unit, the Juvenile Aid Bureau. Detailed instructions have been issued in relation to cautions. A first offender should normally be cautioned but cautions are not limited to first offenders. An admission of the offence is a prerequisite (Queensland Police Service, General Instructions, 9.500). Outside the Brisbane, South Brisbane and Fortitude Valley Districts, the decision to caution is the responsibility of the officer in charge of each police station, but the matter may be delegated to the Juvenile Aid Bureau if there is one at the station, or to the local Criminal Investigation Branch. In Brisbane, South Brisbane and Fortitude Valley either the officer in charge of the police station or the Juvenile Aid Bureau may make the decision to caution or prosecute. It is policy that, where possible, the actual cautioning or counselling be handled by Juvenile Aid Bureau staff. After initial contact with the child, immediate contact with the parents is imperative to inform them of the circumstances if they are not already involved. The police officer should then obtain the facts about the offence and all available information about the child. Every endeavour is to be made to ensure the presence of a parent or guardian at the cautioning session or interview and if they cannot be present they must be notified. The interview should generally be held at police premises. An interview in three stages is advised: first, with the parents alone, then the child, and then the parents and child together when the formal caution is administered. Records of cautions are kept (General Instructions, 9.501–9.505). Detailed statutory provisions relating to cautions are contained in the currently unproclaimed *Juvenile Justice Act* 1992, ss.11–19.

The other Australian jurisdictions use cautioning far less frequently than Victoria and Queensland. In New South Wales and Tasmania, there are detailed procedures for issuing formal cautions in police instructions, but they are rarely used and there are moves to encourage greater use of formal cautions. In New South Wales, the instructions contain the usual requirements for admission of guilt and parental consent, but they are expressly limited to summary offences or summary/indictable offences under the *Crimes Act* 1900 (NSW) ss.476 and 501 and cannot be given for motor vehicle stealing. They are not restricted to first offenders. Procedures require the decision to caution to be made after a cooling-off period, which must not be longer than fourteen days after the arrest. Parental presence at the formal interview administering the caution is required unless the young person is 16 or older and the parents refuse to attend. The Youth Justice Coalition has recommended promotion of diversion by statutory recognition of formal and informal cautioning, policy endorsement, training and state-wide monitoring (1990:244). The system for issuing cautions in Tasmania is set out in Police Standing Orders (Standing Order .109.5 and 109.6) and is currently under review on the grounds it is unwieldy and underutilised. The excluding criteria are numerous, including arrest, previous convictions or caution. Some are vague, such as the exclusion of cautions if court proceedings would be in the best interests of the child. Moreover there is little incentive in saving of police time and paperwork. Instead of formal cautions, police rely heavily on informal cautions. A new system along the lines of the Victorian system is under consideration.

South Australia has a system involving two panels which is unique not only within Australia. Other than in traffic matters alleged against young persons over the age of 16 and homicide cases, a screening panel makes all decisions to prosecute. The screening panel may refer the matter to the children's court, to a children's aid panel, or may decide that no formal action need be taken, in which case there may be a recommendation for a caution by a police officer. A screening panel consists of a police officer and a welfare officer. Their discretion is left very broad by s.7 of the *Children's Protection and Young Offenders Act* 1979 which requires merely that both the needs of the child and the need to protect the community must be considered. The legislation does not restrict referral by screening panels to aid panels on the basis of age, offence or arrest. No appearance or representation is allowed before the screening panel. Both the Police Department and the Department for Community Welfare provide their representatives with guidelines referring to the seriousness of the offence and the child's offending history. Specifically they stipulate that allegations of rape, arson, serious offences against the person or property and serious offences against good order should be referred to the children's court, as should those cases where a child has had at least two prior appearances before an aid panel. Although arrest is not made a criterion of the referral decision, Gale and Wundersitz (1989) have shown that arrest appears to be the primary determinant of a court referral, a fact which has the effect of compounding the disadvantaged position of Aboriginal youth who are apprehended by arrest much more often than their non-Aboriginal counterparts. The ratio of panel appearances to prosecutions is approximately three to two (Seymour, 1988:245).

Like screening panels, a children's aid panel consists of a police officer and a member of the Department for Community Welfare. They have no jurisdiction if the child does not admit the offence or requests that the matter be heard by the children's court. Proceedings before the panel are informal. The only people normally present are the two members of the panel, the child and one or both parents. There is no right to legal representation, but any person who has been counselling or advising the child may make submissions (Seymour, 1988:245). Children's aid panels have the power to warn or counsel the child and his or her guardian; to request the child to give a written undertaking to obey its directions; and to request the child's guardian to give a written undertaking to obey the panel's directions. The undertaking may require the child to accept supervision of a community welfare worker or to attend a training or rehabilitation program. An undertaking to make restitution to the victim or to make good the damage or loss by performing work for the victim may also be required. A second date may be set to monitor compliance with the undertaking (Seymour, 1988:246).

Western Australia combines the systems of cautions and panels. The Children's (Suspended Proceedings) Panel is governed by the *Child Welfare Act* 1947 ss.70–78. Children's panels consisting of a retired or serving police officer and an officer of the Department of Community Services have jurisdiction to deal with first offenders over the age of 10 charged with certain less serious offences which are admitted and which the child or parent elects to have dealt with by the panel. The panel may dismiss the complaint, order supervision for up to six months or refer the matter to court. It is required, in dealing with the child, to have regard to the future welfare of the child.

Legislation for a system of police cautioning was introduced in December 1990 by the *Child Welfare Amendment Act* No. 2, 1990 and was proclaimed in August 1991. The new section 33(1)(a)(i) of the *Child Welfare Act* 1947 gives a police officer a discretion to give either an oral or a written caution. A written or formal caution may be given for any offence other than those in the Fourth Schedule of the *Child Welfare Act* 1947. The cautioning criteria differ from other schemes in a number of respects. Formal cautions are not limited to first offenders and the policy statement indicates that police may caution more than once when there is a lapse of time between offences, the current or previous offence is minor or different, or the record of the child is not serious. In such cases between two and three cautions are envisaged before a different course is taken. No admission of guilt is necessary, nor is compensation or restitution necessary before a caution may be administered. The formal caution involves a verbal warning and the completion and distribution of a written form. The verbal warning can be administered at a police station, at the child's home, or on patrol, but it is desirable to have parents present. A formal caution notice is handed to the child and a copy handed or sent to the parent or guardian as soon as possible.

The report of the Legislative Review Committee recommended the abolition of the panel system on the grounds that a dual diversionary system is confusing and undesirable and the panel system alone, by diverting only 15 percent of offenders from court and so using the formal justice system to deal with juvenile offending at a much higher rate than other states in Australia, had not achieved its diversionary objectives (Legislative Review Committee, 1991:68). But the dual system has been retained with legislative recognition of cautions, and policy directives encouraging them.

Diversion in practice

There has been a policy trend in Australia towards the diversion of young offenders from the courts by means of cautioning schemes and panels. There were two objectives behind such schemes: first, to deal simply and quickly with offenders whose behaviour did not justify court action; and second, to provide early remedial intervention for troublesome but 'pre-delinquent' children (Seymour, 1988:224). It is not an easy task to determine whether either of these objectives has been achieved. Evaluations of diversion do not consistently reveal that levels of delinquency are reduced by diversionary programs (Alder and Polk, 1985). Statistics are available of the number of children formally cautioned and referred to panels. However, such statistics do not necessarily indicate the proportion of offenders who, but for the introduction of cautioning schemes or panels, would have been referred to court. It may be that as a result of the use being made of official cautions and panels, cases are being officially processed which would not previously have entered the system (Seymour, 1988:261; Alder and Polk, 1985:282). Similarly, a large proportion of cautions or panel disposals does not necessarily indicate low formal intervention rates. It is clear that care must be taken in interpreting rates of cautioning and panel disposal and in comparing jurisdictions.

The report of the New South Wales Youth Justice Coalition has reported that in Victoria some 60 percent of young suspects are formally cautioned, in Queensland the figure is nearly 70 percent, while in New South Wales only 20 percent are formally cautioned. In New South Wales there is evidence of an arbitrary and uneven use of cautioning between different areas (Youth Justice Coalition, 1990:130, 243, 244). Statistics supplied by Tasmanian police indicate that in Tasmania only about 5 percent of young suspects are formally cautioned. Cautioning data should be looked at in the context of formal intervention rates. Up-to-date data are not available, but relying on Freiberg, Fox and Hogan's (1988) data, the following can be stated. Victoria and New South Wales have similar formal intervention rates, but despite increasing reliance on cautions in New South Wales, an offender in New South Wales is much more likely to end up in court than one in Victoria. Queensland has somewhat higher total intervention rates, but this is because of higher caution rates rather than court appearances which are similar to Victoria and lower than New South Wales. Western Australia has had a very high formal intervention rate and high rates of court appearances. It remains to be seen whether the diversion rate will increase as a result of the new cautioning scheme. Preliminary indications are encouraging indicating that there has been a drop in the arrest rate and panel referrals while the summons rate has remained static. Tasmania has had a relatively low intervention rate, but a very low cautioning rate. Attempts are being made to increase the latter rate as noted above.

The current policy trend is to favour the promotion of police diversion by statutory recognition of informal and formal cautioning, policy endorsement, training and state-wide monitoring (Youth Justice Coalition, 1990:244; Legislative Review Committee, 1991:68; Department of Community Services, Tasmania, 1991:23). The criteria to be employed should be outlined in the legislation to assist principled and consistent decision making (Seymour, 1988:278; Department of Community Services, Tasmania, 1991:24). Care should be taken to ensure the criteria are not discriminatory (Challinger, 1985). Arrest should not preclude the use of a formal caution and any ambiguity in this regard should be clarified. Finally, the program should be carefully evaluated to ensure that the aims of diversion are being achieved (Alder and Polk, 1985; Youth Justice Coalition, 1990:242).

COMPLAINTS MECHANISMS

There is a well-established process for handling complaints against the police in all jurisdictions. Typically, the procedures involve referral of the complaint to an internal complaints unit with the provision for external review by an ombudsman or other body and there are no special procedures when the complainant is a young person. There is considerable variation between jurisdictions in the extent to which an independent element is built into the system at the stages of receipt, investigation and determination. The procedures for handling complaints in Victoria and Queensland will be outlined as illustrations.

Procedures for complaints against the police in Victoria are governed by the *Police Regulations Act* 1958. A complaint by a member of the public about the conduct of a member of the force may be made to another member of the force or to the deputy ombudsman (*Police Regulations Act* 1958 (Vic.) ss.86L, 86M). If made to a member of the force the complainant must be advised that the complaint may be made to the deputy ombudsman, and the chief commissioner must investigate the complaint unless it is considered trivial, vexatious or not made in good faith. Details of all complaints must be given to the deputy ombudsman in writing. If the complaint is made to the deputy ombudsman it must, subject to a number of exceptions, be referred to the chief commissioner if it warrants investigation (s.86N). Complaints that must be investigated by the deputy ombudsman include cases where the deputy ombudsman considers investigation to be in the public interest or when the conduct complained of is in accordance with established practices or procedures of the force and the deputy ombudsman considers that these practices or procedures should be reviewed. So primary responsibility for investigation for complaints lies with the chief commissioner and is usually done by the police internal investigation department. The deputy ombudsman has an overseeing role and, as well as being informed of complaints made, may request reports in writing on the progress of an investigation, must be given written reports of the results of the investigation (s.86O), and can then request further investigation of a complaint or conduct independent investigations (s.86R). Disagreement between the chief commissioner and the deputy ombudsman can be referred to the minister (s.86S). Disciplinary offences are heard either by the chief commissioner or the Police Discipline Board, comprising a magistrate, the assistant commissioner and a member of the public nominated by the minister.

Queensland has a new system for dealing with complaints against the police. The monitoring of complaints was the responsibility of a police-specific body, the Police Complaints Tribunal, but this has been replaced by the Criminal Justice Commission with duties which include the investigation of complaints of misconduct by the police. A complaint may be made to the Complaints Section of the

Criminal Justice Commission or if it is made to the police, it must be referred to the Complaints Section (*Criminal Justice Act* 1989 (Qld) s.2.28(2)). The Complaints Section assesses all complaints, and recommendations as to investigation are made to the Director of Official Misconduct (s.2.29). Investigations are either done by investigators of the Official Misconduct Division (police officers on secondment and civilian investigators) or may be referred to the Commissioner of Police for investigation by police officers. Reports of investigations must be submitted to the chairman of the Criminal Justice Commission (s.2.24).

Criticisms of investigations by the internal investigation units point out the lack of persistence in investigations by internal units, delays and premature disclosure of charges, dissatisfaction with the lack of or quality of the reporting of findings, and lack of objectivity (Freckleton and Selby, 1989:16). External review has been criticised for the adoption of a purely casework-review response rather than a review of the policy implications of practices and procedures which may, in fact, have given rise to the dissatisfaction which results in individual complaints (Freckleton and Selby, 1989:29).

Reform of complaints mechanisms is a rather blunt instrument for achieving change in the treatment of young people by the police. Nevertheless, improvements to review mechanisms could lead, not only to increased satisfaction in individual cases of alleged police malpractice and an increase in public confidence, but also to external review becoming an informed and effective instrument of change of police practices and procedures (see chapter 4). There is some indication that this is beginning to happen in some States. While the argument has some force that primary responsibility for investigating external complaints against the police should rest with the police, the ombudsman, as an external review body, should be responsible for receiving, reviewing and where necessary investigating complaints. Where complaints reveal a problem with police practices and procedures, re-investigation, with a view to identifying and assessing those practices and procedures, should take place. To this end legislation which clarifies the roles, responsibilities and powers of internal inquiry and external review bodies has been recommended (Freckleton and Selby, 1989:26).

CONCLUSION

Is the current legal framework adequate? The revival of just deserts philosophy has had an impact on the juvenile justice system. The outcome of recent reviews of juvenile justice has resulted in a shift from rehabilitation and welfare to an emphasis on the offence and deserved punishment. At the same time, recognition of the need for a separate system for young offenders has been reinforced by special measures to divert and decarcerate. What has emerged is a system which has pluses and minuses. Attention to due process at the investigatory stage by the recognition and protection of the right to silence and by requirements of the presence of an independent person during questioning is a move forward. Diversion strategies that give legislative recognition and encouragement to police cautioning and discourage the use of arrest by legislative exhortation and the provision of alternative procedures are also positive developments.

In most jurisdictions there have been many improvements to the legal framework of juvenile justice. But nowhere is it adequate. Important matters are only partially or are totally unregulated and the various systems only go a short way to structured decision making. There are glaring omissions at the investigatory phase. Some important matters are regulated by internal police instructions, but given their ambiguous status (they do not create rights, but rather specify desirable practices), and their inaccessibility, legislation is to be preferred. The absence of a legislative charter of rights for young people has been criticised. This would be particularly valuable at the investigatory stage, for currently what 'rights' that can be implied are found scattered through a variety of statutes, regulations and internal police instructions. Existing requirements for the presence of an independent adult are inadequate in most jurisdictions. Prospective statutory requirements for presence drafted to cover preliminary questioning are necessary with provisions for inadmissibility in the event of non-compliance. A statutory right to the presence of a lawyer is necessary as is the obligation to inform a young person of that right. Criteria for arrest and simple alternatives such as attendance notices should be introduced in all jurisdictions. The ideal of a clear requirement of parental notification of questioning, arrest, charge and caution is not met in all states. Some states lack any effective restrictions on fingerprinting of young suspects. Existing statutory provisions are not adequate to ensure that young people are not detained in police facilities, nor do they sufficiently provide for conditions that distinguish young and adult offenders. Few states have an adequate legal framework for encouraging the use of informal and formal cautioning with clear criteria for decision making.

Evidence of maltreatment and inappropriate processing of young people (Alder and Polk, 1985) has called into question the adequacy of existing complaint mechanisms as a method of redress. Exclusion of evidence in court, complaints to the ombudsman or an internal complaints unit of the police appear to be insufficient to remedy inappropriate treatment of young people by the police. A new mechanism or at least new initiatives are required (O'Connor, 1992:54).

The limits of the formal juvenile justice system as a response to crime should be recognised. It should not be seen as the only solution to juvenile crime, for it cannot hope to deal with the underlying causes. The danger of seeking the answers to juvenile crime in the formal justice system is that it inevitably leads to the superficial response of a 'law and order' solution on the assumption it will be effective or at least will give the appearance of doing something. A broader response which does not ignore the social and economic dimensions of juvenile crime is necessary. 'Getting tough is not an. adequate strategy' (Youth Justice Coalition, 1990:8, 36). It should not be forgotten that only a minority of offences are known to the police and even fewer are 'cleared'. The formal system is only processing the tip of the iceberg. Nor should it be forgotten that far from achieving corrective effect, getting caught up in the criminal justice system seems a primary determinant of a continued criminal career. The system neither rehabilitates nor deters.

There is another reason why the legal framework must not be viewed in isolation. There is little point in giving legal recognition to the rights of children if they cannot be asserted or are systematically ignored. There is little point in legislative exhortations to proceed by way of arrest or to reserve custody as a measure of last resort if they are systematically ignored. And the introduction of a new diversionary method as an alternative to prosecution, or an intermediate level of sanction as an alternative to imprisonment, can have a 'net-widening effect', that is, it may increase the penetration of many young offenders into the juvenile justice system (Alder and Polk, 1985; Freiberg, Fox and Hogan, 1988: para. 132). The limits of a rights-based approach are revealed by evidence that even when young people know of their rights, they are frequently unable to assert them and often suffer harm as a consequence of trying to do so (Brown, 1984; O'Connor and Sweetapple, 1988; O'Connor, 1989; O'Connor, 1992:52). There is evidence that requirements for parental presence during questioning and restrictions on fingerprinting of children are routinely ignored (Cunneen, 1990; Alder, 1992). In the case of legislative measures to encourage police to use alternatives to arrest, there is some evidence that entrenched police behaviour may be more important than legislative framework or policy directives. Changes to the legislative framework are not enough. The operation of the system must be continuously monitored to assess whether the aims of the legislation are being achieved. Currently, the lack of co-ordinated and statistical research effort into what happens when a young person is caught up in the juvenile justice system considerably impedes the development of juvenile justice policy (Freiberg, Fox and Hogan, 1988: 24).

REFERENCES

Alder, C. (1992) 'The Young People' in C. Alder, I. O'Connor, K. Warner and R. White, *Perceptions of the Treatment of Juveniles in the Legal System*. Report to the National Youth Affairs Research Scheme. Hobart: National Clearinghouse for Youth Studies.

Alder, C. and Polk, K. (1985) 'Diversion Programmes' in A. Borowski and J.M. Murray (eds), *Juvenile Delinquency in Australia*. North Ryde, NSW: Methuen.

Australian Law Reform Commission (1981) *Child Welfare*. Report No. 18.

Brown, D. (1984) 'The Centrality of Police Interrogation and the Adequacy of a Discourse of Rights', *Legal Service Bulletin*, 9:184–8.

Byrne, D. and Heydon, J.D. (1991) *Cross on Evidence* (4th Aust. edn.). Sydney: Butterworths.

Challinger, D. (1985) 'Police Action and the Prevention of Juvenile Delinquency' in A. Borowski and J.M. Murray (eds), *Juvenile Delinquency in Australia*. North Ryde, NSW: Methuen.

Cunneen, C. (1990) *A Study of Aboriginal Juveniles and Police Violence*. Sydney: Human Rights and Equal Opportunity Commission.

Department of Community Services, Tasmania (1991) *Corrective Services Legislation for Young Offenders*.

Department of Community Services, Western Australia (1986) *Functional Review: Juvenile justice*.

Faine, J. (1988) 'Just a Phone Call: Privilege or right' in I. Freckleton and H. Selby (eds), *Police in Our Society*. Sydney: Butterworths.

Freckleton, I. and Selby, H. (1989) 'Piercing the Blue Veil' in D. Chappell and P. Wilson (eds), *Australian Policing*. Sydney: Butterworths.

Freiberg, A., Fox, R. and Hogan, M. (1988) *Sentencing Young Offenders*. Sentencing Research Paper No. 11, Australian Law Reform Commission and Commonwealth Youth Bureau.

Gale, F. and Wundersitz, J. (1989) 'The Operation of Hidden Prejudice in Pre-court Procedures: The case of Aboriginal youth', *Australian and New Zealand Journal of Criminology*, 22:1–22.

Higgins, W.L. (1982) Cautioning of Juvenile Offenders: A study of the Victorian police cautioning programme. Unpublished Masters thesis, University of Melbourne.

Legislative Review Committee (1991) *Laws for People*. A review of legislation administered by the Western Australian Department for Community Services.

Lipscombe, P. (1989) *Walking the Tightrope: Rights and responsibilities in the welfare system*. Perth: Department of Community Services.

McDonald, E.M. (1981) *Up before the Judge: Perspectives of juvenile defendants in the Children's Court system*. Canberra: Report to Criminology Research Council.

McNiff, F. (1979) *Guide to Children's Court Practice in Victoria*. Sydney: CCH.

O'Connor, I. (1989) *Our Homeless Children: Their experiences*. Sydney: Human Rights and Equal Opportunity Commission.

O'Connor, I. (1992) 'Lawyers, Legal Advocates and Legal Services' in C. Alder et al., *Perceptions of the Treatment of Juveniles in the Legal System*. Report to the National Youth Affairs Research Scheme. Hobart: National Clearinghouse for Youth Studies.

O'Connor, I. and Sweetapple, P. (1988) *Children in Justice*. Melbourne: Longman Cheshire.

Queensland Law Reform Commission (1991) *To Bail or Not to Bail: A review of Queensland's law*. Discussion Paper No. 35. Brisbane: Queensland Government Printer.

Seymour, J. (1988) *Dealing with Young Offenders*. North Ryde, NSW: Law Book Company.

Staden, F. (1986) Police Questioning of Children Project: Draft Report, unpublished. Sydney: Public Interest Advocacy Centre.

Wallace-Bruce, N. (1989) 'The Juvenile Offender in New South Wales and Queensland', *Law Society Journal*, 27(7):57.

Youth Justice Coalition (NSW) (1990) *Kids in Justice: A blueprint for the 90s*. Sydney: Youth Justice Coalition.

CHAPTER 3

Cautions and Appearances: Statistics About Youth and Police

David Tait

INTRODUCTION

'Cautions' and 'appearances' are two of the key terms police use when they process young people who come to their attention. A 'caution' may be given to a young person (particularly first offenders) to warn them off the path of crime. Or charges may be laid and the young person makes an 'appearance' in court. The young people are processed a second time, this time into statistical reports, where 'cautions' and 'appearances' serve as markers of police effectiveness. This chapter looks at this statistical re-processing of young people. How are young people presented in police statistics and those of other agencies which publish police data? What is considered significant information to be presented, and what is left out? What are the questions which law enforcement agencies pose for themselves, and what answers do they come up with?

In considering the meaning of police statistics, it will become clear that this too is a world of cautions and appearances. Comparisons across time, between jurisdictions and between different types of activity, we are warned, must be made with caution (or sometimes not at all). More importantly, the interpretation of increases or decreases in reported crime, or 'cleared' offences, or prosecutions must be subject to scrutiny.

Meanwhile, appearances are the stuff of annual reports, so the various police services around Australia strive to project and sustain an appropriate image of themselves in their statistics. There may not be 'uniform' crime statistics in Australia, but there is a fascinating range of 'uniformed' crime statistics. Criminologists generally express regret that criminal justice statistics in Australia are inconsistent both in quality and definitions. From the point of view of 'reading' the assumptions and images in the statistics, however, such variety provides a rich resource and a priceless opportunity.

Police departments regret that their figures are not always accurate:

> It is an unfortunate fact that crime statistics collated by police have, for some years, been highly questionable. It cannot be asserted that this difficulty is entirely overcome yet, although greater reliance could be placed on this year's figures than previously. (Queensland Police Service, 1991:9)

However, the very 'questionable' character of the statistical reports, in terms of learning about police practices may be one of their most valuable qualities. 'The traces of the storyteller cling to the story the way the handprints of the potter cling to the clay vessel' (Benjamin, 1955:92). Archaeologists of knowledge scratch fruitlessly on the arid soil of census statistics, where the quest for technical perfection and 'technological rationality' (Marcuse, 1968:144–69) has sterilised the categories of their meaning and history. In police statistics on the other hand, the hand of the potter is still there.

MEASURES OF POLICE SUCCESS

Police services are funded by taxpayers and answerable to Parliament for their activities. One form this accountability takes is providing an annual report. Some police services complement this with a special statistical review, with more detail and less gloss than the annual report format. The Victoria Police take this approach, and produce an annual statistical review of nearly 200 pages. The Australian Institute of Criminology has attempted to put together (frequently unpublished) police data from the individual states and territories. Mukherjee (1983) and Mukherjee and Dagger (1990) were able to provide national estimates of crime based on police data. The level of professionalism in the presentation of statistics varies from states with a specialist Bureau of Crime Statistics, where selection and interpretation are included, to those in which 'the facts' are left to speak for themselves. In South Australia, the police annual report provides a statistical review replete with graphs, short tables and commentary; while in the Northern Territory Police annual report, all the statistics are placed in an appendix.

Police statistics are based on a few key concepts. The first of these is the notion of 'clearing' an offence. In popular language, this means that the offender was caught and probably punished. In police terminology, it means only that the police had charged someone with the offence, cautioned them or decided that no offence was committed. (In some 'cleared' cases, no charges would be laid for 'legal reasons', such as that the offender was under the age of 8 (Victoria Police, 1991:4).) So a charge could be laid and the person found not guilty, or perhaps the prosecutor might decide to drop the charges, but from the perspective of official police statistics, the offence was 'cleared'. In a sense it does not matter that police statistical reports choose to give a word their own specialist meaning. But it might be noted that one of the major indicators police reports use to document their success is quite blind as to whether or not the police charged the right person.

This practice might be dismissed as simply an unfortunate choice of words. But it is not an isolated aberration. Consider also that activities reported to the police are treated as 'offences' even if the activity was found by the courts to be lawful. Further, persons charged with an offence are classified as 'offenders', regardless of whether the subsequent court process finds the charges proven or not proven. (Mukherjee, Neuhaus and Walker (1990) tend to use the alternative term 'arrestee' which avoids the assumption of guilt implicit in the term 'offender'.) The police are of course entitled to use words in a way which makes sense to them, but the consistency of the assumptions behind three key statistical concepts ('clear', 'offence', 'offender') provides evidence of an underlying logic. It may reveal what 'the agent does not suspect in them, and which he does not as a rule intend to impart to other people but to keep to himself' (Freud, 1901:247) – in other words, that the person whom the police believe to have been involved in an activity has in fact violated the law. Individual police officers may not 'suspect' this assumption, and may not wish 'to impart to other people' this view. But they use a language laden with the assumption of guilt.

How does this affect young people? Very directly, in the way cautions are used. The assumption of guilt underlies the practice of cautioning young persons (or 'young offenders' as police terminology would express it). In Queensland, the police commissioner instructs police to caution juvenile first offenders where 'the offence is not of a serious nature and where guilt is admitted and satisfactory arrangements are made regarding restitution' (O'Connor, 1992:20). Cunneen points out the implications of this for Aboriginal young people in rural New South Wales is that more of them end up in court:

Almost 20% of the reasons given for issuing citations against Aboriginal youth involved the denial of the offence. What makes this point of particular significance is that for a juvenile to receive a caution he must *admit* the offence. Therefore in a sizeable number of cases Aboriginal youth are being processed by the courts because of a refusal to admit guilt in the first place. (Cunneen, 1988:14)

Formal cautions are in effect an extreme form of charge-bargaining: 'All charges will be dropped if you admit your guilt.' The opportunity of diversion, of avoiding the trauma of a court appearance, and the possibility of the stigma of a conviction: all these are available only to those who are prepared to agree that a crime was committed, and they had some responsibility for it. Diversion is available to those young people who accept themselves as they appear in police statistics, as 'offenders' responsible for 'offences' which can be 'cleared' by accepting a caution.

Diversion does appear to work, in the jurisdictions where data can be obtained, in the sense that most young people apprehended by the police do get filtered out of the system before getting convicted. The use of cautions varies considerably from about 20 percent of juveniles apprehended for summary offences in NSW, to 60 percent in Victoria or 70 percent in Queensland (Youth Justice Coalition, 1990:243). In NSW, 'informal' cautions may also be given for 'minor' street offences, in which case they would probably not even be counted as 'apprehensions' (Youth Justice Coalition:242). The extent to which formal cautions are used varies considerably within states as well, so state averages may conceal considerable diversity (Youth Justice Coalition:130).

The likelihood of a young person being diverted out of the system also varies by type of offence, with homicide naturally being the least likely offence to involve diversion. There were just over 700 young people apprehended by the police for motor vehicle theft in Queensland in 1990–91, and about another 700 for assault (figure 1; these figures are not precise (O'Connor 1992)). About a quarter of those apprehended for car theft and fully a half of those picked up for assault were diverted out of the system by means of a caution. The numbers still in the system dropped to about 500 for car theft and 350 for assault. The difference in the slopes can be clearly seen in figure 1. From the point of view of the magistrate or children's court judge, there were about one and a half times as many juveniles coming to court charged with car theft as with assault, even though

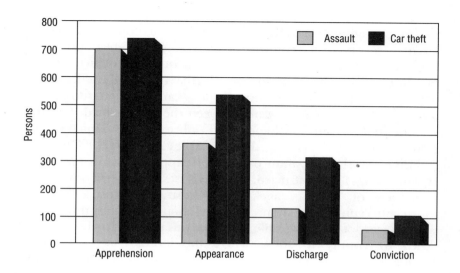

Figure 1   Juveniles apprehended by police: from apprehension to conviction, Queensland 1990–91

the original size of the groups was about the same. Some 200 of each group was 'admonished and discharged', the court's form of a caution. This left about 300 remaining in the system to appear in court charged with car theft and 130 for assault. About a third of each group was convicted, i.e. about 100 for car theft and 50 for assault. With the car-theft group, about 85 percent of the original group of those apprehended were diverted from criminalisation (if a criminal record is considered criminalisation), while with those apprehended for assaults, over 90 percent were diverted.

It might be argued that such high levels of diversion would reflect well on police performance, although as Cunneen implies, closer examination of the handling of Aboriginal young people might cast doubts on the equity of the policy. But levels of diversion are one measure of success police statisticians fail to take advantage of. Why should this be? One possibility is that the concept of the 'clearance rate' avoids the need to consider anything further down the track of the criminal justice system. Solving 'crimes' rather than restoring alleged offenders to their place in the community is the objective of police practice, and the content of police reporting procedures.

DEFINITIONS OF YOUTH AND AGE

Age groupings appear to be among the most neutral and value-free sets of categories which could be used for classifying the population. After all, what could be more objective than one's date of birth? There may be problems about the quality of birth records or the willingness of people to report their age correctly (for example to get into a pub), but surely the number of years between the date of birth and the present are free from ideological and political biases which might be thought to affect class or ethnicity (Miles and Irvine, 1979)?

This comfortable assurance quickly disappears when we see how age groupings are constructed. Early censuses established how many men were of 'military age', while Australian censuses in the nineteenth century were more concerned about how many unmarried women were of 'marriageable age': this was usually further broken down by county to show where the largest surpluses were. Demographers calculate 'dependency ratios' to find out how many people of 'labour force age' there are to pay for the services for everyone else. 'Targeted' government income support brings with it age limits for pensions, cut-off ages for family allowances, and minimum ages for dole payments. All these involve different ways of splitting up the population by age.

'Youth' is defined in various ways. A national longitudinal survey of 'youth' and the labour market included persons between 15 and 24 (Kryger, 1990). This coincides with the United Nations definition of 'youth' (Holden, 1984:5). A broad age-band recognises that maturation is a slow process, and the transition to adulthood is experienced differently according to family background, educational aspirations and the state of the labour market. Or as Max Bingham puts it in a foreword to the Criminal Justice Commission's report on *Youth, Crime and Justice in Queensland,* 'it was considered most useful to investigate the progression of juvenile offenders into adult criminality' (O'Connor, 1992:i). The law prefers clear breaks to fuzzy transitions and in most Australian jurisdictions a distinction is made between those under 17 or 18, and persons over that age. Until that age a person is considered a 'juvenile', and after that an 'adult'. Consequently, police statistics are usually presented with this age break. The distinction recognises that offenders charged by the police will usually be dealt with in a 'children's court' under this age, and by the regular courts after that age. The upper age limit of 'juveniles' is 17 in NSW, South Australia and the ACT (i.e. under 18), and 16 in the other jurisdictions.

The word 'juvenile' itself (at least outside the US) has a harsher ring than the more general word 'youth', or the sociological word 'adolescent'. In a free-association game matching adjectives to nouns, 'juvenile' would probably go with 'delinquency', 'adolescent' with 'problems' and 'youth' with anything from 'homelessness' to 'affairs'. In using the relatively rare word 'juvenile' to identify a particular group of young people, it can be argued that the subtle process of labelling people as deviant has begun. This contrasts with the term 'adolescent', as developed by G. Stanley Hall, which described a period of 'storm and stress' when the growing individual necessarily comes into conflict with the wider society (Hollingshead, 1949). The problems of the 'adolescent' are experienced by all of us as part of a normal transition to adulthood; the difficulties of the 'juvenile' are captured in police statistics.

In Victoria, the 'juvenile–adult' distinction is the first of four dichotomies used to present offender statistics (Victoria Police, 1991). Most tables also distinguish males and females. Within each of the four age/gender groups (male juveniles, male adults, female juveniles, female adults) two further breaks are made: country of birth and prior police contact. 'Foreign born' was used until 1988/89 to distinguish those born outside the old white Commonwealth from others; in the 1988/89 report, this was replaced with 'Australian born'. Those who were 'previously known to police' are distinguished from those of whom the police had no previous knowledge. All three of the other distinctions are presented separately for 'juveniles' and 'adults', thus appearing to confer on 'juvenile' crime a special identity. Australian-born juvenile offenders can be compared with overseas-born juvenile offenders, girls with boys and those known to police with others.

The juvenile–adult distinction is reinforced to some extent by writers who seek to defend young people from the charge that they are a particularly crime-prone group. Mukherjee argues that 'juveniles' are less likely to commit violent crime than adults:

> No matter how one looks at the data, it is eminently clear that juvenile boys and girls, proportionate to their population, are not overrepresented in arrests for violent offences, for example, homicide and aggravated assault. (Mukherjee, 1983:32)

What this claim amounts to is that 'adults' aged 18–24 have very high rates for these offences, leading to higher overall rates for 'adult' offending than 'juvenile' offending. In contrast, South Australian police statistics for 'offences cleared' show that young people under the age of 18 have the highest rate of apprehension for theft (larceny), the largest offence group (figure 2). For the other three large offence groups, burglary (break and enter), motor vehicle theft and serious assault, the peak is slightly later, among people in the 18–24-year-old group. Rape and murder show a similar pattern but with smaller numbers. The modal age in Australia's prison population is about 25, with a sharp decline thereafter (Walker, 1989). So even though Mukherjee is correct that 'juveniles' (as narrowly defined) have lower rates of violent offending than 'adults' (as narrowly defined), it is clear that the adolescent years from about the mid-teens to the mid-twenties is the period when people are most likely to come to the attention of the police. (Some reasons for this are discussed in chapter 5 in this volume.)

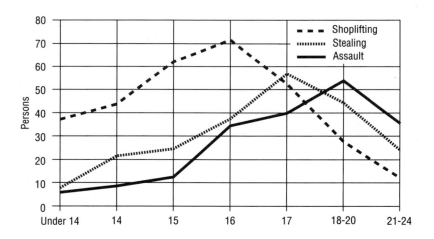

Figure 2   Offenders by age, South Australia 1990–91
Source: South Australia Police Department Annual Report 1990–91

The peak age of different offences can be seen most clearly in the Tasmanian Police Annual Report, where finer age details for young offenders is reported (figure 3). Shoplifting peaks at 16, other 'general' stealing at 17, and assault (including rape, serious and

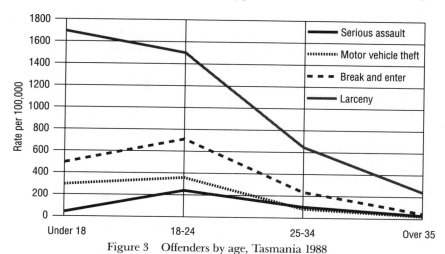

Figure 3   Offenders by age, Tasmania 1988
Source: Tasmanian Police Annual Report, 1988
Note: The 18–20 and 21–24 total divided by 3 to maintain comparability

common assault) at 18–20. These are consistent with US data reported by Mukherjee which puts the peak age for larceny (theft) at 16, robbery at 17, homicide at 19 and aggravated assault at 21 (Mukherjee, 1983:36).

Overall, the size of the youth population coming into formal contact with the criminal justice system is fairly small, about 4 percent according to an estimate by Wundersitz (1992). This ranges from about 10 percent in Western Australia to some 3 percent in New South Wales and Victoria.

CRIMES OF YOUTH

What are the most frequent offences for which 'juveniles' come to police notice? Shoplifting is by far the largest category (table 1), with breaking and entering being also widely reported.

The rates for South Australia and Queensland seem roughly comparable, with almost half of the juvenile 'offenders' listed for these selected offences being identified as involved in shoplifting and just under a quarter in breaking and entering. Crimes of violence are particularly low, with some 5 percent of the South Australian and 6 percent of the Queensland juvenile arrestees being picked up for sexual offences, robbery or assault.

Table 1 *Juvenile 'offenders' recorded by police 1990–91: selected offences, South Australia and Queensland*

	South Australia		Queensland	
Serious assault	144	(2%)	322	(4%)
Sexual offences	98	(1%)	99	(1%)
Robbery etc.	160	(2%)	69	(1%)
Breaking and entering	1758	(21%)	2179	(24%)
Motor vehicle theft	989	(12%)	679	(7%)
Shop stealing	3746	(46%)	4105	(45%)
Other stealing	1296	(16%)	1695	(19%)
Total	8191	(100%)	9148	(100%)

Sources: O'Connor (1992) and South Australia Police Department (1991)

However, there is another group of 'young' offenders who are criminalised because of their age: under-age drinkers. In Victoria in 1990–91, just over 700 juveniles (8–16-year-olds) were recorded by police statistics for this offence, some 3 percent of all juvenile offenders. About 100 of these were eventually convicted in the children's court. Another 500 'adults' (i.e. 17-year-olds) were also apprehended for under-age drinking. Other adults were criminalised in this process as well: 160 adults were charged with supplying liquor to under-age drinkers.

Most of the figures for 'juvenile crime' refer to male juvenile crime. In Victoria, 20,478 of the 24,770 juvenile offenders recorded by Victoria Police in 1990/91 – some 83 percent – were male. Some two-thirds of young women who were apprehended by Victorian police were alleged to have been involved in shoplifting (figure 4). This compares with only 23 percent of male juveniles apprehended for shoplifting by the police in that year. However, even for shop-lifting, male juvenile 'offenders' were more numerous than female 'offenders'. Of the 7500 young people apprehended for shoplifting in Victoria, 4650 (62 percent) were male. Several hundred other young women each year do not get recorded in police statistics, but get charged with not having a valid ticket on a train or using an expired ticket. Indeed at the children's court, twice as many young women appear charged with transit offences (which are mostly ticket offences) as appear on theft charges (which are predominantly shoplifting) (Victorian Attorney-General's Department, 1992).

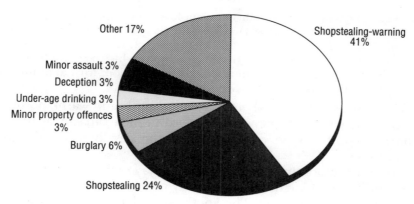

Other 17%

Shopstealing-warning
41%

Minor assault 3%
Deception 3%
Under-age drinking 3%
Minor property offences
3%

Burglary 6%

Shopstealing 24%

Figure 4   Juvenile females apprehended by police, Victoria 1990–91

THE ROLE OF YOUNG PEOPLE IN POLICE STATISTICS

Young people are overwhelmingly presented as 'offenders' in police statistics. They are not seen as students, workers, tenants or lovers. This should perhaps occasion no surprise: after all police are supposed to catch criminals, not run schools or housing programs. But we may learn something about priorities given to 'community policing' or other approaches by examining the assumptions upon which the statistics are based. What is the image of youth they present? Do police have a positive and optimistic view about the young people they come into contact with? Police as well as community service organisations usually develop a way of referring to the members of the public they come into contact with. For example, the Victorian Guardianship and Administration Board refers to those it deals with as 'customers' because the word suggests that they have a right to access the board and to be treated with dignity, although it could also suggest a 'user-pays' ethic. Other organisations refer to those for whom they provide services as 'clients' (which suggests a relationship of patronage), or 'patients'. Police reports refer mostly to 'offenders'.

Even when annual reports describe police contact with young people in innovative ways, the young people are described in their capacity as future or potential offenders. Under the heading 'Youth Diversion', the Queensland Police Department reported that

Police in the Wynnum District of Metropolitan South Region sought to respond to the high level of crime which was being committed by

young offenders, many of them unemployed and with limited prospects
of employment. The program which they developed involved a number
of police and some 29 'at risk' teenagers spending a week together
camping in a bush setting. The camp program, which began in February
1991, is designed to develop a sense of cooperation, trust and mutual
respect. (Queensland Police Service, 1991:13)

While the police-initiated program was described in warm, positive
terms, the young people were described in their capacity as future
offenders rather than contributors to the development of trust
and respect.

Another important role young people play in the criminal justice
system is that of victim. This is barely mentioned in several of the
police statistical reports. The South Australia Police Department
did present some information about victims of crime in its 1991
report. It showed that the age group most likely to be the victims
of robbery were young people between the ages of 15 and 20, and
males were twice as likely to be robbed as females (South Australia
Police Department, 1991:99). More young people had been the
victims of robberies reported to police than had been apprehended
for participating in one.

More than one young person in ten has approached the police
as a crime victim, according to one study (Alder, 1992:20, see also
Alder, 1991:1–14). If one in twenty comes to police notice as an
offender (Wundersitz, 1992), it could be suggested that more police
attention should be paid to the role of young people as victims than
as offenders. A statistical analysis of the housing, employment and
family characteristics of young victims could provide more useful
insights into possible options for crime prevention than rehearsing
the disadvantaged backgrounds of most alleged offenders.

THE OTHER STREET KIDS

Along with the young people frequently targeted by the media, there
is another group of young people who roam the streets at night,
engage in high-speed car chases, and go around looking for trouble.
These are the police themselves. As O'Connor points out, police and
other young people frequently occupy the same public spaces:
'streets, entertainment venues, shops etc.' (O'Connor, 1992:60). Most
of the patrol officers who come into contact with young people are
only a few years older than the 'juveniles' with whom they are
dealing. It is not surprising that police sometimes act a bit like other

young people. According to one study in four Australian states, about a third of young people reported being 'roughed up' by police (Alder, 1992:20). This may be slightly high, given that a third of the sample were contacted in the street or public places. But even so, it does indicate that a substantial minority of young people do experience violence at the hands of the police. Almost half of the males and over half of the Aborigines in the sample reported being 'roughed up' by the police.

What happens to these incidents in police statistics? Probably some of the violence occurs in the context of questioning about alleged offences (Cunneen, 1990:53) and may result in charges or cautions; so the incident appears in the official record with the non-uniformed young person as the 'offender'. However, a few do result in official complaints about police behaviour, and these can be found listed discreetly in annual reports.

In the 1987 report of the Tasmanian Police Commissioner, we are told that the Internal Investigation Unit had 'investigated a total of eighty-nine complaints, and of these, only nine were substantiated ... The most common complaint was of alleged assault. Thirty-five complaints were received, of which only three were substantiated' (Tasmanian Commissioner of Police, 1987:13). The 'only' helps readers to register the gap between the allegations made and the claims which were found (by the police) to be true. The Northern Territory Police reported a similar scale of complaints: 119 in 1990/91, of which 43 were for 'assaults and aggressive behaviour' (Northern Territory Police, Fire and Emergency Services, 1991:67). As with Tasmania, 'only' three were substantiated, but another 25 were still 'pending finalisation'. Four from the previous year's batch of 21 unresolved complaints of assault were also found to be substantiated.

South Australia had a larger volume of complaints, which were handled through a Police Complaints Authority (South Australia Police Department, 1991:161). In 1990/91, 1278 complaints were finalised. Of these 12 percent were 'substantiated', 25 percent 'refuted', and in 61 percent no further investigation was considered appropriate. Most complaints against Queensland police are investigated by the Criminal Justice Commission; altogether there were about 1200 a year, similar to the numbers in South Australia (Queensland Police Service, 1991:33). About 7 percent of these resulted in disciplinary action being taken.

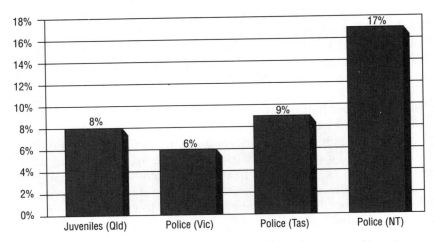

Figure 5   Alleged assaults by juveniles or police: proportion (%) found
'substantiated'

It may help to put these procedures into perspective by comparing
the 'conviction' or 'substantiation' rate for alleged assaults committed
by police with those committed by other young people. Are the
police given easier treatment? Available statistics are not particularly
accurate, but they can give some general idea (figure 5). Somewhere
between 6 and 17 percent of assault allegations result in conviction
or other disciplinary action, both for police officers and juveniles.
The Tasmanian figures give an average over three years. It appears
that most police, like other young people, 'get off' assault allegations.
In other words, police benefit to about the same degree as juveniles
from the 'diversion' practised by the criminal justice system. The
'cautions' available to juvenile arrestees (but not available to adults)
are matched by a similar leniency in relation to police officers against
whom similar offences are alleged.

Of course, the police officers would be on average a few years older
than the 'juveniles' they are being compared with. They are more
into the 'at risk' age for crimes of violence, so perhaps it is not
surprising that allegations of assault were sometimes the most
common complaints made. Whereas juveniles have the highest rates
for property offences, assault and other crimes against the person
are most common among people in the 18–20 (figure 2) or 18–24
age group (figure 1). Another comparison might be with adults

(i.e. predominantly young persons in the 18–24 age group) charged with assault against the police. In Victoria, there were about 1200 adults convicted of assaulting police in 1990–91, compared to 26 police found guilty of assaulting members of the public (Victorian Attorney-General's Department, 1991; Victoria Police, 1991). This ratio of 46 to 1 is rather surprising in the light of the prevalence of 'roughing up' reported in the Alder study described above.

The difference is less surprising when we recall that many of the allegations come from those whom, we are informed by police statistics, are 'offenders'. Allegations against the police are 'complaints', some of which are 'unsubstantiated'. Allegations against other young people are 'offences' committed by an 'offender'.

CONCLUSIONS

'Juveniles' are more likely to be recorded as 'offenders' in police statistics than adults (per head of population), although most of the 'offences' relate to fairly minor thefts or other property offences, particularly shoplifting. They also generally get filtered out of the legal system, with only about 10–20 percent of young 'offenders' being convicted. But by agreeing to be cautioned, a sizeable fraction carry a 'guilty' tag as the price for this early exit. Even though the legal process has avoided the stigma of a conviction, the police statistical process has effectively criminalised large groups of young people by branding them as 'offenders'. It could be argued that nobody reads official statistics and 'you can't believe what police statistics say anyway'. However, the view presented here is that we can learn something about how important organisations like police forces view the world by examining how they categorise their clients, and how they report their activities. The rather Manichean view of a world divided into offenders and police does not do justice to the complex social context of young people's lives, nor to the attempts of police forces to respond to these changing needs.

REFERENCES

Alder, C. (1991) 'Victims of Violence: The case of homeless youth', *Australian and New Zealand Journal of Criminology*, 24(1), March:1–14.

Alder, C. (1992) 'The Young People', in C. Alder, I. O'Connor, K. Warner and R. White, *Perceptions of the Treatment of Juveniles in the Legal System*. Report for the National Youth Affairs Research Scheme. Hobart: National Clearinghouse for Youth Studies.

Benjamin, W. (1955, reprinted 1973) 'The Storyteller' in *Illuminations*. London: Fontana.

Cunneen, C. (1988) An Evaluation of the Juvenile Cautioning System in NSW. Paper presented to Institute of Criminology seminar, Sydney University Law School, March.

Cunneen, C. (1990) *A Study of Aboriginal Justice and Police Violence*. Report commissioned by the National Inquiry into Racist Violence. Sydney: Human Rights Commission and Equal Opportunity Commission.

Freud, S. (1901, reprinted 1976) *The Psychopathology of Everyday Life*. Harmondsworth, Middlesex: Penguin.

Holden, L. (1984) *Youth: A statistical profile*. Wellington, New Zealand: Department of Internal Affairs.

Hollingshead, A.B. (1949) *Elmtown's Youth*. New York: John Wiley & Son.

Kryger, T. (1990) *The Australian Longitudinal Survey: 1985 to 1988 – Dynamics of the youth labour market*. Canberra: Australian Government Publishing Service.

Marcuse, H. (1968) *One Dimensional Man*. Boston: Beacon.

Miles, I. and Irvine, J. (1979) 'The Critique of Official Statistics' in J. Irvine, I. Miles and J. Evans (eds), *Demystifying Social Statistics* (pp. 113–29). London: Pluto.

Mukherjee, S. (1983) *Age and Crime*. Canberra: Australian Institute of Criminology.

Mukherjee, S. and Dagger, D. (1990) *The Size of the Crime Problem in Australia* (2nd edn). Canberra: Australian Institute of Criminology.

Mukherjee, S., Neuhaus, D. and Walker, J. (1990) *Crime and Justice in Australia*. Canberra: Australian Institute of Criminology.

Northern Territory Police, Fire and Emergency Services (1991) *Annual Report 1990–91*. Berrimah, NT.

O'Connor, I. (1992) *Youth, Crime and Justice in Queensland: An information and issues paper*. Brisbane: Criminal Justice Commission.

Queensland Police Service (1991) *Annual Report 1990–91*. Brisbane: Queensland Police Service.

South Australia Police Department (1991) *Annual Report 1990–91*. Adelaide: Police Department.

Tasmanian Commissioner of Police (1987) *Annual Report to Parliament*. Hobart: Government Printer.

Victoria Police (1991) *Statistical Review 1990–91*. Melbourne: Victoria Police.

Victorian Attorney-General's Department (1991) *Magistrates' Courts Victoria 1990*. Melbourne: Management Information Section, Attorney-General's Department.

Victorian Attorney-General's Department (1992) *Children's Courts Victoria 1991*. Melbourne: Management Information Section, Attorney-General's Department.

Walker, J. (1989) *Australian Prisoners 1988*. Canberra: Australian Institute of Criminology.

Wundersitz, J. (1992) Some Statistics on Youth Offending: An inter-jurisdictional comparison. Adelaide: Australian Institute of Criminology Juvenile Justice Conference.

Youth Justice Coalition (NSW) (1990) *Kids in Justice: A blueprint for the 90s*. Sydney: Youth Justice Coalition.

CHAPTER 4

Young People and Their Rights

Ian O'Connor

> The concept of children's rights brings together two of the most important twentieth century developments in the history of ideas. The first is the widespread, if not universal acceptance of the idea that every individual, solely by virtue of being human, is entitled to enjoy a full range of human rights. The second is the recognition of the idea that children shall be treated as people in their own right and not as mere appendages of, or chattels belonging to, the adults under whose responsibility they fall. By combining these two ideas it becomes clear that children are entitled to be treated as holders of human rights and that any qualification to the range of rights they are accorded by society has to be justified by reference to other human rights principles rather than to the predilections, prejudices or narrowly conceived self interest of others. (Alston, 1991:2)

The focus of this chapter is a narrow category of rights – the rights of young people in their interactions with police and the criminal justice system. The establishment, preservation and protection of these basic rights is fundamental to the ideology of the democratic state, which holds,

> that the relationships between the state and the individuals of civil society is one governed not by the arbitrary exercise of power but by power exercised within the constraints of the law. The criminal justice process is the most coercive apparatus of the state and the idea that police and courts can interfere with the liberties of citizens only under known law and by means of the *due process* of law is thus a crucial element in the ideology of the democratic state. (McBarnet, 1981:8)

In this chapter the rights of young people in regard to police are identified. The limited scope of these rights, and the gap between the actuality and the rhetoric of rights is discussed. It is argued this gap results from the lack of enforceable rights, young people's limited knowledge of their rights and the fact that respect for rights is not part of the routine policing of young people. Additionally the structures developed to assist with the assertion and protection of rights, the provision of legal assistance, the courts and police complaints authorities, are inadequate for the task.

RIGHTS

The ideology of the rule of law within a liberal democratic state implies the establishment and respect of certain basic rights of the citizen in the criminal justice system. In abstract terms, the implied rights derive from the restriction of state interference in the liberty of the citizen to those circumstances laid down in law, according to the due processes of the law. Thus, within the Australian criminal justice system, the individual is presumed innocent of wrongdoing, should not be intimidated or overborne in any investigation of wrongdoing, does not have to incriminate him or herself and may only be detained in limited circumstances. If charged, allegations must be proved beyond reasonable doubt and the individual may appeal against court decisions to higher courts.

Rights however are not just broad statements of principles. Nor can rights simply be equated with claims. In the context of the criminal justice system in which the state is empowered to use coercive power against the individual, rights must be conceptualised as entitlements which, if necessary, are legally enforceable (Freeman, 1983). To claim a right successfully requires knowledge of the right, acknowledgment of that right by the other against whom the right is claimed, and mechanisms to enforce the recognition of the right and remedies for any breach of the right.

The rights and responsibilities of young people are discoverable in a myriad of legislation and case law which apply to citizens of all ages, and in specific legislation and case law applying only to young people (see Freiberg, Fox and Hogan, 1988; Seymour, 1988). For young people, the police constitute the first point of contact with the criminal justice system and the protection and recognition of their rights in their encounters with police is essential to their fair treatment in the criminal justice system. To exercise their rights in interactions with police, young people need knowledge of their rights and acknowledgment and respect of those rights by police. Similarly, police need a clear statement of the rights of young people in the criminal justice system. Yet in no Australian state is there a clear statement of children's rights in interactions with police (Warner, 1992).

The difficulty and complexity of discovering and exercising rights is illustrated by one of the most common situations encountered by young people – being stopped by the police and being requested to provide, at a minimum, name and address. In Queensland, at common law, while a police officer is perfectly entitled to ask for a citizen's name and address, the citizen is perfectly entitled not to supply it. However, there are provisions in at least twenty statutes which enable the police to demand a person's name and address (Criminal Justice Commission, 1991). These statutes range from the *Transport Act* (s.71), the *Local Government (Queensland Street Mall) Act* (s.35) to the *Drugs Misuse Act* (s.22).

The lack of clarity of the rights of young people is further exemplified by the situation of young people who have been apprehended or who 'voluntarily assist police with their inquiries'; that is, the rules related to the investigation of offences and the interrogation of suspected offenders. The courts have recognised that children may be vulnerable in such situations and may not, for example, be able to assert the common law right to silence during police interrogation. Thus, in all Australian jurisdictions, children must be questioned in the ˙presence of their parent or of an independent person (see chapter 2).

However, even in relation to this 'right', the scope and intent is unclear. Doubt remains as to at what point prior to the formal questioning, the independent person should or may be present. There is no clear statement of the role (and the requisite knowledge needed to fulfil the role) of the independent person. The assumption that a parent will adequately safeguard the rights of the child in an interrogation is questionable (Human Rights and Equal Opportunity Commission, 1989). A parent is as potentially likely as the child to be ignorant of his or her legal rights, the legal rights of the child and the legal rights and responsibilities of the independent person in a police interrogation. A parent may also feel intimidated. Alternatively, he or she may see the role of the independent person as one of assisting the police to clear the matter up. Notably, most jurisdictions do not provide a statutory right for the child to make a telephone call or to have a lawyer present for any questioning.

The only controls on police practice in this context are the retrospective exclusion of evidence by courts and/or complaints to police complaints authorities. The efficacy of court review depends, at a minimum, on the matter being brought to the court's attention through the young person challenging voluntariness of the confession. Without a formal statement of rights (and given the existing inadequate standard and availability of legal services), children have nothing by which to judge the appropriateness or legality of their experiences with police, except their own experiences and those of other young people (McMillan, 1992; O'Connor and Sweetapple, 1988:16–29; see also Human Rights and Equal Opportunity Commission, 1989, chapter 21).

Thus, in part, the gap experienced by young people between rights rhetoric and rights practice in the criminal justice system is due to both the lack of rights generally and the ambiguity of existing rights. Within the present legal system, it is simply impossible to specify unequivocally the rights of a young person (or other accused person). The entitlements that young people can confidently claim in their encounters with police are blurred from the outset, discoverable only after detailed consideration of case and statute law. If defining the rights of young people is difficult in the abstract, seeking to claim and enforce rights in reality is even more so.

YOUNG PEOPLE AND THEIR ENCOUNTERS WITH POLICE

The functions of policing

Rights are not exercised in a vacuum: their recognition is negotiated in the many encounters between individuals and the police. In relation to youth, these encounters principally occur in the course of police performing their functions of order maintenance (responding to the perceived threat from youth in their use of public spaces), law enforcement (focusing on the apprehension of offenders and the clearing of crimes) and welfare (Youth Justice Coalition, 1990:231–2). (As this chapter focuses on the rights of young people in the criminal justice system, the welfare functions of police are not discussed, though it is noted that police decisions to divert a young person from the criminal justice system may be influenced by welfare concerns (see James and Polk, 1989:42–3).)

The performance of police functions is influenced by police beliefs about young people generally, and their involvement in crime specifically. In this section the extent of youth involvement in crime is first considered. It is then argued that rights have little or no place

in the routine performance by police of their functions of order
maintenance and law enforcement – functions in which police
activity is primarily focused on the young.

Young people are a problem population for police. They are
overrepresented in crime statistics and are perceived as a threat to
public order in their use of public space. Juveniles are disproportionately involved in the crimes cleared by police in Australia
(Mukherjee and Dagger, 1990; Potas, Vining and Wilson, 1990).
However, the extent of overrepresentation must be closely examined,
for juvenile crime has particular characteristics. Juveniles are overrepresented in property related offences (e.g. stealing, break and enter,
motor vehicle theft, etc.) and underrepresented in more serious
offences, including offences of personal violence (Mukherjee, 1985;
O'Connor, 1992b). This is illustrated by the police records of
juvenile involvement in cleared crime in Queensland. In that state
in 1990/91, 30.6 percent of all juvenile offences involved shoplifting.
Breaking and entering constituted 20.9 percent of juvenile offences,
and other stealing (excluding motor vehicle theft and shop stealing)
accounted for 18.4 percent of juvenile offences. On the other hand,
offences against the person comprised only a small proportion of
juvenile offences (see O'Connor, 1992b:10).

Juveniles' proclivity for involvement in petty property offences is
even clearer when the offender data are examined (rather than offence
data as above). Over half (52.1%) of all juvenile offenders apprehended
by police in 1990/91 were involved in shoplifting or other stealing
(excluding motor vehicle theft). Approximately a fifth (19.6%) of
children apprehended were involved in break and enter offences. The
police data, therefore, indicate that most juvenile offenders are not
involved in the commission of serious offences.

There is a public perception that children are responsible for a
substantial proportion of crime committed in the community.
According to data supplied by the Queensland Police Service in that
state in 1990/91, 33.8 percent of cleared break and enter offences were
attributed to juveniles, as were 31.6 percent of stealing offences
(excluding motor vehicle theft) and 24.4 percent of motor vehicle
theft. In contrast, adults were primarily responsible for offences of
violence against the person. Juveniles were involved in 3.4 percent
of cleared homicide related offences (e.g. murder, manslaughter,
attempted murder and dangerous driving causing death), 8.4 percent
of serious assaults, 8.7 percent of minor assaults, 4.1 percent of rapes

or attempted rapes and 4.9 percent of other sexual offences (see O'Connor 1992b:73–9 for police crime data 1985–86 to 1990/91).

Caution must be exercised in extrapolating from the cleared crime figures to the overall responsibility of juveniles for crime in the community. Police arrest figures record the age of offenders for crimes cleared, but not the age of offenders for crimes reported but unsolved. In 1990/91 only 13 percent of break and enter offences in Queensland were cleared by police. This means that less than 5 percent (4.4%) of all break and enter offences reported to police were cleared and attributed to juveniles by police.

It is not tenable to conclude that juveniles are responsible for the vast majority of uncleared property offences. This is so for a number of reasons. There is evidence that juveniles are more likely to be apprehended for the property offences for which they are responsible, and the value of the property involved in crimes committed by juveniles is substantially less than that involving adults (Mukherjee, 1983). In contrast to adults, juveniles tend to offend in groups. In consequence, for each offence cleared a number of juvenile offenders may be charged with a number of offences (Mukherjee, 1986). Children tend to offend closer to their own place of residence, again increasing their chances of apprehension. A recent analysis of reported and cleared crime in Australia concluded that 'contrary to the prevailing wisdom juveniles commit a small proportion of total crimes in Australia' (Mukherjee, 1991:15).

Despite these statistics, juvenile involvement in crime is frequently misrepresented in media campaigns calling for tougher policing of the young. These campaigns are associated with enactment of laws specifically designed to crack down on youth offending (e.g. the enactment by Western Australia of the *Crimes (Serious and Repeat Offenders) Sentencing Act*; see White, 1992a). They also lead to fear of crime and specifically fear of youth crime. The extent of fear of youth crime was evident in a 1987 Australian Bureau of Statistics survey of Queensland householders which found that the most commonly perceived crime problems were 'housebreaking and burglary' (21%) and 'louts or youths' (18.8%). This survey found that an estimated 235,000 persons (16.9%) had seen or heard someone acting in a suspicious manner in the previous six months (Australian Bureau of Statistics, 1987:14). The most commonly observed problems were prowlers (101,500 persons) and louts or youth (76,400 persons). There is a clear perception that youth, especially youth in public places, pose a risk to public safety.

This perception of the extent and severity of youth crime provides the context within which police perform their functions. Police do not simply react to this context. They are active players in shaping it through their use of the media. For example, in 1991/92 the Queensland Police Service announced an operation to reduce crime. The target of this operation was children. Children 'loitering on foot paths and at milkbars' were to be stopped and questioned and were to have their personal details recorded (*Courier Mail*, 28 November 1991). The police spokesman stated 'we are trying to protect property by nipping things in the bud'. The officer justified the program by stating that 80 percent of property crime was committed by juveniles – a clearly nonsensical claim (O'Connor, 1992b).

The belief that youth are both criminal and disorderly is coupled with the belief that young people are disrespectful of authority in general and police in particular. The NYARS project found that 44 percent of police believed that most young people had little respect for authority or the police. A further 32 percent believed about half had little respect for police (White, 1992b). James and Polk noted that the reliance on authority, or the threat of its application, 'is the primary means by which police have to deal with offenders and troublesome people' (James and Polk, 1989:49). Youth are perceived by police to challenge, or actively to refuse to recognise their legitimate authority.

The performance by police of their functions is framed within their beliefs about the criminality and attitude of young people. In relation to the function of order maintenance, the perception that youth occupying public spaces are a threat leads to the police frequently stopping and questioning young people. The young people are often directed to move on by the police. Such routine encounters call into question the right of citizens not to answer police questions and to peacefully carry on their activities unimpeded.

Rights talk, however, has no place in such interactions. Where the legitimacy of the police approach is contested, the encounter frequently escalates into conflict and/or the arrest of the querulous youth for street or other minor offences (Flowers, McIntyre and Loughman, 1992). The young person who stands on his or her rights and refuses to answer police questions directly contests the authority of the police and is perceived to impede the performance of their functions:

These points can be illustrated by the following account (from a police statement) of an encounter between officers and a male juvenile. His 'suspicious activity' was to watch a police car which drove past him. The officers (P) turned back and approached him (S):

P: What's your name?

S: I don't have to tell yous nothing, my lawyer said to tell you nothing . . .

P: How come you were so interested in what we are doing?

S: I'm not telling you anything . . . I know my rights . . .

P: Look mate don't play silly buggers alright, all we want to do is search you for some ID. You seemed pretty agitated when you saw us back there . . .

S: I know me rights you can't do this . . .

P: All right mate, do you know what section 357E of the Crimes Act is? Well you've given reasonable cause to believe you are in possession of something you shouldn't be and that gives us the power to stop search and detain you . . .

S: Yous are going to get shit for this, I'm telling my lawyer, yous are going to get a false arrest against yous . . .

P: Look mate you don't seem to know your rights like you keep telling us. You've resisted and hindered us in our duty so I'm taking you to (a police station) where we can sort this out. (Youth Justice Coalition, 1990:235)

As the Youth Justice Coalition (1990) notes, in the context of order maintenance, police regard narrowly defined rights and legal provisions as out of place. Indeed, the attempt to claim rights is itself regarded as indicative of previous contact with police and therefore warranting further investigation.

Young people also figure centrally in the performance of the police's law enforcement function. Young people are overrepresented in the arrest figures for property crime. But as noted above, despite claims to the contrary, most juvenile crime is petty. It is also routine work for police. The clearing of crimes committed by juveniles primarily results from juveniles being caught in the act, and/or their confessing or otherwise acknowledging guilt. Thus, the routine processing of young offenders is underpinned by the acknowledgment of guilt by the young person which circumscribes the need for a detailed investigation of an offence and the construction of a case to prove the guilt of the young person beyond reasonable doubt in court (McBarnet, 1981). Just as standing on rights is out of place in street policing, it is equally out of place in routine clearing of juvenile crime. The routine investigation and the bulk clearing of crime by police relies heavily on the child not exercising his or her rights. In the next section, it is argued that the nature of the encounter between young people and police is structurally not conducive to claiming rights.

Young people's experience of being policed

The belief that police (and other authority figures) respect the rights of young people is not part of the taken-for-granted world of young people (Cunneen, 1990; O'Connor, 1989; O'Connor and Tilbury, 1986; O'Connor and Sweetapple, 1988). The nature of the encounter between young people and police, and the context in which the encounter occurs ensures the waiving of rights by the suspect.

The NYARS report on the treatment of juveniles in the legal system was based on interviews with children, police and lawyers in Queensland, Victoria, Tasmania and Western Australia (Alder, O'Connor, Warner and White, 1992). The purposive sample of young people aged 16 and 17 years was drawn from schools (40%), malls and public places (30%) and youth services (30%). Eighty percent of this group of young people reported being stopped and questioned by police (Aboriginal young people, unemployed young people and young males had higher rates of contact). A third of those interviewed reported being roughed up and a half reported being taken to a police station. Of those who were taken to the police station 28 percent reported being told about their rights, 21 percent were allowed to make a phone call and 35 percent reported being fingerprinted. Seventy percent stated that the police yelled or swore at them and 40 percent said they had been hit by police (see Alder, 1992).

Lawyers and legal advocates who had extensive involvement with children were also surveyed in the NYARS project (O'Connor 1992a). They reported a pattern of police–youth interaction similar to that reported by the young people. Seventy percent of respondents indicated that most young people were not well treated during police investigation of offences and many young people were not warned of the right to remain silent. Most had been denied access to legal advice (though not to their parents) and most had been verbally intimidated prior to or during questioning. Seventy percent of lawyers and legal advocates indicated that they did not believe that young people could assert their right to remain silent during police questioning. They believed this was primarily because the power imbalance between police and young people was too great. Two-thirds of those interviewed knew of specific incidents where young people had suffered negative consequences for asserting their rights during questioning. These negative consequences included physical and verbal abuse, increased charges and ongoing harassment.

The NYARS results were consistent with other recent studies which have considered police–youth interactions and which have found that threat and violence are not uncommon elements of police–youth encounters (Alder and Sandor, 1990; Cunneen, 1990; Federation of Community Legal Centres [Victoria], 1991; McMillan, 1992; O'Connor and Sweetapple, 1988; Youth Justice Coalition, 1990). Elsewhere (O'Connor and Sweetapple, 1988) on the basis of a series of in-depth interviews with children appearing before children's courts in Brisbane, I argued that the language and logic of threat, violence and intimidation formed the backdrop to all young people's interactions with police. The degree of un-pleasantness of the encounter with police was directly related to the degree of acquiescence by the child (O'Connor and Sweetapple, 1988). Children who confessed, who did not seek to exercise the right to remain silent or seek to call a lawyer and who voluntarily accompanied the police to the station received, from the child's point of view, good treatment. This treatment was only 'good' in the context of the child's own expectations of normal treatment by police. None of those who received 'good treatment' questioned the appropriateness of their arrest rather than summons, of being fingerprinted, photographed and processed through the watch-house.

Not all young people experience direct violence or threats, but that it occurs is part of their taken-for-granted knowledge of the world. Such expectations are functional for they ensure that many children commence their encounters with police from a position of fear and submission:

Q: What about the police who arrested you?
Luke: Oh, they were good
Q: Did they say anything to you when they arrested you [for stealing as a servant with three other boys]?
Luke: Oh, they said, told me to tell Dad what I'd done, and I did, and they said, me, that I took $2,000, and I was scared so I said I did, which I didn't.

Q: The police told you that you'd taken $2,000?
Luke: Yes.
Q: And you were so scared that you agreed, even though you hadn't
          done it?
Luke: Yeah.
Q: But you still reckon they were OK?
Luke: Yeah.
Q: Why do you reckon they were OK when they said to you that
          you did something that you didn't do?
Luke: Because I thought that the police yell at you and all that. They
          didn't.

Paul, who reported being threatened by police, also emerged from
questioning satisfied he had been well treated by police:
Paul: Considering, yeah, they did treat us quite well. Once they got
          what they wanted, they did treat us quite well.
Q: Once they had got you to answer questions?
Paul: Yep. (O'Connor and Sweetapple, 1988:24–5)

In the O'Connor and Sweetapple study, children who did not
comply with police demands were subject to intimidation and/or
overt violence; as a result confessions and compliance were extracted.
This paved the way for the non-problematic processing of the child
by the court. More importantly, such occurrences provided the
context for ongoing interactions between police and young people.

> The gross power discrepancy between child and police and the belief
> that the exercise of police power was unreviewable, regardless of any
> excess in its exercises formed part of the child's taken for granted world.
> In this context children were accepting of all but the grossest abuses of
> power. Given these conditions consent and submission flowed naturally
> from most children and there is no need to exercise physical force.
> (O'Connor and Sweetapple, 1988:29)

Leaving aside the issue of violence, the nature of the investigatory
process is essentially a hidden one. Citizens who accompany or are
taken by police to the station are there alone. Their access to others,
including lawyers, is only with the permission of the investigating
police. For all intents and purposes, permission to leave the station
resides with police. Unlike the court room, what happens in
the police station is hidden from public view. The Criminal Justice
Commission (1991:33) has noted 'that once in the station, he/she is
less likely to exercise his/her right to silence than if he/she
were elsewhere'. Citing McBarnet (1981) the commission further
pointed out:

Alone with the police, the accused is exposed to only one version of how the law defines his behaviour, how the evidence looks against him, be he innocent or guilty, and what his chances are in court. Given their own involvement, interests and indeed beliefs in the case, the police are likely to create, with the best will in the world a sense of pending conviction which makes co-operation, not silence, the only sensible reaction. (McBarnet in Criminal Justice Commission, 1991:33)

McBarnet (1981) and the Criminal Justice Commission (1991) were discussing adults. The circumstances they describe can only be exacerbated when the accused person is a child (see also Human Rights and Equal Opportunity Commission, 1989, chapter 21).

Police exercise extensive discretion in their processing of young offenders. Out of one incident, they may decide to deal with the matter formally (e.g. arrest or summons) or informally (caution, panel or no action), to press one or a number of charges, to arrest or summons, to oppose bail and so on. The manner in which police exercise this discretion is influenced by structural and personal factors and by the extent to which the young person is perceived to have co-operated with the police, their attitude to the offence and their attitude to police. Police officers interviewed for the NYARS research indicated that the degree of co-operation (96%), the seriousness of the offence (97%), and the young person's attitude (89%) were very important factors in influencing their decision to deal with a young person formally or informally. 'In other words, police use of discretion is not only the product of the nature of the offence but is also very much influenced by the nature of the direct interaction between young people and themselves' (White, 1992b:32).

The process by which police effect their functions of order maintenance and law enforcement results in covert and overt breaches of the rights of the young. Our legal system does, however, provide for assistance in the claiming of rights, and mechanisms for the protection and enforcement of the rights of young people. It is the adequacy and efficacy of these mechanisms that are considered next.

THE PROTECTION AND ENFORCEMENT OF THE RIGHTS OF YOUNG PEOPLE

The existence of a right in no way guarantees an individual's ability to exercise that right. A precursor to the exercise of a right is

knowledge of the existence of the right. There are three main
mechanisms by which the recognition of rights are enforced and
breaches remedied:
(a)   legal services for young people;
(b)   the operation of the courts as review mechanisms; and
(c)   police complaints systems.
As a mechanism for protecting and safeguarding rights of young
people each alternative is presently flawed.

Legal services

Our system of criminal law explicitly acknowledges that lone
individuals are not in a position to enforce their rights and safeguard
their interests in legal proceedings. Knowledge of the law and legal
processes and strategies for enforcing and safeguarding legal rights
are the occupational preserve of the legal profession. While the law
impacts on every aspect of daily life, access to lawyers is not as
universal. Theoretically, any person may avail him/herself of the
services of a legal advocate, but the reality of the free market is that
legal advice and representation is available on demand only to those
with economic means. For the rest, assistance is not available, or only
available on more limited terms and conditions as dictated by the
state or by non-government organisations.

The mere provision of general legal services will not ensure either
their appropriateness for, accessibility to, or utilisation by young
people.

> Accessibility is not a passive concept in legal aid policy. It is natural
> to think of access in terms of 'allowing' entrance or admittance to a
> system. In fact legal aid policy must 'create' access, it must create paths
> to services and enable people to use services. (Australian Council of
> Social Services, 1980:43)

Accessibility to legal services for young people would be enhanced
by ensuring that appropriate services are provided in conditions
where they may be utilised. At present, young people, and disadvantaged young people in particular, are confronted with a series
of structural barriers to accessing appropriate legal services. Five of
these barriers are discussed below: cost; young people's lack of
knowledge; youth workers' lack of legal knowledge; non-provision
of legal assistance for police questioning; and the duty lawyer system.

Lawyers cost money. Few young people are in a position to retain a lawyer. Their access to lawyers is primarily through the services provided by legal aid commissions and community legal centres. The legal needs of young people are peripheral to legal aid commissions and most community legal centres (Human Rights and Equal Opportunity Commission, 1989; National Legal Aid Advisory Committee, 1990; O'Connor and Tilbury, 1986; O'Connor, 1992a). It is worth noting that one of the small advances made since the Legal Aid Needs of Youth research was undertaken (O'Connor and Tilbury, 1986) is that there are increased numbers of specialised children's lawyers either employed by the commissions or by specialist children and youth legal centres. However, across Australia the total numbers still remain very small (less than fifteen).

Second, though knowledge of rights is a precondition to their exercise, no legal aid commission provides a comprehensive community legal education program for young people. Commissions continue to provide community legal education in a relatively ad hoc manner, responding to individual requests and individual issues. This is not to deny that individual commissions do sponsor or undertake some useful projects (e.g. the Legal Aid Commission of Victoria produced a booklet on police powers). A number of community legal centres and specialist youth legal centres are more actively engaged in creative educational strategies such as, for example, the Streetwize Legal Comics and Youth Advocacy Centre's legal education game 'Take Control'. (See O'Connor and Tilbury, 1986 and O'Connor, 1992a for discussion of community legal education for young people in Australia.) In the NYARS research, only five legal centres in Australia reported involvement in legal education programs for youth in detention centres – those youth most at risk of conflict with the criminal justice system. Only one centre reported regular involvement for programs for youth in detention (O'Connor, 1992a:47). Until there is a comprehensive and co-ordinated legal education for young people, youth will continue to express ignorance of their legal rights and their prime source of knowledge will remain their own and their friends' lived experience of interactions with police.

The third barrier hindering young people's access to legal service is that access to legal resources is frequently provided by way of intermediaries – friends and professionals. Just as there is no comprehensive legal rights education for young people, there is a similar dearth of education for youth workers. Legal aid commissions and community legal centres provide education to youth workers on an ad hoc basis. Thus youth workers are often ignorant of their own and their clients' legal rights and are pessimistic about potential legal solutions (O'Connor and Tilbury, 1986; but see also Underwood, White and Omelczuk, 1993; and White, Underwood and Omelczuk, 1992).

Fourth, even if young people were knowledgeable of their rights they would experience considerable difficulties accessing legal assistance when it is needed. The services delivered and the manner in which the services are delivered are not conducive to the protection of rights. Legal services are available primarily in office hours and consequently are not available at night and on weekends when young people are most likely to be at police stations (Human Rights and Equal Opportunity Commission, 1989; National Legal Aid Advisory Committee, 1990). In the NYARS survey, only one legal aid commission, the South Australian Commission, reported that it provided assistance for young people during police interrogations. Such assistance was provided only for serious offences which involve only a very small proportion of juvenile offenders. No commission routinely provided assistance in police questioning. Only six legal centres attended police questioning out of office hours (O'Connor, 1992a).

It is during apprehension, interrogation and questioning that most violations of young people's rights occur. This is the most hidden aspect of the child's contact with the criminal justice system and the stage at which the child is most vulnerable. As discussed above, the disability children suffer in the interrogation has long been recognised by the courts:

> many people because of subjective matters such as immaturity, illiteracy or backwardness, or senility or alcoholism suffer pressures in police interviews that can result in errors and injustices in the later judicial processes. Some of these people are suggestible and will agree to things that are not correct. (Committee of Inquiry into the Enforcement of the Criminal Law in Queensland, 1977:103)

At the very point at which young people most need legal assistance, such assistance is not available. The admissions gained at this stage provide the basis for guilty pleas and hence the subsequent non-problematic processing of children in court.

Finally, most children's access to legal services is by way of duty lawyers at the court at which they appear on the day on which they appear. The young person's interview with a duty lawyer is usually his or her first contact with a lawyer over the particular offence. In most states, duty lawyers deal with guilty pleas and bail applications. Most young people meet the duty lawyer shortly before entering court and the duty lawyer will represent a number of children on any one day. There are substantial time pressures on the duty lawyer to interview the accused child quickly, ascertain their legal situation and obtain instructions. Such interactions are not conducive to a detailed discussion of the child's treatment at the hands of the police. As children expect rough treatment, only excesses of police violence are raised with the duty lawyer. The 'informal' questioning prior to the arrival of the independent person, the photographing, fingerprinting and the processing through the watch-house are rarely discussed (see Flowers et al., 1992 for summary of critiques of duty lawyer services; McMillan, 1992).

Thus, the primary mode of providing legal assistance to the young is premised on the assumption of the young person's guilt and aims to provide speedy and (cost) efficient legal services to the young person in court. Far from leading to an active contesting of the elements of the case, or indeed focusing upon the context in which admissions were made, the duty lawyer system facilitates the smooth and routine processing of guilty pleas by juvenile offenders. Additionally, few lawyers have specific expertise in dealing with young people. Some share the community attitude of hostility to the young. Others trivialise the importance of the jurisdiction or the potential outcome for young people. Those specialist children's lawyers or aberrant duty lawyers who do not take the guilt of the child for granted quickly feel the social pressure of other members of the court for slowing down the wheels of justice (McMillan, 1992).

The courts

Courts stand at the symbolic heart of the criminal justice system – they protect the poor and vulnerable, ensure that the rights of the accused are protected and that the innocent walk free. It is in court that individuals may seek retrospective remedies for breaches of their rights as a suspect. Courts may review the voluntariness of confessional evidence and circumstances surrounding any admissions by the defendant. Improperly obtained evidence may be excluded. The correctness of police decisions and the appropriateness of police behaviour in apprehending a young person for a street offence may be scrutinised by pleading not guilty and requiring the police to prove the offence.

There is, however, little evidence that courts play a significant role in monitoring and remedying abuses of young people's rights by police. Many situations (for example, some street altercations between police and young people, or where a child has been interviewed and released) in which young people believe their rights have been infringed never come before the courts because no charges are ever laid. The reasons for the courts' failure to play a monitoring and protective role flow directly from the manner in which offences are constructed and dealt with in court.

The criminal courts in Australia are supposedly adversarial. The adversarial contest is primarily reflected in the trial process where allegations must be proved beyond reasonable doubt. Trials are, however, the exception rather than the rule in summary courts (McBarnet, 1981; Naffine, Wundersitz and Gale, 1990). Most offences are dealt with summarily and are resolved by way of a plea of guilty. For children, 'not guilty' pleas and acquittals are rare events. For example, in Queensland in the five-year period 1986/87 to 1990/91, over 95 percent of matters were dealt with summarily by children's courts. In nearly all of these cases, the young person pleaded guilty. In 1990/91 in only 2.5 percent of appearances was the most serious charge withdrawn or discharged (O'Connor, 1992b). Naffine, Wundersitz and Gale note that the trial is not at the centre of summary justice, rather the main task of summary courts is one of sentencing: 'In other words, the task of the court is simply to decide what to do with confessed offenders' (1990:204).

For courts to play any, let alone an effective role in enforcing respect for children's legal rights in their encounters with police, it is necessary for the matter to be brought to the court's attention. Most children come to court believing or accepting that they are legally guilty. Most legal services are provided on this assumption. The routine processing of the children by duty lawyers and the courts hinders the performance of any monitoring role by the court.

The manner in which cases are constructed and processed by courts further limits any monitoring role by the court. In dealing with a guilty plea, the court focuses on the event defined as the offence and mitigating or aggravating factors surrounding such. Many young people acknowledge guilt for the specific event(s), but want surrounding matters placed before the court. Duty lawyers, in constructing pleas of mitigation, often warn children against bringing irrelevant matters to the court's attention on the grounds that such comments may aggravate the court:

> Children commonly report making allegations against police and other authority figures during their initial interview with the duty solicitor. Even if they plan to plead guilty, many children believe it is only fair that the whole story surrounding their misbehaviour is aired in court. Yet this is not often done, even when children allege that misbehaviour by police was the cause of their own misbehaviour. Some lawyers may be reluctant to repeat children's allegations against others in court since they rarely contribute to the traditional form of a plea of mitigation. The focus of the court and of the lawyers who staff them is on the alleged misbehaviour of the child before the court and the child's allegations are therefore dealt with in a vacuum if they are aired at all. (O'Connor and Sweetapple, 1988:55–6)

In nearly all cases involving young people, courts do not review the evidence, the circumstances surrounding the appearance or the appropriateness of the plea. Thus, its role is to sentence rather than to monitor or safeguard the child's rights during the investigatory phase. Most young people are not repeat players in the court system. They cannot pick and choose which cases they will defend and which cases they will concede to protect future legal prospects. Indeed, defendants who are repeat players in criminal courts are disadvantaged in that they are known criminals, are likely to receive harsher penalties and so on. (See, for example, White, 1992a, on repeat offender legislation in Western Australia.)

Though police are repeat players, they are not disadvantaged by this status. They enter all encounters with young people with the foreknowledge that nearly every matter that proceeds to court is disposed of by way of a guilty plea and/or finding of guilt. A 'not guilty' plea and an acquittal is an *extra*ordinary event – the policing of young people is constituted by ordinary, everyday events. The police know it is a rare incident that will be scrutinised by the court. Thus, the court does not operate as an effective mechanism to enforce or safeguard the rights of the young person.

Police complaints

The second major institutional mechanism that retrospectively reviews and potentially remedies abuses of the rights of young people in their encounters with police and the criminal justice system is the various police complaint bodies and tribunals. The NYARS research found that while young people, legal services and legal advocates all reported that abuse of young people and their rights was a regular occurrence, young people rarely complained to these bodies. Similarly, lawyers, legal advocates or youth workers rarely lodged complaints on behalf of young people (O'Connor, 1992a).

This failure to resort to complaints mechanisms is partly explained by those factors which accounted for the failure of courts to effectively review police behaviour. Thus, those who are most at risk are already most disadvantaged: economically disadvantaged young people, ethnic youth and Aboriginal and Torres Strait Islander youth. Their first access to legal advice is duty lawyers whose primary task is to deal with guilty pleas. Unless the individual has been badly abused, his or her treatment by the police will not even be raised with the lawyer. Most encounters with police are in private. Any complaints depend on the individual child's or their friends' words against the representatives of legitimate state authority.

In some states (e.g. Victoria, Western Australia and Tasmania), police complaints systems are not independent of the police. In other states some young people and their advisers do not believe that the complaints system, though independent in name, is independent in practice (O'Connor, 1992a). Because of the perceived lack of independence, they do not expect their complaints to be taken seriously or believed; they believe that the police version of events will always be preferred to their own – especially as there are rarely independent witnesses to police–youth interactions.

Many young people believe that there will be negative consequences if they complain about their treatment. For example, a study of homeless youth in Melbourne concluded: '[They do not] report incidents of police assaults to anyone: they fear retaliation, feel they will not be able to prove their allegations, and they believe nothing will be done in any case' (Alder and Sandor, 1990:49). Such beliefs are consistent with their experiences of the consequences of challenging police practices on the street and endeavouring to assert their rights prior to and during formal questioning. Most young people have to continue interacting with the same police in their local area and believe that complaints will provoke retaliatory action from the police (O'Connor, 1992a).

Finally, complaints mechanisms are individually based. They inquire into specific allegations about a specific occurrence made by a particular aggrieved person. Frequently the issue is not one incident, but a series of interactions between police and a number of young people. Because of fear of victimisation, most young people wish to remain anonymous. But anonymous complaints are not considered – and more importantly complaints made by youth workers or other representatives on behalf of groups of individuals are not considered unless the details of specific occurrences are provided, thus enabling the complaint to be proceeded on the normal case-by-case basis. In many situations, it would be more fruitful to consider the pattern of interactions between police and young people, rather than a specific incident. Incidents need to be examined in the context of the ongoing skirmishes between police and the particular group of young people.

Police complaints mechanisms are established to investigate 'extraordinary' events where it is alleged that police have failed to carry out their tasks and functions appropriately. As was argued above, many abuses of young people's rights occur in the process of police routinely carrying out their functions. It is these routine practices of policing which are in question, but complaints systems are not designed to review 'ordinary' events.

CONCLUSION

The focus of this chapter has been a narrow category of rights – the rights of young people in their interactions with police and the criminal justice system. These basic rights, which seek to ensure that individuals are not subject to arbitrary exercises of state power, are fundamental to the ideology of the democratic state.

For the purposes of this chapter, rights were defined as legally enforceable claims. They are entitlements which the citizen can expect to be respected. The examination of the rights of young people in interactions with police and the criminal justice system calls into question the scope and extent of rights enjoyed by young people in such interactions. The non-existence of clearly defined legal rights in encounters with the police undermines the existence, respect and enforcement of the rights of young people. This occurs for two reasons. First, much police contact with young people occurs in the context of street policing and order maintenance. Police enjoy wide powers under legislation which creates street offences (e.g. the right to demand name and address, to stop and question, to move young people on, the power to arrest, etc.). Such powers are used to achieve the order maintenance function of policing. Additionally these powers are utilised by police to assist in their law enforcement and crime clearing function (e.g. detaining a young person on a petty offence, such as resisting arrest, to facilitate the investigation of another offence where the person would not voluntarily accompany the police to the station).

Second, in relation to police contact during the investigation of crimes, there are no clear statements of a young person's rights. In most states there is no statement regarding *if* and *when* a young person has a right to a lawyer, the right to a telephone call and so on. The existence and the establishment of the breach of such rights are discoverable only by challenging the process in court. Thus, all practices stand as correct unless challenged.

It was argued that rights should be examined in the context of their application, in the day-to-day interactions between police and young people. Currently, the rhetoric and practice of rights has no place in the performance of police functions of order maintenance and law enforcement. Indeed, police may argue the performance of routine police work would be hindered by successful efforts by young people to assert rights. Young people's lived experience of policing is that attempts to assert rights are actively rebuffed.

The structural mechanisms for facilitating the exercise and enforcement of the rights of the young person, and for monitoring and reviewing breaches of their rights in their encounters with police, do not achieve their purpose. Young people have very limited rights to legal assistance during police questioning. Even if this right was routinely acknowledged, legal services are generally not available out of hours or for police questioning. The situation in which the individual is most vulnerable – alone and at the police station – is the very situation in which the person has most need of, and least access to, a lawyer.

Legal services are provided on the basis that most young people are guilty and will plead guilty. Given young people's expectations of treatment by police, it is only the most severe abuses that are reported to, or acted on by, their legal representatives. Most young people plead guilty. The routine processing of guilty pleas by courts means that courts rarely review any inappropriate aspects of the interactions with the police associated with the investigation of the offence. For similar reasons, complaints mechanisms have proved ineffective.

The lack of clear statements of young people's rights in their encounters with police, the broad range of police powers, and the lack of any effective review of the exercise of those powers results in young people having few rights which they can claim 'without having to grovel, plead or beg or to express gratitude when we are given our due, and to express indignation when what is our due is not forthcoming' (Bandman cited in Freeman, 1983:32).

A further factor in the equation is that many young people are ignorant of their rights (Flowers et al., 1992; Alder, 1992; O'Connor and Sweetapple, 1988; O'Connor and Tilbury, 1986; Youth Justice Coalition, 1990). The lack of knowledge of rights and of the processes for ascertaining and assisting in the enforcement of rights clearly disadvantages young people in their interactions with police.

Knowing about rights and being able to exercise rights are two different matters. Children who ask to make telephone calls or see a lawyer are frequently told that they have been watching too much television (Faine, 1988). The power differential between police and the young person, the nature of routine policing and the lack of adequate mechanisms for reviewing police activity are barriers to claiming rights. Education of young people will not remedy those barriers.

Rather, it is necessary to address those aspects of the police approach to work and police culture which are fundamentally disrespectful of the rights of the individual. Mukherjee (1991) notes that the police have actively used the media, and their media units, to promote concern about 'law and order' which in turn feed calls for more resources (e.g. police) to combat crime. The focus on juvenile crime fulfils an important function for police – it enables both a boosting of the numbers of reported crimes which justifies the need to continue the war on crime, and provides a rationale for police claims for more resources to combat crime. At the same time, the mass clearing of crimes committed by juveniles bolsters the police crime clear-up rates which is used by police to promote confidence in their ability to wage the war on crime successfully if they are adequately resourced.

It is young people who have suffered most from the mis-representation of crime statistics. The community is constantly exposed to misrepresentation of the extent of youth crime and the notion that they are knowledgeable of rights, and indeed that the police are powerless in the face of these rights. As one police officer stated in his regular weekly column in a local newspaper: 'The police are at a standstill because we can't talk to these kids without a solicitor or social worker present' (*Westside News*, 14 February 1990).

Police education and training should aim to develop a respect for the rights of, and an understanding of young people.

> What is required is a change in police attitudes towards the policing of young people. Police training, already undergoing substantial change, should stress the skills which are needed in dealing with young people and should communicate information about juveniles, and their attitudes to law and police, which will help to challenge some of the entrenched cultural stereotypes and misconceptions. (Youth Justice Coalition, 1990:236)

There is a similar need for community education concerning the nature and extent of young people's crime, the transitory and petty nature of much of that crime, young people's need for and usage of public space, and respect for their rights.

It is necessary to envisage alternative methods of accountability, besides courts and complaints bodies. Such an orientation would imply structures where young people and their representatives could have greater input on the nature of policing. For example, many ongoing skirmishes between police and groups of young people could usefully be conceptualised as conflicts and be resolved by alternative dispute-resolution processes. The existing dispute-resolution structures (courts and complaints bodies) do not redress the existing power differentials between police and young people. Current dialogues between police and youth are conducted on the streets and in stations on a 'one up–one down' basis. Commitment from police to resolve interactional difficulties through mediation or other dispute-resolution processes requires a willingness on the part of police to set aside some of their power so that a joint solution to disputes may be reached. The notion of listening to young people, of engaging in discussions on neutral territories and reaching joint solutions rather than imposing solutions would alter the dynamics of police–youth interactions.

The media promote the mythology that young people enjoy a broad range of legal, social and welfare rights. Indeed, it is often suggested that the tasks of law enforcement and other authorities are impeded by manifold rights exercised without restraint by the young. In reality, in their encounters with the police and criminal justice system, young people enjoy few rights. The façade of rights is the screen behind which the real business of policing young people is able to proceed unhindered.

REFERENCES

Alder, C. (1992) 'The Young People' in C. Alder et al. (eds), *Perceptions of the Treatment of Juveniles in the Legal System*. Report for the National Youth Affairs Research Scheme. Hobart: National Clearinghouse for Youth Studies.

Alder, C., O'Connor, I., Warner, K. and White, R. (1992) *Perceptions of the Treatment of Juveniles in the Legal System*. Report for the National Youth Affairs Research Scheme. Hobart: National Clearinghouse for Youth Studies.

Alder, C. and Sandor, D. (1990) *Homeless Youth as Victims of Violence*. Melbourne: Criminology Department, University of Melbourne.

Alston, P. (1991) 'Australia and the Convention' in P. Alston and G. Brennan (eds), *The UN Children's Convention and Australia*. Canberra: Centre for International and Public Law, Australian National University.

Australian Bureau of Statistics (1987) *Community Crime Prevention Attitudes (Queensland)*, Catalogue no. 4506.5.

Australian Council of Social Services (1980) *Framework for Accountability and Accessibility Review*. Canberra: Commonwealth Legal Aid Commission.

Committee of Inquiry into the Enforcement of the Criminal Law in Queensland (1977) *Report of the inquiry into criminal law enforcement in Queensland*. Brisbane: Government Printer.

Criminal Justice Commission (1991) *Police Powers in Queensland*. Brisbane: Criminal Justice Commission.

Cunneen, C. (1990) *A Study of Aboriginal Juveniles and Police Violence*. Sydney: Human Rights and Equal Opportunity Commission.

Faine, J. (1988) 'Just a Phone Call: Privilege or right' in I. Freckelton and H. Selby (eds), *Police in our society*. Sydney: Butterworths.

Federation of Community Legal Centres (Victoria) (1991) *Report into the Mistreatment of Young People by Police*. Melbourne: Federation of Community Legal Centres (Victoria).

Flowers, R., McIntyre, J. and Loughman, J. (1992) *The Nature of Legal Support Work: A Young Person's Perspectives*. Sydney: Marrickville Legal Service.

Freeman, M.D.A. (1983) *The Rights and Wrongs of Children*. London: Francis Printers.

Freiberg, A., Fox, R. and Hogan, M. (1988) *Sentencing Young Offenders*. Canberra: AGPS.

Human Rights and Equal Opportunity Commission (1989) *Our Homeless Children*. Canberra: AGPS.

James, S. and Polk, K. (1989) 'Policing Youth: Themes and directions' in D. Chappell and P. Wilson (eds), *Australian Policing: Contemporary Issues*. Sydney: Butterworths.

McBarnet, D. (1981) *Conviction: Law, the state and the construction of justice*. London: Macmillan.

McMillan, A. (1992) A National Approach to Juvenile Justice. Paper presented to the Australian Institute of Criminology, National Conference on Juvenile Justice, Adelaide, 22–24 September.

Mukherjee, S. (1983) *Age and Crime*. Canberra: Australian Institute of Criminology.

Mukherjee, S. (1985) 'Juvenile Delinquency: The dimensions of the problem', in A. Borowski and J.M. Murray (eds), *Juvenile delinquency in Australia*. Sydney: Methuen.

Mukherjee, S. (1986) 'Nature and Extent of Burglary in Australia' in S. Mukherjee and L. Jorgensen (eds), *Burglary: The Social Reality*. Canberra: Australian Institute of Criminology.

Mukherjee, S. (1991) Confronting Crime: An evaluation of Australia's crime problems and a consideration of crime control strategies. Paper presented to the second Melbourne Criminal Justice symposium, University of Melbourne, 16 March.

Mukherjee, S. and Dagger, D. (1990) *The Size of the Crime Problem in Australia* (2nd edn). Canberra: Australian Institute of Criminology.

Naffine, N., Wundersitz, J. and Gale, F. (1990) 'Back to Justice for Juveniles: The rhetoric of law reform', *Australian and New Zealand Journal of Criminology*, 23:192–205.

National Legal Aid Advisory Committee (1990) *Legal Aid for the Australian Community*. Canberra: AGPS.

O'Connor, I. (1989) *Our Homeless Children: Their Experiences*. Sydney: Human Rights & Equal Opportunity Commission.

O'Connor, I. (1992a) 'Lawyers, Legal Advocates and Legal Services' and 'Conclusion' in C. Alder et al., *Perceptions of the Treatment of Juveniles in the Legal System*. Report for the National Youth Affairs Research Scheme. Hobart: National Clearinghouse for Youth Studies.

O'Connor, I. (1992b) *Youth, Crime and Justice in Queensland*. Brisbane: Criminal Justice Commision.

O'Connor, I. and Sweetapple, P. (1988) *Children in Justice*. Melbourne: Longman Cheshire.

O'Connor, I. and Tilbury, C. (1986) *Legal Aid Needs of Youth*. Canberra: Australian Government Publishing Service.

Potas, I., Vining, A. and Wilson, P. (1990) *Young People and Crime: Costs and prevention*. Canberra: Australian Institute of Criminology.

Seymour, J. (1988) *Dealing with Young Offenders*. Sydney: Law Book Co.

Underwood, R., White, R. and Omelczuk, S. (1993) *Young People, Youth Services and Legal Issues*. Perth: Edith Cowan University.

Warner, K. (1992) 'Legislative and Policy Overview' in C. Alder et al., *Perceptions of the Treatment of Juveniles in the Legal System*. Report for the National Youth Affairs Research Scheme. Hobart: National Clearinghouse for Youth Studies.

White, R. (1992a) 'Tough Laws for Hard Core Politicians', *Alternative Law Journal*, 17(2):58–60.

White, R. (1992b) 'The Police' in C. Alder et al., *Perceptions of the Treatment of Juveniles in the Legal System*. Hobart: National Clearinghouse for Youth Studies.

White, R., Underwood, R. and Omelczuk, S. (1992) 'Legal Problems and Youth Workers', *Youth Studies Australia*, 4:41–45.

Youth Justice Coalition (NSW) (1990) *Kids in Justice: A blueprint for the 90s*. Sydney: Youth Justice Coalition.

CHAPTER 5

Street Life: Police Practices and Youth Behaviour

Rob White

The crucial elements of the relationship between young people and the police – whether these be positive or negative – are forged on the street. The climate of fear, mistrust and conflict characteristic of this realm is often seen as simply being due to the personal fault or whim of particular young people or to the attitudes and behaviour of the police themselves. However, as this chapter will show, such factors also need to be linked to specific structural conditions pertaining to the position of young people in society, and to the routines and practices of the police as a whole.

The chapter begins by outlining police–youth interaction in terms of the location of contact and the nature of the relationship between the police and different groups of young people. The concern of this section will be to discuss the issue of police harassment and the violence directed against young people, to indicate those groups which are more likely to be subjected to this violence, and to explore the reasons for the development of mutually antagonistic relationships from the perspective of young people and of the police themselves.

The second part of the chapter looks at the general issue of how 'public spaces' – such as the streets, malls and shopping centres – are socially constructed and institutionally regulated. The issues of public order and of the youth street presence will be explored, particularly as these relate to the economic position of young people and their visibility in the public domain. The main concern here is to outline where young people fit within the larger framework of urban life and the urban political economy.

In the third section, the focus is on the nature of police powers and police culture as these impact upon young people. Issues such as the relationship between official and informal departmental policies, the practical exercise of police powers, and denial of the rights of young people are examined. As part of this, the legislative context, the ways in which 'normal police practices' are constructed, and the general task orientation of the police will be investigated. It will be argued that any improvement in the relationship between young people and the police is contingent upon significant shifts in the use of police power and in what is seen to constitute 'good policing'.

The chapter concludes with a summary of the reasons why the negative relationships between young people and the police cannot be reduced to simply a 'public relations' problem or be explained solely through a critique of either police practices or the behaviour of young people. What occurs on the street is fundamentally influenced by shifts in the relationship between the state and community; this, in turn, is shaped by the specific character of commercial activity and the state of the economy.

STREET LIFE, YOUNG PEOPLE AND THE POLICE

The street is both the main site of police–youth contact and the target of police intervention. It is here where young people are most likely to congregate in groups, and it is here where they can be both visible and anonymous at the same time.

The relationship between young people and the police is very much 'territorial' in nature. That is, interaction between the police and young people tends to be shaped by physical location, the group activities of young people and the specific types of intervention by police within a particular locale. The fact that so much of the contact occurs on the street is significant in any examination of youth–police relations.

The concept of 'street' refers to both a specific feature of the urban landscape (e.g. avenue, footpath, roadway) as well as to more general 'open' public spaces (e.g. malls, shopping centre entrances, parks). Broadly defined, the 'street' constitutes the most frequent area within which police–youth contact takes place.

This is indicated in figures from a recent National Youth Affairs Research Scheme (NYARS) survey (Alder, O'Connor, Warner and White, 1992) which show that young people from a wide range of economic and social backgrounds, and of both sexes, have been stopped by the police on the street. The survey found that of the young people interviewed (in Tasmania, Queensland, Victoria and

Western Australia), 80 percent had been stopped by the police, and of these all but 17 percent had been stopped on the street. It was further reported that 25 percent had been stopped while in a public building such as a train station, and 23 percent in a shopping mall (Alder, 1992:21).

The study asked police officers where they thought young people were of particular concern. The most frequently specified places were malls (53% of police officers) and shopping centres (60% of police officers). Although the question was not posed in terms of 'the street', it was clear from the findings that the officers were basically referring to places where young people are especially visible to the general public (White, 1992a:31).

What actually happens on the street is, of course, a major factor in determining the specific interaction between police and young people. The character of the relationship between young people and the police will be reflected in the attitudes and activities of both parties, and in the patterns of contact. With reference to the young people interviewed for the NYARS study, it was pointed out that:

> Most (80%) had been stopped and spoken to by the police at some time, fewer (50%) had been taken to a police station, almost one quarter had been 'officially cautioned', and a third of the young people claimed that they had been 'roughed up' by the police. (Alder, 1992:19)

Given that this survey included young people from a range of different backgrounds, the findings show an extraordinary degree of police intervention in young people's activities.

The actual nature of police–youth contact will, however, be shaped by situational variables such as the appearance, activities, attitudes and behaviour of the young people. From 'trendies' to 'street kids', young women to Aboriginal young people, the use of the street will vary (e.g. ranging from a place where 'fun' and entertainment are paramount, to where 'survival' is the name of the game), as will the trappings of youth subcultural fashions, jargon and degrees of adherence to dominant gender, class and ethnic stereotypes (White, 1990; Brake, 1985).

So too the police response to particular young people varies according to the sort of young people with whom they come into contact. Aboriginal and homeless young people are especially vulnerable to police intervention and harassment. Likewise groups of young people perceived to be 'gangs' are subject to constant surveillance and police contact. Racism, at both a structural and personal level, certainly plays a major part in the nature of police–Aboriginal relations (Cunneen, 1990a; Gale et al., 1990). But so do the concepts of 'dangerousness', 'worthlessness' and 'troublemakers'. And these in turn are very often linked to how 'public space' and 'public order' have been socially constructed.

From the point of view of specific groups of young people, there is growing evidence that Aboriginal and Torres Strait Islander juveniles, and 'street kids', are particularly vulnerable to aggressive police intervention. The NYARS study, for example, found that 'the police were more likely to be 'heavy handed' in their dealings with young men, Aboriginal youth and marginal youth' (Alder, 1992:20). This was indirectly corroborated by the police responses to a question regarding which groups of young people they found most difficult. Again, it was 'gangs', 'street kids' and Aborigines and Torres Strait Islanders who were seen as causing the most problems from the point of view of the police (White, 1992a).

Harassment, discrimination, maltreatment and abuse of legal rights have been well documented in relation to police dealings with Aboriginal young people (see Cunneen, 1988, 1989; Carrington, 1990; Gale et al., 1990). The work by Chris Cunneen for the Human Rights and Equal Opportunity Commission (1990a) is perhaps the most systematic survey of police violence against young Aborigines ever undertaken in Australia. This work, plus other material collected as part of the Human Rights Commission National Inquiry into Racist Violence and the Royal Commission into Aboriginal Deaths in Custody, substantiates long-standing claims that Aboriginal and Torres Strait Islanders have suffered greatly at the hands of officers of the criminal justice system (see especially, Johnston, 1991; Moss and Castan, 1991; and chapter 6).

In the case of 'street kids' and 'homeless youth', there are a number of recent studies which show that these groups of young people are subject to various kinds of police violence, intimidation and harassment (see O'Connor, 1989; Alder and Sandor, 1990; Alder, 1991; Cowie, 1991; White et al., 1991). A Salvation Army report on young homeless people found that:

The overall picture drawn by these findings is that of the most vulnerable and unprotected young people in society being taken advantage of by a misuse of authority. This picture is emphasized by the finding that under 16 year olds and under 18 year olds generally claim a greater incidence of abuse by the police than do the older age groups. The apparent advantage taken of vulnerability is further expressed by the finding that young women, while claiming a significantly lower incidence of straightforward physical abuse, claim a greater incidence of psychological abuse and sexual intimidation. (Hirst, 1989: 62)

The surveys and investigations undertaken in the last few years – in most states and territories, and nationally – provide powerful evidence not only of police harassment of young people generally, but also of the particular vulnerabilities to this style of intervention by the most dispossessed, oppressed and marginalised sections of the youth population.

Some idea of the nature of the relationship between the police and young people on the street can be ascertained by referring briefly to various studies which have examined issues of harassment and violence. These studies indicate that intimidation is a significant aspect of police involvement with young people generally, and that any challenge to police 'authority' by a young person will be harshly dealt with by them (see O'Connor and Sweetapple, 1988; White, 1990; Youth Justice Coalition, 1990; Federation of Community Legal Centres (Victoria) 1991). A recent parliamentary select committee report into Youth and the Law in Western Australia commented that:

> Evidence given to the Committee suggests that there are some problematic issues in police youth relations. In fact, a number of serious allegations were made to the Committee about police mistreatment of young people; mistreatment that is suggestive of a disregard for both Standing Orders and the rights of young people. The nature of this evidence also suggests that, in some instances, young people can be goaded into unlawful activity in response to police harassment. (Watkins et al., 1992:29)

In the light of figures which show that Western Australia has the highest rate of police–youth contact in the country (Watkins et al., 1992), it is little wonder that the nature of these relations is a matter of grave concern.

It is important at this stage to make a distinction between 'contact' and 'harassment' as two separate dimensions of police–youth interactions. As pointed out earlier, there is a considerable amount of contact between young people and the police on the street. This, in itself, need not be a bad thing. However, the question which needs answering is why is there so much antagonism on the street between the police and young people?

Part of the reason for this lies in the fact that police harassment is part of a cycle of response and counter-response of the police and young people to the actions of each other. Young people are not passive automotons: they react to the police, just as the police in turn respond to the actions and behaviour of young people. According to the police, officers are themselves often subject to harassment by young people. In the NYARS study, it was found that 98 percent of the police interviewed said that they had been assaulted or harassed by young people in the course of their work:

> The kinds of harassment most commonly referred to included verbal taunts (73%), being shouted at (68%), and swearing (62%). Fewer officers reported being assaulted with a weapon (16%), having an object thrown at them (27%) or being kicked (36%), although a majority (52%) did say that at some time they had been punched by a young person. (White, 1992a:33–34)

This suggests that the street is a 'testing' ground, physically and psychologically, for the police, as well as for many of the young people with whom they come into contact.

How or even whether the street is a testing ground for police and for young people is contingent upon several factors. Certainly the experiences of different groups of young people on the street vary considerably depending upon social characteristics, use of the street, visibility, and general perceptions regarding the attitudes and behaviour of some young people (e.g. as being 'troublemakers' or 'undesirables'). But it also very much depends upon the perceptions that the police have of the job they have been assigned to do, and of the policy context within which they work.

At some stage, most young people are likely to have contact with the police while on the street. This is partly due to the specific age-construction of the law, which targets young people through a series of 'status offences' based upon age, including requirements regarding school attendance and general 'welfare' protection measures. Police intervention in general can be seen to be based upon apparently benign welfare objectives or as the result of established legal strictures regarding permissible youth activities, as well as ordinary criminal law matters. Whether this is appropriate, adequate or just is a matter beyond the scope of this chapter. Nevertheless, given the intervention that does occur, we need to understand why many young people consider and resent this as an intrusion, and why certain groups are particularly vulnerable to sustained police harassment.

In essence, the police are often called upon to perform contradictory functions and to perform their tasks across a range of institutions (James and Polk, 1989). For instance, in a number of states they have been increasingly involved in various school-based programs, as well as in recreation and leisure areas. Police are involved in schools in a positive and non-threatening manner insofar as they engage in things such as talks on safety or road rules. Simultaneously, however, they may be called upon to play a role based upon surveillance and coercion – as in the case of truancy patrols and the policing of amusement and leisure centres (White, 1989a). This can lead to obvious tensions, arising from the dual role of the police in both assisting young people and exerting power over them.

Significantly, it is when the police partake in activities within the physical grounds of the school that perhaps they are seen as less threatening and more 'friends' than 'foes'. Fear and anxiety related to the anonymity of police authority can be broken down by personal interaction and the development of trust relationships involving individual police officers in a non-policing environment. But schooling policies, as legally defined and enforceable, also lead the police at department level to pursue actively the perceived educational interests of the young by policing them outside of the boundaries of the schoolyard *per se*.

Currently in some states, and across time in most states, police have been responsible for the regulation of young people who are outside of school during normal school hours. The NYARS study found that 50 percent of police–youth contact was during the afternoon period (White, 1992a:31), indicating a time of day when many young people are not supposed to be seen in venues where otherwise they may have a legitimate right to be. From a police perspective, their intervention is entirely legitimate from the point of view of social objectives and pursuit of a desired social good – namely, education for all young people. However, it not only reinforces their 'authority' role, but it also puts them into contact with large numbers of young people who do have a right to be in public spaces during daytime, and this in turn can be a source of potential friction.

The second most frequent time that police have contact with young people is in the early parts of the night (White, 1992a:31). At this time of day, policing tends to revolve around facilitating the normal operation of commercial enterprises and the work of transit authorities. This can mean moving young people away from shopfront doors, monitoring the flow of human traffic to ensure there is no disorderly behaviour or obstacles to movement, or simply assisting people in getting from point A to point B. Again, from a police perspective, the exercise of police power is designed first and foremost to protect shopkeepers and to prevent any harm arising from the mass movement of people from one location to another. How the police perform such duties is of course crucial to the relationship they subsequently may develop with young people.

A third area in which the police have been concerned with young people particularly is that of general social welfare. Until recently in most states, the police have been, by law, obliged to step in and assist those young people whom they deemed to be in need of 'care' and 'assistance'. To intervene in the lives of 'street kids', for example, was not simply a matter of 'having a go'. It was statutorily based. Regardless of current legislation, the presence of young persons in public places who are in obvious social distress and who are suffering economic misfortune is, nevertheless, worrisome, both in terms of electoral and organisational politics, and with regard to genuine humanitarian concerns.

While the police could argue that they are simply 'doing their job' by stopping and questioning young people on the street, the reverse perception is usually quite different. The 'street' represents for many young people a place to express themselves without close parental or 'adult' control, at little or no cost in commercial or financial terms. It is also a sphere or domain where 'things happen', where there are people to see, and where one can be seen by others. In short, for many young people the street is an important site for social activity (see White, 1990). And the intrusion of 'authority' into one's social affairs can and does create resentment and resistance, especially if this is done in a heavy-handed fashion.

Different perceptions of the nature of the street, and of different uses of the street, are one source of the friction between police and young people. Another is the general fear and apprehension among young people generated by the actions of the police in relation to specific groups of their peers, and occasionally confirmed by their own direct experiences of police intervention. What happens on the street, and what happens to particular young persons, is not a matter confined to the immediate protagonists – it permeates the wider youth population in the form of stories, myths, legends and tales. Instances of police 'bashings' or particularly nasty 'run-ins' with the forces of 'authority' will be relayed far beyond the immediate vicinity or youth population involved in a particular incident. Personal experience is not a necessary requirement for one to feel the repressive impact of police powers.

COMMERCIAL SPACE AND PUBLIC ORDER

The ways in which young people use the street differ according to factors such as gender, class and ethnic background. How particular groups of young people define the street – both in terms of territory (e.g. identifying a particular storefront, park or avenue as being their patch or turf) and with respect to activity (e.g. a meeting point or simply a point of passage) – is subject to constant negotiation involving peers, parents, police, businesspeople and others. Ultimately the 'master' definition of the street will be determined by those who have the power to control the use and passage of people in a particular geographical area.

It is highly significant that a frequent point of contact between young people and the police is malls and shopping centres. If we are to understand the dynamics of police–youth interaction, we need to know the attractions of such venues for young people, and the reasons why the state (in the form of the police) and proprietors (in the form of managers and business owners) wish to discourage certain young people from using these 'public' spaces the way they do (White, 1992b). As well, it is important to bear in mind that policing varies in substantively different ways depending upon the city area one is speaking about, the category of people most directly involved in the use of a particular urban area, and the approach adopted by the police to regulate social behaviour and communal relationships (see Cohen, 1979).

It is necessary, for instance, to distinguish the policing of certain communities (e.g. Aborigines, migrant, working class) and neigh-bourhoods (e.g. Redfern, Balga, St Kilda), and the policing of public sites where diverse crowds of people tend to congregate (e.g. malls, shopping centres). The concern of this chapter is less with the former than with the latter sort of policing pattern. Nevertheless, it is important to bear in mind that particular communities and neighbourhoods are often subject to over-policing and a form of police practice which is especially aggressive in nature (see Cunneen, 1988, 1990b). This is due to a combination of historical conflicts between workers or Aboriginal people and the police, the prevalence of 'street crime' in poorer urban areas, and the politics of visibly being seen to be doing something about the 'law and order' problem. The same people, usually the more marginalised or oppressed in society, tend to be the main targets of general policing practices across the community, neighbourhood and public venue spectrum.

The use of urban malls and shopping centres by young people generally stems from a range of social and economic factors. The 'bright lights' of city centres, the lack of recreation or leisure facilities in one's own neighbourhood, no money to pay for alternative forms of entertainment, proximity to public transport services, the reputation of certain places as good ones at which to 'hang out', the danger and excitement associated with interacting with young people from many types of backgrounds – these are some of the reasons why young people are to be found in urban centres of this nature. In addition, and as mentioned above, the 'street', including malls and shopping centres, provides a place where young people can feel secure in their activities by having numbers of like-minded peers around them and yet being relatively anonymous and free in terms of close parental or other adult control.

While various social and economic factors influence the decisions of young people to seek out certain venues for their activities, the broader question still remains as to why the mall or shopping centre, in particular, is so often chosen as the gathering point. Such centres have been popularly construed as being 'public' places, open to all and sundry, as evidenced by the fact that they are serviced by the main transportation and communication lines (White, 1992b). Whereas the 'village common' might have been the model site for community activity in the past, the mall, public square or shopping centre represents the main community focal point in the late twentieth century.

However, there are fundamental differences between the public common and the modern shopping centre or mall. As one reviewer commented regarding a specific shopping mall:

> The so-called 'public spaces' are all movement channels. The places specifically designed for sitting, waiting and meeting people are all private. Essential to maximise consumption, there are no places at the mall for people to meet that do not require them to spend money. (McManus, 1991:4)

The presence of security guards and/or police patrols to deter 'undesirables', restrictions on the use of such spaces for handing out political literature or for public demonstrations, the fact that the design and control over shopping centres and malls is not subject to meaningful or participatory democratic control, and the locking up of some malls at night, all constitute elements of a system which effectively precludes such venues from truly representing 'public' spaces at all (McManus, 1991). A more precise categorisation is to see them as 'commercial' spaces, spaces designed with one purpose specifically - to make profits for the owner.

Public space in the modern urban environment thus embodies the central elements of the capitalist market. It exists to facilitate the exchange of goods and services for money and credit. It exists first and foremost to bring a return to the business community. The atmospheric trappings of the mall or shopping centre - in the form of glossy advertising, musical jingles, consumer contests, (respectable) community stalls, and clever shopfront displays - are designed to bring people into the consumer spaces. And once there, the role prescribed for the patron of such centres is to buy something, not to use the space for other purposes.

For many young people, however, the central logic of the shopping mall - to consume - is either not realisable or is not the primary reason for their use of this space. Other motivations for young people to congregate in such centres have already been mentioned. To this we need to add several qualifications.

Social responses to young people will be shaped by their position as consumers, and as producers, in the context of general street life. For example, young people who do purchase goods and services, or who exhibit a level of affluence which makes them appear as potential consumers, are rarely seen as problematic from the point of view of businesses or the police. A certain amount of leeway will exist in terms of which kinds of behaviour will be censured.

In the case of the dispossessed, the obviously poor and visible minority groups, their social position is usually mirrored in the suspicion and confrontative attitudes of those around them, as various studies and reports have indicated (see Burdekin, 1989; Johnston, 1991). From the point of view of 'consumption', these young people are virtually 'worthless'. They are unable or unwilling to purchase the goods and services so tantalisingly displayed. Meanwhile, they are using the 'consumer' space as public space for uses of their own. This offends against the social construction of such places as being primarily and solely for the benefit of consumers (and businesses).

Young Aborigines, the young homeless and 'street kids' are seen as threats in other ways as well. On the one hand, their presence is seen as disruptive to the normal course of commerce. The territory they occupy, and the activities and behaviour they exhibit, are seen to dissuade other patrons from consuming what the shopping mall has to offer. They are also visible reminders of the failures of capitalism to deliver the goods to everyone, of the deficiencies of a welfare system which is not able to meet basic human needs. These young people are perceived as 'threats', partly because the conditions of their lives are so alien to many people in the wider society, and partly because of the strong association between poverty and the 'criminal classes'.

Social inequalities have been exacerbated through successive years of 'deregulation' and 'economic rationalism', with major effects in terms of youth unemployment, poverty, alienation and general reduction of social welfare provision. The pool of visible, unemployed, young people is currently very large and is growing. In the present circumstances, they are also more vulnerable to state intervention of some kind or another in their lives, whether this be aimed at shaping their welfare–employment activities (e.g. as in the Newstart Allowance scheme) or monitoring their spare-time activities (e.g. as in police campaigns aimed at keeping them off the streets).

On the other hand, for many young people beyond and including these groups, 'doing nothing' (in the sense of not consuming) involves activities such as petty vandalism, fights, the setting of dares and associated risk-taking, making noise and minor shoplifting. In other words, what young people do with their time involves activities which have long been seen as simply a 'normal' part of growing up (while recognising significant gender, class and ethnic differences in this process). The production of 'noise' through listening to music, of a visible identity via dress and language, of 'style' by acting in particular ways, is part of a process of establishing themselves in the world around them (Hebdige, 1979; Brake, 1985). What could be seen as a 'normal' aspect of teenage life very often rests upon appeal to the 'abnormal' in cultural terms.

What young people do with their time, and money, is therefore of concern to the owners and controllers of the shopping centre or mall. The rise of the 'youth consumer' in the 1950s and the ability of business to incorporate previously rebellious fashions and fads into their commercial orbit were important elements in the changing pattern of relationships between young people and the commercial sphere (Stratton, 1992). The importance of the youth market, however, has diminished in relative terms in recent years due to the impact of the deepening economic recession which has extended into the 1990s (see Australian Youth Policy and Action Coalition, 1992).

The general perception of young people in society is a crucial part of how they will be treated in the public domain. Insofar as 'youth' is associated with disruption, rebellion, alienation or other generally dismissive or negative appellations (Graycar and Jamrozik, 1989), they will not be made welcome in venues such as malls or shopping centres. In a similar vein, media-generated 'moral panics' regarding youth 'crime waves' and the stereotyping of certain young people as being particularly 'troublesome' or 'dangerous' can stimulate a general fear or anxiety at a popular level (see Cohen, 1972; Pearson, 1983; White, 1990). This has implications for all young people who use the street, in addition to any particular group which is the target of such campaigns. It also provides a ready justification for police intervention insofar as the police see their role as responding to such requests for action.

Those who run the commerical enterprises also, of course, have the political power to see that their particular economic interests are protected. And it is the attempts to control the behaviour and actions of the young generally, and the marginalised in particular, which set in train the conflicts between young people and the police.

The concerns raised here open the door to discussion of wider issues relating to the private ownership of 'public' spaces, and how the legal construction of property rights can impinge upon such things as freedom of expression and freedom of association. They are also linked to questions regarding the nature of state regulation of 'consumer' spaces, and how the use of surveillance cameras, rules and various regulations of behaviour and access impinge upon such things as democratic participation and citizen rights in society. For present purposes, however, the main concern is to consider the role of the police in relation to the specific issue of youth activity in the 'commercial' spaces. To understand this fully, we need to briefly explore the cultural foundations of police practices.

POLICE POWERS AND POLICE CULTURE

The police occupy a very ambivalent position in society. They have been granted the ability to wield force 'legitimately' and are able to exercise great powers to intervene in many facets of the lives of Australian citizens. They ostensibly exist as an occupational group whose purpose is to serve the public and to protect citizens from harm. And yet, they are constantly subject to problems of undervalued status, in terms of both financial reward and public esteem.

There is no doubt that tensions exist between the police and the wider community. These stem in large measure from the nature of police work itself. It has been pointed out that many police 'enter an insular environment where they work and socialize almost exclusively with their colleagues' (Fitzgerald et al., 1989:201) and, on the other hand, 'the community has unfavourable perceptions of police behaviour, attitudes, efficiency and competence' (Fitzgerald et al., 1989:210). The problem appears to be one of relating the objectives of police work to the exercise of authority in the course of this work.

Broadly speaking, police work involves elements of law enforcement, peace-keeping and social welfare (Brannigan, 1984). The first area generally refers to combating serious crime. It is popularly conceived of in terms of an emphasis on using force and physical methods to 'uphold the law' and thus bears all the hallmarks of an American style (or Hollywood version) of policing. The second area makes reference to the police role in restoring disruptive situations to normalcy without necessarily arresting anyone. The idea is to maintain order without resort to further criminal justice sanctions. This approach is often linked in practice to various conceptions of 'community policing'.

The third area of police work involves officers in providing social welfare, counselling and mediation services, as well as doing things such as searching for lost children, responding to road accidents, and so on. The social welfare aspect of policing is particularly relevant in terms of the traditional rationale for police interference in the lives of working class and Aboriginal children. That is, a concern with 'social welfare' (including the moral welfare of young people) meant that very often the police were not only required, but were largely expected, to intervene regularly and actively in the affairs of young people on welfare grounds.

There is often tension between the different task orientations of the police. This is due to the manner in which official police policy frames the objectives and methods to be used at any point in time. It is also because, at an operational level, there are different perceptions, and disagreements, among police officers regarding the main aims of policing, and to whom and how they should be accountable. This has been expressed in the following way:

> Some police officers are trying to engage in a form of 'community policing' which acknowledges the participation of all citizens and residents in real decision-making. But many others are still pre-occupied with policing the community, and are using methods which are unjustified and heavy-handed in doing so. Rather than maintaining social order, these police officers are disrupting communities, particularly through over-policing those groups which are the most oppressed and least powerful in Australian society. Rather than forging respect and moral authority by engaging in peacekeeping activity and intelligent use of discretion, many such officers are treating the general public as 'the enemy', subject to continual suspicion and constant surveillance. (White, 1992c)

It is the latter part of this passage which is of particular interest in regards to the relationship between young people and the police. For, in addition to general perceptions that the public is apathetic and that people cannot be trusted, the police occasionally express their frustration concerning the apparent reluctance of the courts to 'enforce the law' in the case of young people (White, 1992a).

The reasons for this frustration stem partly from the paradoxical situation where, on the one hand, supporters of a strong 'law and order' approach to crime and offending behaviour stress greater intervention, while on the other hand the structures and processes of the courts are designed to take into account the special needs and welfare of young people in any sentencing decision. Just as importantly, however, are the ways in which the 'enemy' – i.e. young people – have been ideologically constructed in the debates over juvenile justice, and how the police have responded to these debates.

The advocates of 'law and order' tell us that the primary threat to 'freedom' and private property is the 'criminal'. The criminal is seen as abnormal, and as an alien force which threatens our institutions from the 'outside'. This is expressed in language which describes young people as 'louts', 'larrikins', 'no-hopers', 'gang-members', 'dole-bludgers', 'hooligans' and so on. This is a part of the process whereby one section of the population is separated off from the 'law-abiding general public'. As Cunneen describes it:

> The public individual is reconstituted in opposition to the hoodlum as a classless, genderless and raceless 'citizen'. The citizen by definition is policed by consent because the citizen is law-abiding. On the other hand the hoodlum will never be policed by consent because, by definition, the hoodlum is outside the consensus. And of course the hoodlum at certain moments in history displays particular sectional interests: unemployed youth, trade unionist, Black. (Cunneen, 1988:191)

The targeting of young people as a group warranting police intervention and increased surveillance has been marked by sustained ideological campaigns establishing youth as 'the enemy'. In the context of high levels of youth unemployment and the increased visibility of young people in the public sphere, this is hardly surprising, especially given the potential for offending that such circumstances generate (White, 1989b).

The use of evocative language and lurid headlines in the media, plus political support from government leaders and within the police hierarchy, have provided legitimacy for the police to use 'whatever means necessary' to do their job. And 'the job' in this instance has been defined as 'cleaning up the streets', to 'keep young people in line', and to 'manage' the unemployed, the poor and the black – all for the sake of the largely mythical 'average citizen'. In several states this has been accompanied by legislative changes which directly enhance police powers at the point of contact (see Carrington, 1990; White, 1992d).

In order to illustrate the manner in which the extension of police power can occur, we can briefly examine recent legislation in Western Australia aimed at juvenile offenders. The *Crime (Serious and Repeat Offenders) Sentencing Act* 1992 greatly enhances the powers of the police. Simultaneously, it reduces the ability of certain targeted young people to resist the imposition of harsh penalties, even in circumstances where the imposition of such penalties is manifestly not warranted. In essence, the Act provides the police with a greater capacity to directly influence the sentencing options available to the court. And it is the nature of police practices at the grassroots level which is the linchpin of these new-found sentencing powers.

The institutional basis for such powers lies in the sections of the Act which provide that a repeat offender convicted of a violent offence will face a mandatory term in prison or detention, with time of release decided on an 'indeterminate' basis; that a 'repeat offender' is one who has been convicted on six or more separate occasions of one or more prescribed offences; and that in the case of 'violent offences', it only has to be shown that the offender had appeared in court and been convicted on three or more occasions before being subjected to mandatory incarceration.

In practical terms, this gives the police a significant role in sentence decision making. Much will depend upon how they exercise their 'discretion' to charge or not to charge particular young people, the choice of particular offences with which they charge the young person, and the manner in which charges are processed in relation to conviction appearances. How precisely the police will exercise their responsibilities in relation to these new institutional powers is indeed a crucial issue.

The cultural context for the use of police power is therefore an issue of importance. For example, the impetus for police to act in a heavy-handed fashion while performing their duties is linked to certain aspects of 'police culture'. These include the routine use of force in dealing with young people, and the antagonisms that can develop over time due to the violence, racism and abuse all too often associated with 'normal police practices' (see Fitzgerald et al., 1989; Cunneen, 1990ab). A clear illustration of this was provided in the 1992 ABC television documentary, 'Cop It Sweet', which focused on policing in the Sydney suburb of Redfern.

In Western Australia, highly suggestive comments which appeared to approve the harassment of potential offenders made by an assistant commissioner of police (and the defence of this officer and strategy by government ministers) served to remind the public that the 'big stick' approach to policing was by no means out of fashion in that state. Given the youth and relative inexperience of many police on-the-beat and in contact with other young people, such statements were inflammatory to say the least. They also gave credence to the view that the police should impose their 'authority' as a first resort and that they need not be overly bothered with the safeguards normally associated with the 'legitimate' wielders of force.

In the context of both institutional enhancements of and cultural justifications for extended police powers, young people are extremely vulnerable. Given the existing relationship between young people and the police as described earlier in the chapter, any legal measure which is designed to take away court discretion must be regarded as highly contentious. This is because the construction of the legal categories of 'repeat offender' and 'violent offender' in the WA legislation means that the ways in which police undertake their work ultimately determine the sentencing option available. For example, 'resisting arrest' is an easy, common and serious offence with which to charge young people, and is one which appears to fit that section of the Act earmarked for the 'violent offender'. This has implications that bode ill for many young people caught up in the web of police intervention and harassment.

The exercise of police power is contingent upon a variety of factors. It has been shown, for instance, that police believe that the degree of co-operation shown by the young person, the seriousness of the offence and the young person's attitudes are important influences in the nature of the direct interaction between young people and themselves (White, 1992a:33). The frequency, style and location of the contact also have a bearing on both police and young people's responses to each other (Youth Justice Coalition, 1990). Furthermore, it has been shown that the police develop a set of cues or expectations regarding the potential threats or trouble posed by certain groups of young people. This leads the police to pre-empt possible trouble by harassing those young people whose demeanour, dress and language identify them beforehand as being of potential concern (James and Polk, 1989; Piliavin and Briar, 1964; Smith, 1975).

In terms of the policing of street life, the work tasks of the police will also be influenced by such factors as the level of institutional contact between the police and local businesses (e.g. through Business Watch types of schemes), the focus of political attention on certain urban areas (e.g. as in the 'City Safe' initiative in Perth), and the allocation of police resources to particular zones (see White, 1992b). The use of technology in the form of surveillance cameras, golf buggies and two-way radios in specified locations also bolsters the perception that such areas are 'important' and must be 'protected' from the predations of potential juvenile offenders.

The police have recourse to a range of options and techniques in 'persuading' young people not to use the street as they do. At a formal level, police have discretion in areas such as whether or not to intervene, whether or not to offer a formal or informal caution, and whether or not to arrest or issue a court summons. But the exercise of their powers in practice is a process involving different types of actions and different sorts of strategies.

It has been pointed out, for example, that the practice of 'name checking' (asking young people their name and address) is used, especially around commercial centres, as a method of moving young people away from these areas. In their submission to a parliamentary select committee in Western Australia, one youth work agency told the committee of how its youth workers sat with a group of young people outside a restaurant in Northbridge for two hours. According to the youth workers, during this time the group was approached by at least ten different police officers and on a number of occasions the young people were name-checked or questioned. As the youth workers pointed out: 'Yet at no stage were the young people acting in a disruptive, abusive or "criminal" manner. Other evidence indicates that some young people can be name-checked multiple times in one night' (quoted in Watkins et al., 1992:30). As commented on in this parliamentary report and elsewhere (Watkins et al., 1992; Youth Justice Coalition, 1990), the constant hassle of the name-check can eventually lead to resistance and backlash on the part of young people. Situations can thus deteriorate rapidly as the young people grow tired of the continual attention and implied 'suspicion' regarding their activities and status.

A related tactic of police intervention is to question and detain young people without apparent good cause or the usual legal safeguards. In the same report cited above, for instance, another youth worker told how three or four young people will be singled out in a group by the police in public areas like amusement centres and the police will:

> take them out to the car park, split them up, ask them to stay there, and walk around and interview each one without arresting them, without giving them a reason other than that they just want to talk to them . . . They are made to stand publicly in a car park with the police walking around saying, 'Stand by that car, stand by that car'. The police just walk and interview them in front of shopping centres where people are leaving. (Watkins et al., 1992:31)

Clearly this represents a situation which is highly intimidating and perhaps embarrassing for the young people involved. It would certainly do little to engender a respect for the police as a whole.

The use of force is one of the distinguishing characteristics of police work. That is, it is only the police who, under normal circumstances, have the statutory power to use force against another citizen. However, the question arises whether or not the actual exercise of force by the police is entirely warranted or justified in a number of instances involving young people. In this respect, there is mounting evidence that many young people are subject to physical and verbal abuse from the police, as distinguished from the legitimate use of force in the course of an arrest or peace-keeping operation (see Youth Justice Coalition, 1990; Cunneen, 1990a; Alder, 1991; White et al., 1991; Alder et al., 1992; Watkins et al., 1992). For present purposes, our main concern is to highlight the fact that to 'rough up' young people on the street can be seen as yet another police technique to keep them away from the more public commercial venues.

Characteristics of the police officer have a part to play in an analysis of police violence. The age, sex and experience of the police appear to have some impact on their behaviour on the street (Youth Justice Coalition, 1990; White, 1992a). So too does the perception on the part of some police officers that the courts are 'too lenient' and therefore they will hand out the 'punishment' themselves (Watkins et al., 1992; Alder et al., 1992). The lack of training in areas such as police–youth relations and Aboriginal history and culture, racism and work stress are other factors in the poor relationships on the street.

Another cause of concern on the part of young people is that they often have great difficulty in exercising their legal rights in encounters with the police. In some cases those who do talk of their rights are considered to be 'smart-asses' by the police and subject to 'special treatment' in terms of charges laid and the juvenile justice process from the point of contact onwards (Youth Justice Coalition, 1990; O'Connor and Sweetapple, 1988). Police have enormous discretionary powers. Young people who challenge their authority are vulnerable to a wide range of potential charges, ranging from swearing and public order offences through to resisting arrest. Under such circumstances, an appeal to abstract 'rights' may be more than disadvantageous at an immediate practical level.

The police, then, have a wide range of powers and routine techniques for ensuring that public order is maintained and that young people will not intrude upon the commercial relations of the shopping centre and mall. The ways in which they regulate the activities and space of young people directly impacts upon the police–youth relationship in general.

CONCLUSION

The antagonisms and conflicts between young people and the police on the street are not simply a matter of personal whim or due to the presence of particularly nasty individual personalities. The relationship between young people and the police is structured through a combination of three broad influences:

- the *social background* of the young people, and particularly those who have been marginalised in the areas of production (e.g. employment), consumption (e.g. income) and community life (e.g. family and peer networks), heavily influences the extent and nature of police intervention in their lives. The more vulnerable sections of the youth population – the unemployed and Aborigines – in essence constitute the primary targets of the police. As perceived 'threats' to public order, attention on these young people and the techniques used to control them set up a wider dynamic which affects how police respond to any gathering of young people regardless of background or the activity in which they are engaged.

- the *constriction of social space* for young people, especially in the light of the commercialisation of public spaces and the calls by businesspeople and older consumers to regulate 'consumer space', which in turn constitutes one of the few venues available for young people to congregate *en masse*, is a further condition for potential conflict. The planning and design of urban space has tended to favour commercial activity over and above general social and communal activities. This has impacted upon the opportunities of young people to assert their autonomy and interests in a less visible manner.

- the political and occupational *pressures on the police* to be seen to be 'doing their duty' and to be 'protecting the public', and in particular defending those sections of the 'public' which have direct economic interests in specific geographical and cultural localities, is a further factor in the structural relationship between police and young people. The methods and operations of the police in carrying out their tasks tend to be based upon an 'authoritarian' rather than 'co-operative' model of intervention. A lack of respect on both sides leads to an escalation in the use of even more heavy-handed methods and more fierce resistance on the part of certain groups of young people.

From the point of view of the police, the question may be seen as one of just 'doing their job'. For young people, however, the issue is often one of being able to 'hang out' without being hassled. They are not the 'criminals' as portrayed in the more sensationalised media reports, and the committing of minor offences by young people generally does not reflect any sort of deep anti-social character traits.

If what happens on our streets is to change in any significant fashion, then a range of initiatives will have to be undertaken. As the above analysis suggests, however, any proposals for reform will need to take into account the structural contradictions of a society in economic recession, institutional conflicts arising out of the opposing demands placed upon the police, and the personal actions and responsibilities of both young people and police officers.

At a social-structural level, it is clear that policies directed at providing greater social justice and social welfare are badly needed if the problems of youth alienation and marginalisation are to be overcome. These problems tend to become culturally entrenched over time in the form of various youth subcultures. Thus, the drift into and out of illegal behaviour – which is a generalised phenomenon across the teenage population – may occasionally harden into consistent patterns of offending behaviour for those sections of the youth population which do not have a stake in the current economic, political and social institutions of Australian society. The street can be a 'hard' place. And it takes 'hard' people to establish their position in one of the few spaces in society which is open to them and which, through force of numbers and cultural symbolism, they can make their own.

At the level of institutional practices, the police are often caught up in contradictory roles and are left without adequate resources to become a positive part of particular communities or neighbourhoods. For example, police have indicated that they feel that meeting with young people in a non-threatening atmosphere (and perhaps out of uniform) would do much to break down the barriers between themselves and young people (see White, 1992a). This implies a significant shift in police department resources and orientation if it is to occur in practice. Simultaneously, however, they are often called upon to actively intervene in the lives of young people in a directly coercive and regulating manner, as in the case of truancy patrols and the enforcement of curfews. Also, the forceful exercise of police powers and instances of over-policing in some localities work against the ideals of fostering a more constructive relationship with young people at the grassroots level.

Part of the impetus for 'law enforcement' types of approaches to policing comes from the demands of business proprietors to have something done about non-consumers whose presence may upset those wanting to buy goods and services. Rather than attempting to simply close off commercial space to these young people, which can engender running wars between the young people and shopkeepers and shopping complex managers, creative alternatives are needed. For a start, businesspeople could try to engage in a dialogue with the young people concerned, and try to work out various compromises in the use of the 'public spaces' in the commercial centres. Or, pressure can be put on local councils, including offers of financial assistance from business interests, to open up new areas where young people could congregate without the hassles of police, parents, shoppers or businesspeople. Given the dearth of other alternatives and until new 'community commons' are created, young people will be forced by circumstance and existing property relations to seek out commercial venues for their 'spare-time' activities.

The commodification of public space (via the extension of private ownership and control), and the commercialisation of public activity (by privileging monetary exchange relations over casual social interaction), set the immediate context for police–youth relationships. Until the 'street' is reclaimed as a community resource, and police practices are subjected to community scrutiny and control at the local area level, it cannot be expected that things will greatly improve. So too, only when there is a shift from 'policing the community' to police becoming part of the community, will the relationships between young people and the police perhaps be able to develop on the basis of mutual respect, understanding and recognition of the rights and obligations of the other.

REFERENCES

Alder, C. (1991) 'Victims of Violence: The case of homeless youth', *Australian and New Zealand Journal of Criminology*, 24(1):1–14.

Alder, C. (1992) 'The Young People' in C. Alder et al. (eds), *Perceptions of the Treatment of Juveniles in the Legal System*. Hobart: National Clearinghouse for Youth Studies.

Alder, C., O'Connor, I., Warner, K. and White, R. (1992) *Perceptions of the Treatment of Juveniles in the Legal System*. Report for the National Youth Affairs Research Scheme. Hobart: National Clearinghouse for Youth Studies.

Alder, C. and Sandor, D. (1990) *Homeless Youth as Victims of Violence*. Melbourne: Criminology Department, University of Melbourne.

Australian Youth Policy and Action Coalition (1992) *A Living Income: Income support for young people* (plus assorted media releases and information packages). Sydney: Youth Action and Policy Association (NSW).

Brake, M. (1985) *Comparative Youth Culture*. London: Routledge and Kegan Paul.

Brannigan, A. (1984) *Crimes, Courts and Corrections*. Toronto: Holt, Rinehart and Winston of Canada.

Burdekin, B. (1989) *Our Homeless Children*. Report of the National Inquiry into Homeless Children by the Human Rights and Equal Opportunity Commission. Canberra: Australian Government Publishing Service.

Carrington, K. (1990) 'Youth: The right police?', *Arena*, 91:18–24.

Cohen, P. (1979) 'Policing the Working-class City' in B. Fine et al. (eds), *Capitalism and the Rule of Law*. London: Hutchinson.

Cohen, S. (1972) *Folk Devils and Moral Panics: The creation of the Mods and Rockers*. Oxford: Martin Robertson.

Cowie, M. (1991) Struggle for the Streets. Paper presented to the Annual Conference of the Australian and New Zealand Society of Criminology, October, Melbourne.

Cunneen, C. (1988) 'The Policing of Public Order: Some thoughts on culture, space and political economy' in M. Findlay and R. Hogg (eds), *Understanding Crime and Criminal Justice*. Sydney: Law Book Company.

Cunneen, C. (1989) 'Constructing a Law and Order Agenda: Conservative populism and Aboriginal people in North West New South Wales', *Aboriginal Law Bulletin*, 2(38):18–20.

Cunneen, C. (1990a) *A Study of Aboriginal Juveniles and Police Violence*. Sydney: Human Rights and Equal Opportunity Commission.

Cunneen, C. (1990b) *Aboriginal–Police Relations in Redfern: With special reference to the 'police raid' of 8 February 1990*. Sydney: Human Rights and Equal Opportunity Commission.

Federation of Community Legal Centres (Victoria) (1991) *Report into Mistreatment of Young People by Police in Victoria*. Melbourne.

Fitzgerald, G. et al. (1989) *Report of the Commission of Possible Illegal Activities and Associated Police Misconduct*. Brisbane: Queensland Government Printer.

Gale, F., Bailey-Harris, R. and Wundersitz, J. (1990) *Aboriginal Youth and the Criminal Justice System: the injustice of justice?* Cambridge: Cambridge University Press.

Graycar, A. and Jamrozik, A. (1989) *How Australians Live: Social policy in theory and practice*. Melbourne: Macmillan.

Hebdige, D. (1979) *Subculture: The meaning of style*. London: Methuen.

Hirst, C. (1989) *Forced Exit: A profile of the young and homeless in inner urban Melbourne*. Melbourne: Salvation Army.

James, S. and Polk, K. (1989) 'Policing Youth: Themes and directions' in D. Chappell and P. Wilson (eds), *Australian Policing: Contemporary Issues*. Sydney: Butterworths.

Johnston, E. (1991) *National Report* (vols.1–4). Royal Commission into Aboriginal Deaths in Custody. Canberra: Australian Government Publishing Service.

McManus, P. (1991) 'Not Just A Better Shopping Environment: A study of social issues pertaining to malls'. Perth: School of Architecture and Planning, Curtin University of Technology.

Moss, I. and Castan, R. (1991) *Racist Violence: Report of the National Inquiry into Racist Violence in Australia*. Human Rights and Equal Opportunity Commission. Canberra: Australian Government Publishing Service.

O'Connor, I. (1989) *Our Homeless Children: Their Experiences*. Sydney: Human Rights and Equal Opportunity Commission.

O'Connor, I. and Sweetapple, P. (1988) *Children in Justice*. Melbourne: Longman Cheshire.

Pearson, G. (1983) *Hooligan: A history of respectable fears*. London: Macmillan.

Piliavin, I. and Briar, S. (1964) 'Police Encounters with Juveniles', *American Journal of Sociology*, 70:206–14.

Smith, G. (1975) 'Kids and Coppers', *Australian and New Zealand Journal of Criminology*, 8:221–30.

Stratton, J. (1992) *The Young Ones: Working-class culture, consumption and the category of youth*. Perth: Black Swan Press.

Watkins, J. et al. (1992) *Youth and the Law*. Discussion Paper No.3, Select Committee into Youth Affairs. Perth: Western Australia Government Printer.

White, R. (1989a) 'Making Ends Meet: Young people, work and the criminal economy', *Australian and New Zealand Journal of Criminology*, 22:136–50.

White, R. (1989b) 'Reading, Writing and Repression: Police in the schools', *Legal Service Bulletin*, 14(2):58–62.

White, R. (1990) *No Space Of Their Own: Young people and social control in Australia*. Cambridge: Cambridge University Press.

White, R. (1992a) 'The police' in C. Alder et al., *Perceptions of the Treatment of Juveniles in the Legal System*. Hobart: National Clearinghouse for Youth Studies.

White, R. (1992b) Young People, Community Space and Social Control. Paper presented at the Australian Institute of Criminology Conference on Juvenile Justice, Adelaide, September.

White, R. (1992c) 'Policing the Community', *Melbourne Report*, February 2–3.

White, R. (1992d) 'Tough Laws for Hard-Core Politicians', *Alternative Law Journal*, 17(2):58–60.

White, R., Underwood, R. and Omelczuk, S. (1991) 'Victims of Violence: The view from the youth services', *Australian and New Zealand Journal of Criminology*, 24(1):25–39.

Youth Justice Coalition (NSW) (1990) *Kids in Justice: A blueprint for the 90s*. Sydney: Youth Justice Coalition.

CHAPTER 6

Enforcing Genocide?
Aboriginal Young People and the Police

Chris Cunneen

THE HISTORICAL BACKGROUND

What is different or unique about the relationship between Aboriginal young people and the police? After all, there are continuities in the type of police intervention into working-class lives and the intervention into Aboriginal communities. There are also continuities in the gender-specific treatment by the police of non-Aboriginal young people and Aboriginal young men and women. However the relationship between Aboriginal young people and the police is also structured by the processes of colonialism and neo-colonialism. Indeed the determinant factor historically in the relationship is that Aboriginal young people are indigenous people, while the police have been part of a state apparatus which is colonial.

In broad terms, it is possible to categorise police relations with Aboriginal young people into three distinct phases: the period of open warfare and resistance; the period of 'protective' legislation; and a contemporary period of criminalisation. The different stages of colonial expansion and control across the continent from the end of the eighteenth century through to the early twentieth century have overlapped and existed side by side in different parts of the country. Indeed, these distinct phases are most usefully conceptualised as modes of intervention rather than simply as periods of time.

For instance, at the same time as the Native Mounted Police had the effect of institutionalising violence on the frontier in Queensland, the Victorian government introduced the 1869 'Act to Provide for the Protection and Management of the Aboriginal Natives of Victoria'. Thus open warfare and protective legislation existed contemporaneously in different parts of the country.

A common element to these modes of intervention has been the attempted implementation of a process of genocide. Under

international law, genocide is defined as those acts committed with
the intent to destroy, in whole or in part, a national, ethnic, racial
or religious group. Such acts may involve deliberate violence or
policies aimed at cultural destruction.

Aboriginal young people and infants were treated the same as
Aboriginal adults in the frontline of colonial warfare. Murder by
state forces (Elder, 1988; Evans, Saunders and Cronin, 1988) and
settlers was largely either legitimated or ignored by the colonial
government, although on some occasions the government attempted
to distance itself from the behaviour of its police (see Neal,
1991:150-4). The massacre of Aboriginal tribal and kinship groups
meant that Aboriginal young people were killed alongside older and
younger members of the group. Age was irrelevant at this level of
state intervention: an overriding concern was Aboriginality. Groups
of people were murdered *because they were Aboriginal*, that is,
because they were the indigenous people in possession of the land
and because they resisted colonial expansion. Thus, the accounts of
various massacres by mounted and other police suggest that the
killing was indiscriminate in terms of age.

In particular areas of Australia, massacres by state police extended
well into the twentieth century. In 1926 in the Kimberley region of
Western Australia, a punitive party led by two police officers was
responsible for killing up to thirty Aboriginal people of various ages,
including children (Markus, 1990:3). During 1928 in Coniston, some
sixty to seventy Walbiri people were killed over several weeks by a
Northern Territory police party. The officer in charge openly
admitted to a policy of shoot to kill. The victims were of both sexes
and all ages (Elder, 1988:141-53). According to a missionary who
spoke to survivors of the killings, 'The natives tell me that they
simply shot them down like dogs and that they got the little children
and hit them on the back of the neck and killed them' (cited in
Markus, 1990:163).

During the early periods of colonisation, children and young
people were also often the explicit target of other, ostensibly more
humane, policies by both the state and the church. These policies
were aimed at the removal of Aboriginal children from their families
and kinship groups (Attwood, 1989; Markus, 1990). The purpose of
that intervention was to effect genocide. 'From the earliest period
of contact, those seeking to absorb Aborigines into European culture
have looked to children as their best hope' (Markus, 1990:22). Some

of the earliest 'Aboriginal' institutions established by whites were designed to remove Aboriginal children from their families. The Parramatta Native Institution established in 1814 is one example (Brook and Kohen, 1991). In Victoria, missionaries by the mid-1800s were concentrating on the removal of Aboriginal children from their families to dormitories as a way of attempting to prevent the transmission of Aboriginal culture (Attwood, 1989:18). Legislation in Victoria in 1869 facilitated this process by giving the Aborigines Protection Board considerable power including care and custody of children (Attwood, 1989:84). Read has noted that 'by 1850 all the half-dozen missions which had come and gone in eastern Australia had ... tried to raise Aboriginal children separated from their parents' (Edwards and Read, 1988:xi). Police were involved in enforcing the separation from families as demanded by the missionaries.

The scale of removal by the missionaries was relatively modest compared to the more direct state-organised policies of removal under various pieces of state protection legislation in the late nineteenth and twentieth centuries. A major function of the New South Wales Aborigines Protection Board was to gain control over Aboriginal children. The aims have been identified as

> The reduction of Aboriginal birth-rate by removal of adolescents, particularly girls; [the] prevention of Aboriginal children's identification with the Aboriginal community by isolating them from their families and communities through adolescence; [and] preventing or hindering their return to their families or the Aboriginal community. (Wootten, 1989:8–19)

Thus, the primary purpose for the administration was that 'whatever else the children grew up to be, they should not be allowed to grow up as identifying Aborigines' (Edwards and Read, 1988:xiii). Indeed the Royal Commission into Aboriginal Deaths in Custody has noted that 'such a policy would today be internationally condemned as genocide' (Wootten, 1989:19).

This interventionist policy was gendered. Goodall has argued that between 1900 and 1940 Aboriginal girls bore the heaviest impact of removal policies: pubertal girls were targeted and, in its early years, some 80 percent of the children removed were female, the majority of whom were 12 years and older (Goodall, 1990b:6).

According to one historian the purpose of child removal was to counter the 'positive menace to the State' which the ever-increasing and non-assimilated Aboriginal population was supposed to represent (Read, n.d.:5). The legislation, although varying in degrees and timing from state to state, legitimated police intervention into Aboriginal life in an unprecedented manner.

The original NSW protection legislation of 1909 was found to be too constricting because it had to be shown before a magistrate that the child or young person was actually neglected prior to removal. However, Goodall (1990b) has demonstrated that the children the board wanted to remove were not neglected. Indeed, the board failed in a series of court cases because it was unable to demonstrate neglect. The legislation was amended in 1915 to allow removal of Aboriginal children without a court hearing if the Aborigines Protection Board considered it to be in the interest of the child. The legislative change was achieved through a public campaign aimed at convincing parliament and the public that Aboriginal parenting was, *by definition*, negligent. The board gained greater powers and, in the process, reinforced racist assumptions about Aboriginal parenting. Goodall (1990b:7) has argued that such assumptions about the incompetence of Aboriginal child-nurturing were to permeate police views in their carrying out of the Protection Board policies.

In the Northern Territory, the police were responsible for implementing the Commonwealth policy of segregating 'light-skinned' children. In Alice Springs in 1914, the local chief protector (who was the police sergeant) took an active role by initiating the establishment of a government institution for Aboriginal children and young people. Accordingly, police on patrol were instructed to seize children and bring them back to the institution (Markus, 1990:22–36). During the 1930s, Cecil Cook, the chief protector for the Northern Territory, greatly expanded the practice of child removal by police (Markus, 1990:100).

In New South Wales the police played a fundamental role in the operation of the Aborigines Protection Board, both in terms of its bureaucratic structure and in its day-to-day activities. It was noted that: 'It is difficult to decide whether the police should be regarded as agents of the Board or whether the Board itself should more properly be seen as an arm of the Police Department' (Goodall, 1982:190). The commissioner of police was *ex officio* chairman of the Protection Board and all police were appointed 'guardians' of Aborigines after the 1909 legislation.

Contemporary newspaper reports note the anxiety created by child removal, particularly when children were often literally stolen from unsuspecting parents (see, for example, the *Sydney Morning Herald,* 9 January 1925, p.8 for an account of four children being removed by police from parents at Grafton). The removal of Aboriginal children was resisted by parents at every step (Goodall, 1982:73). Early Aboriginal political organisations in south-east Australia, such as the Australian Aborigines Progressive Organisation, drew attention to the forcible removal of Aboriginal children and the role of police as 'guardians' (Markus, 1990:176–7). Along with the demand for land and full citizenship rights, the question of policing and incarceration of Aboriginal young people was seen as a key political issue by Aboriginal people from the 1920s.

FROM PAST TO PRESENT

The policy of child removal has deeply conditioned the Aboriginal view of what the 'rule of law' has meant for their families and kin. The long-term social and political ramifications of the policy are still being felt. It has been estimated that in Australia today there may be 100,000 people of Aboriginal descent who do not know their families or communities (Edwards and Read, 1988:ix). Specifically in relation to police, it has been noted that 'the fear that police were arriving to take the children meant that all the Aboriginal community treated any arrival by police with fear and suspicion' (Anti-Discrimination Board, 1982:125). Some of the children removed by the police are now the adults being arrested for street offences. 'It is therefore not surprising that there are many levels of tension and conflict between the two groups' (Anti-Discrimination Board, 1982:125).

The historical relationship between police and Aboriginal young people has consequences which compound and influence the contemporary relationship. In a most obvious sense young people grow up, and their early contacts with police at a youthful age influence later interactions. Aboriginal young people are also recipients and bearers of their own culture and their own history which has been, and continues to be, handed down through oral traditions, and increasingly through written materials. A central part of these oral traditions revolves around the conflict with police as enforcers of a repressive and racist political and social structure which denies Aboriginal people basic human rights. The point is illustrated in the comments of an Aboriginal woman in Bourke discussing the 1950s and 1960s in rural New South Wales.

> *Woman:* They had those welfare laws over them in the sixties. In 1967 they abolished the Dog Tag Act. My father's got one. He was the only black person in Bourke who held one of those certificates ... which allowed him not only to drink but to walk the streets as a citizen. If he didn't produce it he was locked-up ... If he was on the street and if he didn't have his dog tag, well he was 'vagged'. They put a vagrancy charge on him.

> *Interviewer:* Is that something which is constantly talked about amongst Aboriginal people?

> *Woman:* Yes. But then this is why the people feel like they do with the police. For instance I saw the police come to my house, we used to live in an old shack down the reserve, and drag my father out and kick and kick and kick him. I saw that. I'm only 32 years of age and that is still on my mind. And yet I try not to show it or pass it on to my kids.

> *Interviewer:* But the kids are obviously aware of all this?

> *Woman:* Of course they are. Their parents have told them things. Look at my husband. He lived out at Wanaaring. They were told, my husband's mother and father were told, to move their old tin humpy from where they had it. And they didn't because my father-in-law was out of town at the time. My mother-in-law was there with eight little kids. So the police came down driving a bulldozer and knocked the house on top of them. It didn't happen generations ago. We are still part of what happened. My husband was in that house when it was knocked down by the police. And all this is passed on to the kids. (Cited in Cunneen and Robb, 1987:267)

Despite the attempts at cultural genocide and the amnesia which pervaded 'our' official histories, the story of oppression and resistance has been passed on from one generation to another in Aboriginal families and communities. That story has provided both a reservoir of knowledge for understanding contemporary situations and a basis on which at least some current modes of resistance have been formulated.

THE PROCESS OF CRIMINALISATION

In 1991 the Human Rights and Equal Opportunity Commission's National Inquiry into Racist Violence found that the issue of relations between Aboriginal juveniles and police was of concern in Aboriginal communities. Central to those concerns were both the extent to which Aboriginal juveniles are still placed in custody, and their treatment while in custody. Allegations of harassment and violence by police were submitted to the inquiry from across Australia. For example, of the sixteen incidents of alleged police violence which were documented in the Pilbara region in Western Australia, nine involved serious violence against Aboriginal male and female juveniles (Human Rights and Equal Opportunity Commission, 1991:94).

Since the late 1960s the removal of Aboriginal children from their families and kinship networks, as a result of either welfare complaints or specific legislation aimed at Aboriginal people, has increasingly fallen into disrepute. However, Aboriginal children continue to be incarcerated in juvenile institutions at a rate which is nothing less than a national scandal (see Cunneen and Libesman, 1990). For example, in Western Australia in early 1990, some 73 percent of inmates in juvenile detention centres were Aboriginal, yet Aboriginal youth comprised a little over 4 percent of the state's youth population. In that state an Aboriginal young person was sixty-two times more likely to be incarcerated than a non-Aboriginal youth (Cunneen, 1990b:15–16). Gross levels of overrepresentation were typical of other states (D'Souza, 1990).

Aboriginal overrepresentation in the juvenile justice system increases at the most punitive end of the system: courts are more likely to incarcerate Aboriginal youth than non-Aboriginal youth. In Western Australia, Aboriginal male youth were nearly eight times as likely as non-Aboriginal male youth to be sentenced to detention (15.6% compared to 2% of court outcomes), and Aboriginal female youth were some twenty-one times more likely to be sentenced to detention than non-Aboriginal young women (4.3% compared to 0.2% of court outcomes) (Broadhurst, Ferrante and Susilo, 1991:74). Similarly in South Australia, Aboriginal young people made up 8 percent of police apprehensions, but 28 percent of young people in detention. Aboriginal youth in that state were also more likely to receive a detention order as a sentencing outcome than non-Aboriginal youth (Gale, Bailey-Harris and Wundersitz, 1990:4–5).

Thus, the processes of removal and institutionalisation of Aboriginal young people have not stopped during the later part of this century simply because legislation has been altered and particular practices have been defined as unacceptable. Aboriginal youth are still institutionalised at a truly extraordinary rate as a result of the processes of criminalisation. It is important to recognise the continuities with earlier policies which legitimated the removal of Aboriginal children from their families. Indeed, the process of criminalisation has replaced the previously overt genocidal doctrine of 'breeding out' Aboriginality. Aboriginal youth are no longer institutionalised because they are Aboriginal, but rather because they are criminal. It is also important to consider the change in the gendered processes of intervention. Goodall (1990b:6,9) has argued that the post-war period saw a change from a focus on Aboriginal girls to a focus on boys. Such a gendered shift has been further pronounced with law and order campaigns which by and large have focused on Aboriginal males.

While the earlier welfare practices in relation to Aboriginal youth were self-consciously based on race, the practices of the justice system remain committed at an ideological level to the rule of law. The rule of law places central importance on equality before the law, due process and the protection of rights, and a system of law which prevents the arbitrary use of power and discretion. Since police practices provide substantial latitude in the use of discretion, it becomes particularly important to scrutinise the role of the police in the process of criminalisation and state intervention. Further reason for examining police practices in particular is provided in the research by Gale, Bailey-Harris and Wundersitz (1990) which indicated that police decisions have significant implications for the young person's later career through the juvenile justice system. Thus, the police continue to be at the forefront in exercising the control functions of the state.

The empirical evidence shows that Aboriginal young people are disproportionately the focus of police intervention. For example, Aboriginal young people made up some 40 percent of all Aboriginal people arrested in Western Australia during 1990. This comprised about twice the juvenile to adult ratio typical of non-Aboriginal arrests (Broadhurst, Ferrante and Susilo, 1991:29, 35).

There is also evidence that formal police intervention occurs at an earlier age with Aboriginal young people, and that Aboriginal overrepresentation is greatest at the earliest age of intervention. For example, in Western Australia in 1990, some 14 percent of adult arrests were of Aboriginal people. However, in the same year, some 25 percent of all juveniles who were arrested were Aboriginal. The level of Aboriginal overrepresentation increases dramatically among the youngest group under the age of 14-years-old. The majority of young people under 14 who were arrested were Aboriginal: some 72 percent of girls under 14 arrested by police were Aboriginal, and some 66 percent of boys under 14 who were arrested were Aboriginal (adapted from Broadhurst, Ferrante and Susilo, 1991:44–6).

The criminalisation of Aboriginal young people necessitates increased scrutiny of the functions of police in their dealings with Aboriginal young people. During earlier historical periods, police intervened into Aboriginal life under clearly articulated racist legislation. During the current period, however, the justice system removes and incarcerates Aboriginal young people on the assumption that they are criminal. It is assumed that as criminals they are treated, assessed and judged the same as any other person in society. It is both imperative and difficult to examine the way in which a system, which legitimates itself on liberal notions of equality, might simultaneously be engaged in practices which are racist. The processes of institutional racism may not be immediately apparent. In fact, the dominant ideology of liberalism which informs the legal system logically denies that the system itself could be engaged in methodically reproducing racist oppression.

ENTERING THE SYSTEM: CAUTIONING, SUMMONS AND ARREST

Police determine the entrance into the juvenile justice system. Police decisions whether to caution, charge, proceed by way of arrest or by summons influence later judicial decisions made about the young person. Indeed, decisions made about adult offenders are influenced invariably by previous criminal records which themselves reflect proceedings as a juvenile (Walker, 1987). As a result, there is a compounding effect where early punitive decisions negatively influence later decisions in the juvenile and criminal justice process. A chain of continuing escalation in the level of intervention is established.

The acquisition of a criminal record also enables and legitimates ongoing police surveillance and intervention. As Edmunds has astutely observed, a police record

maintains individuals . . . within the area of vigilance of the police. [The record] operates like the old convict markers: whoever the person is, his or her record ... marks the limits of their ability to redefine their place in the community. To have been noticed by the law is to remain subject to the law's scrutiny. (Edmunds, 1989:104)

For a young person, the acquisition of a criminal record becomes a primary determinant of the court's decision to sentence him or her to detention (Gale et al., 1990:6–7).

It is also necessary to understand the nature of all of the stages of police intervention because, as Feeley (1979) has argued, the pre-adjudication process may constitute the real punishment for those caught in the web of criminal justice intervention. The events which occur between apprehension by police and the final sanctioning by the court may be more punishing in terms of loss of liberty and other forms of personal hurt and suffering than any punishment meted out by the court. The issue raised by Feeley of 'process as punishment' is particularly important in relation to Aboriginal young people. The empirical evidence presented below relating to arrest rates, the nature of charges, bail conditions and the incidence of harassment and police violence in custody all suggest that Aboriginal young people are given a particularly difficult time in negotiating the processes of juvenile justice. To the extent which the system can be one which engages in various forms of punishment prior to the sanctioning by the court, Aboriginal young people receive the more punitive options.

Available evidence shows that Aboriginal youth have less chance of receiving the diversionary police option of cautioning. In New South Wales, a study of the use of cautioning for Aboriginal young people found that in a number of towns in north-west NSW, Aboriginal young people received slightly more than half of the cautions which were issued, slightly less than half of the citations (summons), but over two-thirds of arrests on criminal charges (Cunneen, 1988; see also Luke, 1989). Once Aboriginal youth were detained they were less likely to receive a caution than non-Aboriginal juveniles. 'Around 5% of Aboriginal juveniles detained received a caution compared to slightly more than 10% of non-Aboriginal juveniles. Conversely nearly 90% of Aboriginal youth were arrested and charged compared to 75% of non-Aboriginal youth' (Cunneen, 1988:36).

Luke (1989) analysed police apprehensions in seven New South Wales towns during 1988. He found that, of those apprehended,

31 percent of non-Aboriginal youth received cautions compared to 10 percent of Aboriginal youth. Considerable differences in treatment were found even where the offences were the same. For instance, of those apprehended by police for shoplifting, some 91 percent of non-Aboriginal youth were cautioned compared to 74 percent of Aboriginal youth. Similarly, there were differences in the treatment of first offenders: 49 percent of non-Aboriginal first offenders were cautioned compared to 29 percent of Aboriginal young people who were first offenders. In NSW generally, Cunneen and Luke (1992) found that Aboriginal young people had a higher chance of being charged rather than given a court attendance notice and had a higher likelihood of being refused bail.

The fact that Aboriginal young people had less opportunity of receiving cautions in New South Wales is alarming given that there has been a decline in the use of cautioning generally. In 1986/87 the 4863 cautions issued comprised 25 percent of formal interventions. By 1990/91 the number of cautions had declined to 1142 or 7 percent of formal interventions (NSW Bureau of Crime Statistics and Research, 1992). The scenario for Aboriginal young people in NSW would appear to be one of double disadvantage: a general decline in cautioning, with Aboriginal youth not receiving the benefits of those cautions which are issued.

A similar picture of the failure to use adequately cautions for Aboriginal youth emerges when the use of summons or court attendance notices instead of arrest is considered. The use of a summons or court attendance notice is a less punitive way of bringing a young person before the courts on a criminal charge. Summonses do not involve detention at the police station or the determination of bail.

In Western Australia, Aboriginal people (both adults and juveniles) were about half as likely as non-Aboriginal people to be proceeded against by way of summons (13% of Aboriginal people summonsed compared to 24% of non-Aboriginal) (Broadhurst, Ferrante and Susilo, 1991:33).

After having decided to proceed against a young person, police in South Australia have the choice of either apprehending by way of arrest or filing a report which results in the issuing of a summons. Aboriginal youth are much more likely to be arrested than non-Aboriginal youth. It has been noted that despite a general reduction in the use of arrest by police as a means of apprehension, Aboriginal youth are now more likely to be arrested than they were in previous periods. 'In 1972–73, young Aborigines accounted for 10.6% of all appearances brought about by way of arrest, but by 1985–86 this has risen to 19%' (Gale, Bailey-Harris and Wundersitz, 1990:31).

The International Commission of Jurists (ICJ) recently completed a report on justice issues relating to Aboriginal people in western New South Wales. The ICJ report found that it was the 'invariable practice' for police to arrest and charge persons for summary offences rather than proceed by way of summons. 'It is apparent that summonses are used infrequently by police in summary prosecutions in north west New South Wales' and that this 'inflexible approach is contrary to law and practice' (ICJ, 1990:30). The practice of proceeding by way of arrest for minor offences occurs despite the law. Superior courts in New South Wales have said that summary prosecutions should be commenced by summons unless there is a real concern that a person will not appear to answer the summons (ICJ, 1990:36–7). Given the nature of relatively small communities, with many of the alleged offenders known to police, such a concern seems unwarranted.

The Royal Commission into Aboriginal Deaths in Custody was particularly concerned with the issue of police arresting Aboriginal juveniles rather than cautioning or issuing a summons or court attendance notice. Recommendation 239 of the Royal Commission calls on governments to review legislation and police instructions to ensure that police only proceed by arrest when there are reasonable grounds for believing it to be necessary. The commission recommends that

> the general rule should be that if the offence alleged to have been committed is not grave and if the indications are that the juvenile is unlikely to repeat the offence or commit other offences at that time then arrest should not be effected. (Johnston, 1991a:183)

BAIL

The issue of police bail for Aboriginal youth is important because the conditions which are set may lead to further criminalisation. The Royal Commission into Aboriginal Deaths in Custody has sought, in recommendations 90 and 91, a review of the appropriateness of bail criteria in relation to Aboriginal people, particularly juveniles. The Royal Commission identified numerous problems with bail including that 'unreal conditions are regularly broken, meaning that young people are recycled through the courts ... [in addition] available evidence shows that police are more likely to refuse bail to an Aboriginal than a non-Aboriginal in similar circumstances' (Wootten, 1991b:353). Many of the bail conditions placed on Aboriginal young people are unnecessarily oppressive: both banishment and curfews have been used as bail conditions against young people. In cases of banishment, bail conditions are imposed which require the young person to leave the town and reside elsewhere until the time of the court appearance. In New South Wales, banishment has been used against Aboriginal juveniles in Bourke, Wilcannia, Brewarrina and Walgett. The use of such orders could be said to violate basic international standards on human rights in relation to freedom of movement. They impose enormous pressures on the young person and his or her family. Bail conditions which restrict movement outside the home between 7 p.m and 7 a.m. have also been placed on Aboriginal young people. Such restrictions, in practice, amount to a curfew (Cunneen, 1990a).

In the report on the death of Lloyd Boney, Commissioner Wootten made some important observations concerning bail.

> Conditions should not be set which obviously will not or cannot be complied with. Unrealistic conditions simply set the defendant up for failure, and produce the result that bail is at the discretion of the police, who can arrest the defendant for breach of conditions whenever they choose not to turn a blind eye to the breach. (Wootten, 1991a:177)

The setting of unrealistic and non-compliable bail conditions is a way of further extending the control of police over Aboriginal young people. It is a way of both punishing the defendant (if he or she should try to comply with the conditions), and of extending surveillance over the individual to the point of determining his or her location (to walk the streets at a particular time or in a particular place may be to commit an offence). It is also a way of extending power by allowing the defendant freedom at the discretion of police officers. Power is maintained through the threat of potentially arbitrary arrest for breach of bail at any time.

Such legal relations enable a principle of 'compulsory visibility' to be operationalised. In relation to prison Foucault stated, 'It is the fact of being constantly seen, of being able always to be seen, that maintains the disciplined individual in his subjection' (1979:187).

Similarly the use of some bail conditions legally constitutes the subject within a gaze which can determine both spatial and temporal location.

POLICE REFERRAL TO CHILDREN'S PANELS

Both South Australia and Western Australia have a formalised diversionary system which relies on children's panels as an alternative to the court. A recent parliamentary report in New South Wales has recommended the establishment of a children's panel in that state (NSW Legislative Council Standing Committee on Social Issues, 1992:94–101). The aim of the panels is to divert minor and/or first offenders from the formal processes of the court. Those appearing before the panels do not have a criminal conviction registered against them, although their appearance before the panel is recorded.

Why might the role of panels be an issue to be addressed in a discussion on police and Aboriginal youth? Quite simply because police play a major role in deciding who goes before panels and in the composition of the panels themselves. It has been repeatedly demonstrated that those decisions impact negatively on Aboriginal young people. In other words, decisions made by police mean that Aboriginal young people do not receive the benefit of diversion.

In Western Australia, the children's panel is made up of two members, one representing the Police Department and the other representing the Department of Community Services. In the Perth area, the police representative is usually a retired police officer; however elsewhere the officer is a serving police officer. Seymour (1988:248) noted that in small towns the officer who apprehended the child may also sit on the panel. Wilkie (1991) has noted that no Aboriginal police officer had been authorised to sit on panels. Referral to a panel instead of the children's court is at the discretion of the police.

Wilkie (1991:135–6) has shown that Western Australian Aboriginal young people are much less likely to be referred to a children's panel than non-Aboriginal youth. During the first half of 1990, Aboriginal young people comprised 22 percent of children's court appearances and 12.6 percent of children's panel appearances. One in three non-Aboriginal young people was referred to a panel compared to one in eight Aboriginal youth. The Western Australian evidence does not tell us why police chose not to refer Aboriginal young people to panels: it may or may not be because they did not fulfil certain eligibility requirements. It does however indicate that the system operates in a way which further criminalises Aboriginal youth and that the police are the gatekeepers of the system.

The South Australian system of panels is slightly more complicated than the Western Australian model. In South Australia there is a screening panel which makes the initial decision to refer the juvenile to a children's aid panel or to the children's court. The screening panel is comprised of a police officer and a representative from the Department of Community Welfare. The screening panels were more likely to refer Aboriginal young people directly to the children's court rather than to the children's aid panel, the less punitive option.

Gale (1990) and her colleagues matched Aboriginal and non-Aboriginal young people who were referred from the screening panel to the children's court by demographic, residential and socio-economic criteria as well as prior appearances and the number of charges. They found that because Aboriginal youth were more likely to be arrested in the first instance rather than reported, they were more likely to be referred to court rather than the aid panel. The authors suggest that because of the police presence on the screening panel, there is pressure to refer arrested juveniles directly to the court. As a result, Aboriginal young people were being denied the opportunity of diversion offered by the panels because they had been arrested in the first place. The original punitive decision to proceed by way of arrest, rather than other methods, compounds into an escalating level of intervention.

POLICE VIOLENCE AND HARASSMENT

An important part of the dynamics of policing Aboriginal young people is the use of violence and harassment. The use of such measures should be seen in the context of the extent to which police constitute a semi-independent penal regime enforcing their own systems of punishment. In addition, there is also an historical continuity in the use of violence by the state against indigenous people.

In recent years, there has been a growth in the literature discussing the issue of violence and harassment of Aboriginal young people by the police, including government reports (Equal Opportunity

Commission, 1990), royal commission inquiries and reports to non-government human rights organisations (Burger, 1988). Such reports have presented a similar picture. For instance, in a study for the London-based Anti-Slavery Society, Julian Burger noted that 'a most disturbing feature of police relations with the Aboriginal community was the report by Aboriginal legal services officers and solicitors of mistreatment of minors' (Burger, 1988:55). The study concluded that complaints concerning police mistreatment had been largely ignored by the authorities, while the police themselves had claimed that the allegations were exaggerated or fabricated. However, Burger noted that juveniles generally do not come forward with the complaints themselves and discuss such mistreatment only incidentally.

The most extensive research on the question of police violence and Aboriginal young people was conducted for the Human Rights and Equal Opportunity Commission's National Inquiry into Racist Violence. The report portrayed a damning picture of the interaction between police officers and Aboriginal young people (Cunneen, 1990b). The research was based on interviews with 171 Aboriginal juveniles in detention centres in three states (Queensland, Western Australia and New South Wales). Overall 85 percent of the juveniles interviewed reported being hit, punched, kicked or slapped by police. In NSW 82 percent of juveniles reported being assaulted, while in Queensland 90 percent and in Western Australia 94 percent of juveniles reported being assaulted by police.

Some 63 percent of juveniles reported being hit by objects by police. The most common object was a police baton (49%), but also other objects included telephone books (23%), torches (14%) and bats, golf clubs and brooms. Many of the juveniles who reported being hit with batons stated that the incidents occurred, not during arrest as might be expected, but at the police station and often in the police cells. For instance of the thirty-six Aboriginal juveniles who were interviewed in Mt Penang Detention Centre (NSW), some fifteen stated that they had been hit with police batons. More than half (9) of the fifteen stated that they had been hit by batons at the station, usually while detained in the cells. Aboriginal girls had similar complaints of violence to the Aboriginal boys. Eleven of the fourteen girls interviewed alleged that they had been assaulted. There were also allegations of sexual harassment.

The alleged assaults reported in the research occurred on the street, during arrest and at the police station. Complaints about violence and harassment in public places came particularly from suburban and business centres (see also chapter 5). Most of the juveniles interviewed had complaints concerning violence while they were detained in police stations and were being questioned about alleged offences.

Some 81 percent of the juveniles said that they had been subjected to racist abuse by police officers. Many of the Aboriginal girls who were interviewed stated that they were abused with language which was both racist and sexist. The use of such derogatory language, besides being racist in its content, is also important in relation to the provocation involved and the likely consequences of further charges (assaulting police, resisting arrest, offensive language) should the Aboriginal young person retaliate in some manner. In addition, the psychological effects of such racist abuse (and, in the case of females, linked with sexist abuse) should not be underestimated.

A number of juveniles said that while they were in police custody, suggestions had been made by police officers in relation to committing suicide and that threats had been made by police in relation to hanging. One example from NSW included a 17-year-old youth who alleged that he had been kicked and hit with batons by five police in the cells at an outer-metropolitan Sydney police station in mid-1989. After the alleged violence, he was given a sock and told, 'you may as well use it'. It was not possible to examine this issue comprehensively in all the states surveyed. However, in Western Australia some 21 percent of the juveniles interviewed alleged that such suggestions and/or threats had been made by police officers.

Few of the juveniles interviewed had made any form of complaint in relation to the alleged assaults. Where there was some form of complaint made, the actual nature of that complaint was often ambiguous: it may simply have involved telling a welfare worker or solicitor about the alleged assault. There were a number of reasons given for not complaining about alleged assaults, including a sense of futility ('what's the point?'); ignorance of procedures ('I didn't know you could complain'), fear of retaliation and harassment ('I didn't want to get into any more shit with the coppers'), and a sense in which the violence was something 'normal' and to be expected. A Western Australian Aboriginal Legal Service solicitor in evidence before the Royal Commission into Aboriginal Deaths in Custody similarly noted in relation to police violence that 'children seem to think it's normal. They don't report it, they don't even think it's worth their mentioning it. That's one of the problems, another is fear of later harassment once they've complained' (Royal Commission into Aboriginal Deaths in Custody, 1990:173). For those who do notify the legal service of being assaulted, solicitors may be reluctant to raise the issue because of the lack of substantive evidence, their own sense of frustration and futility in relation to police complaints mechanisms and a lack of resources to follow through complaints.

There would appear to be two primary situational factors involved in the use of police violence against Aboriginal juveniles. One situational factor revolves around the use of violence in police stations and lock-ups. Violence in this situation is directly related to gaining admissions from individuals who have been arrested; however, it can also include a routine form of summary 'punishment'. Many of the statements by Aboriginal young people referred to above indicate the extent to which violence was used while the young person was in custody. The second situational factor relates to the use of violence in the policing of public places. Public places are also areas of social space. The use of such space can involve a contest over the definitions of legitimate public behaviour. The resort to violence by authorities can be seen as a way of maintaining the authority of the dominant order. This issue is discussed further below.

ABORIGINAL YOUNG PEOPLE AND POLICING PUBLIC PLACES

The policing of Aboriginal young people in public places is a critical component in the interaction between Aboriginal youth and police. The question of police harassment is commonly raised.

The Royal Commission report (Johnston, 1991b) into the death of John Pat shows a not untypical scenario of policing in Aboriginal communities. Police patrolled the town every 15 minutes to an hour, particularly around the riverbank and the hotel. They often entered the hotel to 'show the flag', as one police officer put it. Such a metaphor captures succinctly the image of an occupying colonial force. Hostility was apparent. The circumstances leading up to the death of John Pat show how the surveillance, resentment and provocation spill over into open confrontation. A group of

Aboriginal people were requested to leave the vicinity of the hotel, they were provoked into a fight, which then led to their arrest. A number were later assaulted while in custody. John Pat, a 16-year-old Aboriginal boy, died of head injuries.

There are also important gendered aspects of policing Aboriginal youth in public places (see chapter 7). Much of the debate around Aboriginal youth and criminalisation has neglected the specific nature of the relationship between Aboriginal young women and the criminal justice system. The challenges of black youth to authoritarianism, particularly in the policing of public places, have been assumed to involve male youth. Yet there is evidence that Aboriginal girls in public places are also represented as posing a threat to good order. It has also been argued that particular definitions of black femininity come into play:

> Popularised male discourses, mythologies and fantasies about the black female body underscore the hysterical fears expressed by extra-judicial agencies that the publicly visible presence of Aboriginal girls is somehow 'harmful to the local community' ... Aboriginal girls are subject to additional forms of regulation and surveillance. (Carrington, 1990:8)

Today many of the most intense and largest public confrontations with police involve the participation of Aboriginal young people. For example on the night of 28 August 1986, three police cars responded to an incident involving the breaking of a shop window in Bourke. The police had rocks and bottles thrown at them. The local police inspector went to the scene, withdrew the police present, called out other off-duty police and issued all police with riot equipment. Police were then ordered to clear the streets down into the Aboriginal section of Bourke (Cunneen and Robb, 1987:182).

Observers estimated that there were between fifty and eighty Aboriginal people present, of whom about 80 percent were juveniles. The spark for the confrontation had been an incident the previous night where an Aboriginal youth had been seriously injured after being apparently deliberately run over by a non-Aboriginal driver. Rumours quickly spread that the driver had been treated leniently by police. Tensions were already high in the town as a result of the distribution of racist literature earlier in the week.

As a result of the riot some sixteen Aboriginal people were arrested. Of those sixteen, eleven were juveniles. The youngest person arrested was 11-years-old. Ten of the juveniles were charged with common law riot (Cunneen and Robb, 1987:183-4). At the time, common law riot was the most serious public order offence available to police and carried a potential for life imprisonment (Cunneen and Findlay, 1986). Of the ten juveniles charged with common law riot, two were 14-years-old and four were 15-years-old. Some three days later the Aboriginal community organised a demonstration to coincide with the appearance of the young people for their initial court hearing. In anticipation of the demonstration, the Bourke police inspector requested that members of the Tactical Response Group (TRG) be airlifted some 700 kilometres from Sydney. In the presence of the TRG the Aboriginal youth were escorted, handcuffed, across to the court house.

ABORIGINAL YOUTH AS A LAW AND ORDER PROBLEM

A significant number of reports have indicated that Aboriginal young people have been targeted as constituting a 'law and order' problem (for example, see Cunneen and Robb, 1987:121; Dodson, 1991, vol. 1; White, 1991). The implied remedy is more punitive intervention in terms of legislation, police practices and sentencing options.

In 1988 the NSW state government introduced new public order legislation ostensibly as a result of conflict between young Aboriginal people and the Tactical Response Group in Redfern. The media were also quick to pick up on Aboriginal youth as a 'law and order' issue. According to the *Sydney Morning Herald*,

> The State Government will rush through new laws to deal with rioters more quickly in the wake of Friday night's clashes between Aborigines and police at Redfern. During Friday night's confrontation, about 50 police armed with batons and led by Tactical Response Group officers with riot shields stood in line facing an increasingly angry group of some 50 young Aborigines (29 August 1988, p.1).

The new riot legislation (s.93b NSW Crimes Act) has been criticised for its unsatisfactory definition of violence, its vagueness and the fact that it includes private as well as public behaviour (Brown, Neal, Farrier and Weisbrot, 1990:1036).

In addition to the substantial penalties involved, it is significant that such a major change in public order legislation should be associated with the alleged public order disturbances by Aboriginal youth. The redefinition of the problem as being one of Aboriginal criminality was reinforced when the premier announced the legislation as part of a government response so that Redfern would not become a 'no-go' area.

With changes in legislation and more punitive police actions comes the constant denial that racism is the issue. Punitive legislation such as the NSW *Summary Offences Act* 1988 or the Western Australian *Crime (Serious and Repeat Offenders) Act* 1992 reinforce particular styles of police intervention and differentially impact upon Aboriginal young people. The first young people arrested for violent disorder under the *Summary Offences Act* were Aboriginal youth in Bourke (Cunneen, 1990a). In Western Australia, the Department of Community Services estimated that over half the juveniles to be affected by the new legislation would be Aboriginal (Wilkie, 1992).

Law and order campaigns aimed at Aboriginal young people are often localised and may, in some cases, explain apparent variations in the number of apprehensions of Aboriginal juveniles by police. Local non-Aboriginal power-brokers can directly influence the nature of police intervention (Cunneen, 1990a and Goodall, 1990a). One consequence of increasingly punitive interventions may be the provocation of further resistance from the young people themselves. The construction of Aboriginal youth as a 'law and order' problem diverts attention away from the structural conditions of institutional racism. To the extent that race is problematised, it is to reinforce the view that Aboriginal young people as a race are the cause of public order disturbances and criminal activity.

EXPLAINING THE DYNAMICS OF POLICING ABORIGINAL YOUTH

James and Polk (1989:42) have suggested that to understand how young people are policed it is necessary to consider the reciprocal concepts of police discretion and the police prediction of trouble. We have analysed data which demonstrate that the substantive discretionary choices made by police impact negatively on Aboriginal young people. The literature on how police predict trouble suggests that police develop and act upon sets of expectations. Such expectations are formulated around the symbols of subculture, class and race (Piliavin and Briar, 1969; see also Reiss, 1973 and Skolnick, 1966).

Piliavin and Briar (1969) dealt specifically with the issue of 'race'. They observed that black Americans and youth who fitted 'delinquent stereotypes' were more frequently stopped and interrogated by police even in the absence of evidence that an offence had been committed, and were given more severe dispositions for the same offences as those committed by other youth. Black youth were observed by the writers to display a more 'recalcitrant demeanour' than other youth. Police interpreted such demeanour as a confirmation of criminality. The police justified their selective treatment of black youth by arguing that such youth were more likely to commit offences. While the evidence supported over-representation among offenders, black Americans were also overrepresented among those who were stopped and subsequently cleared of any wrongdoing.

Some Australian studies (Alder and Sandor, 1990, and O'Connor and Sweetapple, 1988) have also concluded that the police response to young people is determined in part by the young person's perceived co-operation with police. Violence by police is an attempt to address the non-recognition of their authority. In considering homeless youth, Alder (1989:52) noted that 'the fact that encounters between police and these young people are likely to commence on the street further aggravates the initial situation, as the public arena intensifies the need of police to maintain an image of control'.

The use of police violence as an exercise of power may have a gratuitous element not easily explained by the rationale of a 'threat to authority' or the 'prediction of trouble'. By providing a sense of rationality to the use of violence and harassment, such explanations may also implicitly provide a legitimation to police actions. It may also be used to account for harassment and violence arising from particular situational confrontations and not pay sufficient detail to broader structural and historical conditions for selective enforcement procedures against particular social groups.

However, attention to the social dynamics through which police develop their 'predictors of trouble' does have the advantage of focusing on the use of discretion, selective enforcement, violence and harassment as components of day-to-day police work. It draws our attention to the way in which policing is operationalised. Hogg (1991:14–16) has argued that police power is exercised according to norms which are unarticulated and grounded in a police 'common sense'. Such common sense is the knowledge which forms the basis of selective enforcement and enables the 'sanctioning of marginal offences and offenders'. The knowledge is transmitted through the organisation and through the occupational culture. It is a knowledge which is reinforced through formal and informal training to identify 'what is suspicious, potentially troublesome, etc. based on time, place, circumstance, demeanour, gesture, character, social location, and so forth and modes of sanctioning that could be utilised to deal with such problems' (Hogg, 1991:16).

To what extent do police practices in relation to Aboriginal youth reflect police knowledge of Aboriginal offending rates? Such a question has certainly been argued heatedly in Britain in relation to policing minorities (Lea, 1986), but only more recently has become contentious in Australia. The position which is adopted on Aboriginal offending rates has important implications as to how we might explain police discretion, selective enforcement and harassment in relation to Aboriginal youth. If 'race' is seen as an indicator of criminality then police practices in relation to Aboriginal youth could be explained as rational occupational decisions.

Cunneen and Robb (1987) found that the level of Aboriginal overrepresentation for criminal charges was high for offences like assaulting police, hindering police, resisting arrest and offensive behaviour. Gale and her colleagues (1990:48) made a similar finding. These are offences which can be explained relatively simply through over-policing and the adverse use of police discretion. However, Aboriginal young people are also overrepresented in other charges such as property theft and assault. Such overrepresentation cannot be as easily explained by over-policing. Some recognition that the over-commission of offences, and the relationship of these particular offences to a class or socio-economic position is important.

However, there remains the difficulty of what can be precisely discerned from statistics on arrests of Aboriginal young people. While it is possible at some levels to distinguish between the over-commission of offences and over-policing – for instance, in relatively clear-cut offences like homicide or serious assaults – there are difficulties with a range of other offences. For example, charges for offences against the person may be directly influenced by police strategies. Gale and her colleagues (1990:48) note that in South Australia the proportion of Aboriginal juveniles charged with offences against the person was nearly double that of non-Aboriginal juveniles. However, these differences were almost entirely a result of more charges relating to common assault, which is less serious.

In relation to property offences, a range of factors limit the extent to which we can discuss the over-commission of offences. Quite basic issues such as the extent to which offences are reported can be related to the level of policing and the perceived likelihood of a satisfactory response on the part of the victim. In addition, there is the question of what we might make of police clear-up rates. For example, the clear-up rate is notoriously low for both motor vehicle theft and break, enter and steal. The low clear-up rate means that there is considerable room for speculation about the actual commission of offences. The overrepresentation of Aboriginal people in arrest figures tells us much about detection by police, but it may be of far more limited value in giving us an accurate picture of who commits offences (see chapter 3).

Police work relies to a certain extent on criminal stereotypes, which may themselves be in part derived from dubious statistical analyses. Such stereotypes enable the development of racist practices. It is worth keeping in mind, however, the extent to which those stereotypes might be defined outside of policing. Police knowledge is not formed in a vacuum. To understand how particular knowledges have developed in Australia in relation to policing Aboriginal young people, we need to go full circle, back to the deeper historical and contemporary structural dynamics of policing in a colonial setting.

RACISM, COLONIALISM AND THE POLICING OF ABORIGINAL YOUTH

In drawing together the distinctive features of policing Aboriginal young people I want to draw attention to four aspects of the relationship between Aboriginal young people and police. These are: the historical foundation to the relationship which determines certain structural features; the contemporary imperatives in policing Aboriginal communities; the relationship between police, Aboriginal youth and recorded crime statistics; and the experiences of Aboriginal young people in relation to the police.

This chapter began with a discussion of the various modes or phases of intervention by the state into the lives of Aboriginal young people which were characterised as open warfare, protection and criminalisation. Each phase had its own particular focus on young people and each was gendered in its approach. Overwhelmingly though, the various phases represented a level of police intervention unprecedented in the non-Aboriginal community. The focus of intervention included both the public and private spheres of Aboriginal life. Indeed, an important part of the colonial experience was the denial to Aboriginal people of an existence of a private sphere removed from scrutiny and surveillance.

Such intervention has had a profound and structuring influence on the relationship between Aboriginal young people and the police. Police have been imbued from the protection days with racist assumptions concerning the incompetence of Aboriginal families to care for and nurture their young. In the post-war period, this has been combined with a construction of Aboriginal young people as criminals. The historical structuring of the relationship between police and Aboriginal young people can be seen as offering one level of explanation to police decisions in relation to discretion, selective enforcement, harassment and violence.

The second aspect of the relationship concerns the contemporary imperatives of policing in Aboriginal communities. We need to seriously consider how the economic and political crises over the last decade have been partly reformulated into tough talk on law and order, and indeed how Aboriginal people and youth more generally have come to be defined as a 'law and order' problem (Cunneen, 1990a, 1991). An important part of the discourse on law and order has been a racist doctrine which identifies Aboriginal people as the cause of the 'crime problem'. Along with the growth of 'law and order' politics and the introduction of specific legislation aimed at young (Aboriginal) people, there has been a substantial reorganisation and re-equipping of state police forces which has enabled a more coercive and paramilitarised police response. The sheer numbers of police in some Aboriginal communities have increased dramatically during the last decade (Cunneen, 1992:83–4).

A further dynamic in policing Aboriginal youth has been the pressure placed on police in local areas to take a more 'pro-active' role in containment strategies. Such pressure derives from local business and political interests which have a stake in more punitive enforcement strategies (Cunneen, 1990a; also chapter 5). The contemporary political characterisation of Aboriginal young people as a law and order problem, especially when understood with an appreciation of the historical functioning of policing in a colonial society, provides the structure to the social dynamics of policing Aboriginal youth.

The characterisation of Aboriginal young people as a law and order problem inevitably raises the third aspect of the relationship between police and Aboriginal young people and that is the question of Aboriginal juvenile crime rates. The socio-economic or class position of Aboriginal young people may offer some help in understanding their overrepresentation in police statistics. However, whether Aboriginal young people actually offend more often and seriously than their non-Aboriginal counterparts is difficult to determine. Policing itself plays such a fundamental role in determining the extent and nature of offences and offenders brought before the court that no simple conclusions can be drawn.

Juvenile offending is increasingly discussed in terms of socio-economic disadvantage and there is no doubt that Aboriginal youth are massively 'disadvantaged' on all social indicator scales (Johnston, 1991c, vol. 2). However, it is important to consider two points in relation to disadvantage. Firstly, there are distinct aspects of the relationship between police and Aboriginal young people because of their history and contemporary status as indigenous people. Secondly, while Aboriginal young people experience disadvantage in terms of health, housing, education, unemployment, welfare dependency, etc., there is a need to understand that disadvantage within the context of colonialism, dispossession and the destruction of an Aboriginal economic base. In other words, Aboriginal young people are not simply 'disadvantaged', they are part of a dispossessed nation of people who are oppressed. The concept of oppression is more suitable than 'disadvantage' because it incorporates both the manifestations of disadvantage, such as unemployment, and the active dimensions of policing and the criminal justice system which have been used to control Aboriginal people. Further, an understanding of oppression inevitably demands an explanation of racism.

Oppression and racism are essential components of the fourth and final aspect I wish to discuss concerning the relationship between Aboriginal young people and the police. How do Aboriginal young people experience policing? It is fair to say that police are considered by these young people as racist and oppressive, they are considered as sexist, harassing, intimidatory and violent. The vast majority of youth interviewed in one study (Cunneen, 1990b) claimed they had been subjected to police violence, an equivalent number claimed they had been subjected to racist language by police. In addition,

it was perceived that police were harassing in their responses to
Aboriginal young people in public areas. I have argued elsewhere
(Cunneen, 1990b) that there is a 'vocabulary' of racism which
accompanies police violence and harassment, and transforms such
actions into *racist* violence and harassment. Similarly, one might
consider the language involved in sexist abuse. Other studies have
highlighted sexual harassment by police officers against girls
ranging from the use of sexual comments to strip searches (Youth
Justice Coalition, 1990:254). However the interviews conducted with
Aboriginal young women made clear that the sexist abuse was
always contextualised by race.

The title of this chapter poses the question of whether policing
policies are 'enforcing genocide'. This question is meant to be
neither melodramatic nor rhetorical. Rather, it must be seriously
asked and answered in any analysis of police relations with
Aboriginal young people in Australia. Former policies in relation
to the police and justice were incontrovertibly genocidal. Policies
and practices today may be similarly genocidal in their impact, if
not in their conscious intent. I have attempted to outline a number
of processes which help us to understand the specific way in which
policing impacts on Aboriginal youth. Policing has had an
enormously negative and destructive influence over Aboriginal
family, kinship and cultural ties. Some of those policing policies
have been articulated by the dominant interests of the state in
maintaining colonial control. Policing strategies in relation to
Aboriginal youth have also been determined by local interests,
particularly in rural areas. Indeed, both at local and state level,
Aboriginal young people have been increasingly defined as a law
and order problem which has both legitimised and demanded police
intervention. This chapter has shown the way in which the nature
of police intervention has shifted from one based on government-
authorised removal policies to increasing criminalisation. There has
also been specific focus on the features of criminalisation which
impact on Aboriginal young people including arrest, failure to use
cautions, bail conditions, failure to use diversionary options, and
the use of harassment and violence. Much of current policing
strategies can be understood within the broader historical and
contemporary demands of a colonial order.

Just as we must acknowledge that colonialism has structured
the relations between Aboriginal people and the police, so too we

should see that, ultimately, self-determination and sovereignty will be critical forces in destructuring the oppressive relations imposed by the state. For this reason Mansell's point is important

> Prior to invasion Aboriginal people were a nation of people ... Aboriginal people ought not to sell themselves short by perceiving ourselves in terms of a unit of Australian society – an ethnic group or minority – who are just getting a hard time. We are in fact a nation of people and we ought to stand up and acknowledge it. (Mansell, 1989:5)

Self-determination implies the right to establish and control indigenous justice systems, including policing and juvenile justice. More than any other policy options, it offers a long-term and just mechanism to establishing a non-oppressive relationship between Aboriginal young people and the police.

REFERENCES

Alder, C. and Sandor, D. (1990) *Homeless Youth as Victims of Violence.* Melbourne: Criminology Department, University of Melbourne.

Anti-Discrimination Board (1982) *A Study of Street Offences by Aborigines.* Sydney: NSW Anti-Discrimination Board.

Attwood, B. (1989) *The Making of the Aborigines.* Sydney: Allen and Unwin.

Broadhurst, R., Ferrante, A. and Susilo, N. (1991) *Crime and Justice Statistics for Western Australia: 1990.* Nedlands, WA: Crime Research Centre, University of Western Australia.

Brook, J. and Kohen, J. (1991) *The Parramatta Native Institution and the Black Town.* Kensington, NSW: NSW University Press.

Brown, D., Neal, D., Farrier, D. and Weisbrot, D. (1990) *Criminal Laws.* Annandale: Federation Press.

Burger, J. (1988) *Aborigines Today. Land and Justice.* London: Anti-Slavery Society.

Carrington, K. (1990) 'Aboriginal Girls and Justice: What justice? White justice', *Journal for Social Justice Studies,* Special Edition Series, Contemporary Race Relations, 3:1–18.

Cunneen, C. (1988) 'An Evaluation of the Juvenile Cautioning System in NSW', in Proceedings of the Institute of Criminology, *Changes in Direction of Juvenile Justice,* No. 75. Sydney: Sydney University Law School.

Cunneen, C. (1989) 'Constructing a Law and Order Agenda', *Aboriginal Law Bulletin,* (June):18–20.

Cunneen, C. (1990a) 'Aborigines and Law and Order Regimes', *Journal for Social Justice Studies,* Special Edition Series, Contemporary Race Relations, 3:37–50.

Cunneen, C. (1990b) *A Study of Aboriginal Juveniles and Police Violence.* Report Commissioned by the National Inquiry into Racist Violence. Sydney: Human Rights and Equal Opportunity Commission.

Cunneen, C. (1991) 'Law, Order and Inequality' in J. O'Leary and R. Sharp (eds), *Inequality in Australia.* Port Melbourne: Heinemann.

Cunneen, C. (1992) 'Policing and Aboriginal Communities: Is the concept of over-policing useful?' in C. Cunneen (ed.), *Aboriginal Perspectives on Criminal Justice.* Monograph Series No. 1. Sydney: Sydney University Institute of Criminology.

Cunneen, C. and Findlay, M. (1986) 'The Functions of Criminal Law in Riot Control', *Australian New Zealand Journal of Criminology,* 19:163–78.

Cunneen, C. and Libesman, T. (1990) 'Editorial', *Aboriginal Law Bulletin,* 2(44):2.

Cunneen, C. and Luke, G. (1992) Aboriginal Young People and the Law in NSW. Preliminary Results. Unpublished paper to the Criminology Research Council.

Cunneen, C. and Robb, T. (1987) *Criminal Justice in North West New South Wales.* Sydney: NSW Bureau of Crime Statistics and Research.

D'Souza, N. (1990) 'Aboriginal Children and the Juvenile Justice System', *Aboriginal Law Bulletin,* 2(44):4–5.

Dodson, P. (1991) *Regional Report of Inquiry into Underlying Issues in Western Australia.* Royal Commission into Aboriginal Deaths in Custody. Canberra: AGPS.

Edmunds, M. (1989) *They Get Heaps.* Canberra: Aboriginal Studies Press.

Edwards, C. and Read, P. (1988) *The Lost Children.* Moorebank: Doubleday.

Elder, B. (1988) *Blood on the Wattle.* Frenchs Forest, NSW: Child and Associates.

Equal Opportunity Commission (1990) *Discrimination in Government Policies and Practices, S.82(b).* Report No. 8, Review of Police Practices, Summary of Main Report. Perth: Equal Opportunity Commission.

Evans, R., Saunders, K. and Cronin K. (1988) *Race Relations in Colonial Queensland.* St Lucia, Qld: University of Queensland Press.

Feeley, M. (1979) *The Process is the Punishment.* New York: Russel Sage Foundation.

Foucault, M. (1979) *Discipline and Punish.* Harmondsworth, Middlesex: Penguin.

Gale, F., Bailey-Harris, R. and Wundersitz, J. (1990) *Aboriginal Youth and the Criminal Justice System.* Cambridge: Cambridge University Press.

Goodall, H. (1982) A History of Aboriginal Communities in NSW 1909–1939. Unpublished PhD thesis, Sydney University.

Goodall, H. (1990a) 'Policing in Whose Interest?', *Journal for Social Justice Studies,* 3:19–36.

Goodall, H. (1990b) 'Saving the Children', *Aboriginal Law Bulletin,* 2(44):6–9.

Hogg, R. (1991) 'Policing and Penality', *Journal for Social Justice Studies*, 4:1–26.

Human Rights and Equal Opportunity Commission (1991) *Racist Violence*. Report of the National Inquiry into Racist Violence. Sydney: Human Rights and Equal Opportunity Commission.

International Commission of Jurists (1990) *Report of the Aboriginals and the Law Mission*. Sydney: Australian Section of Law Mission.

James, S. and Polk, K. (1989) 'Policing Youth' in D. Chappell and P. Wilson (eds), *Australian Policing: Contemporary issues*. Sydney: Butterworths.

Johnston, E. (1991a) *National Report, Overview and Recommendations*. Royal Commission into Aboriginal Deaths in Custody. Canberra: AGPS.

Johnston, E. (1991b) *Report of the Inquiry into the Death of John Pat*. Royal Commission into Aboriginal Deaths in Custody. Canberra: AGPS.

Johnston, E. (1991c) *National Report*, vol 4. Royal Commission into Aboriginal Deaths in Custody. Canberra: AGPS.

Lea, J. (1986) 'Police Racism: Some theories and their policy implications' in R. Matthews and J. Young (eds), *Confronting Crime*. London: Sage.

Luke, G. (1989) Aboriginal Young People. Paper presented to the Aboriginal Youth and the Justice System Conference, 4 September. Dubbo.

Mansell, M. (1989) 'Treaty Proposal: Aboriginal sovereignty', *Aboriginal Law Bulletin*, 2(37) (April):4–6.

Markus, A. (1990) *Governing Savages*. Sydney: Allen and Unwin.

Neal, D. (1991) *The Rule of Law in a Penal Colony*. Cambridge: Cambridge University Press.

NSW Bureau of Crime Statistics and Research (1992) *NSW Lower Courts, Criminal Courts and Children's Courts Statistics 1991*. Sydney: Department of Attorney-General.

NSW Legislative Council Standing Committee on Social Issues (1992) *Juvenile Justice in New South Wales*. Standing Committee on Social Issues Report No. 4. New South Wales Parliament, May.

O'Connor, I. and Sweetapple, P. (1988) *Children in Justice*. Melbourne: Longman Cheshire.

Piliavin, I., and Briar, S. (1969) 'Police Encounters with Juveniles', in D. Cressey and D. Ward (eds), *Delinquency, Crime and Social Process*. New York: Harper and Row.

Read, P. (n.d.) *The Stolen Generations*. Sydney: NSW Ministry of Aboriginal Affairs.

Reiss, A. (1973) 'Police Brutality: Answers to Key Questions' in A. Niederhoffer and A. Blumberg (eds), *The Ambivalent Force: Perspectives on the Police*. New York: Rinehart.

Royal Commission into Aboriginal Deaths in Custody (1990) *Transcript of Hearing into Juvenile Justice Issues*, Perth, 29 May.

Seymour, J. (1988) *Dealing With Young Offenders*. North Ryde, NSW: Law Book Company.

Skolnick, J. (1966) *Justice Without Trial*. New York: Wiley.

Walker, J. (1987) 'Prison Cells with Revolving Doors: A Judicial or Societal Problem', in K. Hazlehurst (ed.), *Ivory Scales*. Kensington, NSW: NSW University Press.

White, R. (1991) 'Taking Custody to the Community', *Current Issues in Criminal Justice*, 3(2):171–84.

Wilkie, M. (1991) *Aboriginal Justice Programs in Western Australia*. Research Report No. 5. Nedlands, WA: Crime Research Centre, University of Western Australia.

Wilkie, M. (1992) 'WA's Draconian New Juvenile Offender Sentencing Laws', *Aboriginal Law Bulletin*, 2(55) (April):15–17.

Wootten, H. (1989) *Report of the Inquiry into the Death of Malcolm Charles Smith*. Royal Commission into Aboriginal Deaths in Custody. Canberra: AGPS.

Wootten, H. (1991a) *Report of the Inquiry into the Death of Lloyd James Boney*. Royal Commission into Aboriginal Deaths in Custody. Canberra: AGPS.

Wootten, H. (1991b) *Regional Report of Inquiry in New South Wales, Victoria and Tasmania*. Royal Commission into Aboriginal Deaths in Custody. Canberra: AGPS.

Youth Justice Coalition (NSW) (1990) *Kids in Justice: A blueprint for the 90s*. Sydney: Youth Justice Coalition.

CHAPTER 7

The Policing of Young Women

Christine Alder

INTRODUCTION

Traditionally police work has been considered 'men's work' and the police force has been compared to 'an all male institution such as a rugby club or boys' school' (Reiner, 1985 quoted in Edwards, 1989:26). Organisational forces and occupational values facilitate what has been referred to as a 'cult of masculinity', which has a 'significant influence on police officers' behaviour towards women' (Edwards, 1989:27). However, despite the rapid growth in research on women's and girls' experiences of the criminal and juvenile justice systems, the policing of young women in particular has been left relatively unexplored. This chapter provides an overview of existing research in this area. Beginning with the research on police handling of criminal and welfare matters, the chapter then turns to two issues of specific concern: police violence towards and harassment of young women, and the policing of young Aboriginal women. Before concluding, police responses to young women's victimisation are considered.

POLICE DECISIONS IN CRIMINAL MATTERS

An overview of police statistics immediately reveals that young women account for a relatively small proportion of the total number of arrests (see chapter 3). One of the traditional explanations for these figures drew upon notions of chivalry which suggested that young women were treated more leniently than young men. The assumption that young women are treated with chivalry has been challenged by research which examines young women's experiences in the juvenile justice system. This research reveals that young women are not always treated more leniently, but are in fact, in some circumstances, treated more harshly than young men (Chesney-Lind and Shelden, 1992). However, most of this research has focused on the responses of court officials with less attention having been given to police contact and decision making (Krohn, Curry and Nelson-Kilger, 1983; Visher, 1983).

Studies of police behaviour in the field rarely examined the effect of gender on the decision to arrest. In making this point, Chesney-Lind and Shelden (1992:128) outline the findings of one exception in the work of Monahan (1970 cited in Chesney-Lind and Shelden, 1992:128). This study of police dispositions of juvenile offenders in Philadelphia found that police were more likely to release a girl than a boy they suspected of committing a crime; equally likely to apprehend males and females they suspected of running away; and more likely to arrest girls they suspected of sex offences. These findings revealed a pattern that contradicted the general assumption that police always dealt more leniently with young women than young men. While the findings of this study suggested that the sex of the individual played a role in police decision making, the form and nature of this effect was still somewhat unclear.

In a later American study, which compared self-report data from high school students with official records, Elliott and Voss (1974) found that boys were at least four times more likely than girls to experience police contact for a serious offence. They concluded that the official records reflected a bias in favour of girls.

However, contradictory conclusions were drawn in a more recent study in Miami which involved street interviews with a large number of youths who had frequently engaged in serious offending (Horowitz and Pottieger, 1991). In terms of overall arrest rates the researchers concluded that 'there was no apparent bias against males ... It is even possible to argue that overall arrest patterns demonstrate the opposite: a bias against girls' (Horowitz and Pottieger, 1991:81). In support of this conclusion, the researchers noted that while males reported committing more major felonies and drug sales, they were not significantly more likely to have been arrested in the previous twelve months.

The authors of this study go on to suggest that analyses of overall arrest rates can be deceptive and that the complexity of the ways in which gender and race are involved in arrest decision making requires much more detailed analyses. They suggest that the offence itself is one factor which may affect the direction of the gender bias.

For example, they note that young women engaging in high-volume petty property offending were more likely than similarly involved boys to be arrested. On the other hand, other findings could be interpreted as suggesting that girls were advantaged by gender bias in arrest decisions: 'that no arrests resulted from almost 1,800 major felonies by females is especially striking' (Horowitz and Pottieger, 1991:84).

Gender stereotyping of the offence is one of the factors explored by Horowitz and Pottieger (1991) as a possible explanation for some of these differences. They suggest that perhaps none of the major felonies (a category which included robbery, assault, burglary, and motor vehicle theft) reported by the young women resulted in arrest because such offences are seen as 'male' offences and are 'invisible' to the police and public alike. Similarly, they argue, white females are more likely than white males to be arrested for the 'female' crime of high-volume petty shoplifting.

[marginalia: ♂ crimes]

[marginalia: ♀ crimes]

The possibility that gender stereotyping of offences affects the likelihood of arrest for males and females has been suggested by other researchers in the United States. However the direction of the effect is sometimes thought to be different to that offered by Horowitz and Pottieger. It has been argued that female property offenders may receive some preferential treatment from the police and courts, while women suspected of crimes typically perpetuated by males (such as robbery and assault) are often punished more severely (Chesney-Lind, 1978).

In England, Gelsthorpe observed a juvenile liaison office in a police station and found that police did view girls' and boys' offending differently. While girls were seen as predominantly 'shoplifters', boys were thought to be most often involved in 'taking and driving away' (Gelsthorpe, 1986:129). This view prevailed even though a detailed analysis of the files indicated that both boys and girls were shoplifting and generally engaging in a wide range of offences. Nor did the available detailed information support the view that boys and girls shoplifted different sorts of goods. For example, contrary to police expectations, 'None of the girls in the 1981 referral list had stolen make-up' (Gelsthorpe, 1986:129). It was not possible to determine from these data whether, or in what ways, the gendered view of offending held by police influenced their decision making in regard to young people.

Thus, the evidence regarding the nature of the effect of the gender stereotyping of offences is mixed. In fact, Visher concludes from her American study that 'particular offence types are not labelled as sex-role traditional or sex-role deviant' (Visher, 1983:19). A more strongly supported finding regarding sex-role stereotyping relates to expectations regarding the behaviour of the individual woman. As Visher concludes, 'Police officers respond to female suspects on the basis of the image that they project, rather than the type of offence they have committed' (Visher, 1983:21). A similar observation is made by an English feminist: 'The policing of women, whether in public or private matters, whether as victims or offenders, protesters or campaigners, has been influenced by police stereotypes of appropriate female behaviour' (Edwards, 1989:26).

In an American study of drug arrests, DeFleur found that women who acted in stereotypic ways were 'seldom processed' (DeFleur, 1975:101). Such behaviours included crying, claiming to have been led astray by men, or expressing concern about their children. By comparison, those young women who tended to be aggressive and hostile were more often arrested. Consistent with these findings, Visher concluded from her research that 'young black or hostile women receive no preferential treatment, whereas, older, white women who are calm and deferential toward police are granted leniency' (Visher, 1983:23).

The observation that antagonistic, hostile behaviour is not consistent with the expected behaviour of women and is likely to be responded to negatively in the criminal justice system is supported by Worrall's observation regarding magistrates in England:

> Such 'dumb insolence' was not expected from women defendants since it did not accord with stereotypical expectations of women as guilt-ridden and anxious to please. Defiance manifested in dress, posture, or speech is typically a masculine attribute and women who displayed such an attitude risked alienating magistrates . . . (Worrall, 1990:62)

Of course, young men who are hostile and antagonistic to police are also more likely to be arrested than young men who are 'civil' and co-operative (Smith and Visher, 1981; Piliavin and Briar, 1964; White, 1992). It has been argued that hostile behaviour challenges the authority which police assert by arresting the person concerned. In a recent Australian study, police reported that the degree of co-operation shown by the young person was one of the key factors in their decision to deal formally or informally with that person (White, 1992). The impact of the interplay between gender and demeanour on police responses has not been fully explored in the literature.

In both of the observations above regarding the consequences of hostile behaviour for women, the authors also commented on the relative age of the persons being arrested. In fact, Visher notes that:

> The suspect's age has a significant impact on police arrest decisions for female suspects, but age is not important in encounters with male suspects. Younger females receive harsher treatment among female suspects than do older females ... Police officers adopt a more paternalistic and harsher attitude toward younger females to deter any further violation of appropriate sex-role behaviour. (Visher, 1983:15)

Looking across the few existing studies of police decision making in regard to the criminal activities of young women, it is clear that a complex set of factors is involved. Thus, a simple comparison of arrest rates for boys and girls to determine who is treated more harshly may hide more than it reveals, both of the process and young women's experiences of them.

POLICING YOUNG WOMEN'S WELFARE

In Australia, the USA and Great Britain, juvenile justice legislation allows for a young person whose welfare is deemed to be in jeopardy to be taken into state care. Depending on the wording of the particular legislation, such young people may be deemed to be 'incorrigible', 'in need of care and protection', or 'in moral danger'. In the USA behaviours which are covered by these provisions are frequently referred to as 'status offences'. It is in this area of the juvenile justice process that most evidence has been accumulated regarding the existence of a particularly harsh and paternalistic approach to the behaviour of young women.

Traditionally police have played a key role in identifying and presenting 'care' cases to juvenile court: this has been a feature of the 'welfare' role of police in the community (James and Polk, 1989). The life circumstances of young offenders and those young people identified as being 'in need of care' are frequently similar. Thus, one of the dimensions of discretion for police in dealing with young people has been the decision as to whether it is the criminal or welfare jurisdiction of the children's court which is most appropriate for dealing with the circumstances of the case.

In general, research has found that of those young people who have been formally processed in the juvenile justice system, young women are more likely than young men to be dealt with as 'status offenders'. In a study of juvenile court appearances in Victoria, Hancock found that 63 percent of female and only 8 percent of male court appearances (excluding neglect cases) were presented to court on protection applications (Hancock, 1980). An examination of police records in an American study also found that girls suspected of status offences were more likely than their male counterparts to be referred to juvenile court (Krohn et al., 1983; see also Chesney-Lind, 1977).

A broad range of factors to do with the young person's behaviour and home circumstances is normally considered in determining whether or not a 'care application' is warranted. However, in her study of a police station in England, Gelsthorpe noted that in the case of girls, police showed a particular concern with young women's sexual activity, discussed the possibility of pregnancy and used doctors' examinations to confirm sexual activity. As one officer is quoted as saying, 'For a start, when kids go missing we assume that the girls are "being legged", we assume that boys of 13 and 14 can look after themselves' (quoted in Gelsthorpe, 1986:134).

An American study found that while 70–80 percent of young women being taken to the children's court were given physical examinations, this was true for only 1–10 percent of boys (Chesney-Lind, 1974). The doctors' reports regularly commented on the state of the girl's hymen, even though it was not apparent that this was directly related to the young woman's health or to the behaviour for which she was being held. Such information was used to broaden the original offence or to create a new one. Cases where sexual concerns were added to the original offence, or non-sexual offences were overlooked in favour of sexual behaviour, have also been commented on in England (Gelsthorpe, 1986; Smith, 1978:83).

A concern with the sexual activity of girls was also found in a study of police reports in Victoria. Hancock reports that explicit reference was made to 'sexual intercourse' in 29 percent of female and 1 percent of male cases. Implicit in the reports was an acceptance of adolescent male sexual experimentation as indicated by the use in boys' reports of such terms as 'sowing wild oats', 'over-sexed' and an acceptance of the notion of the irrepressibility of the male sex drive. In the case of girls, there was a concern to protect them from premarital sexual activity and perception of female 'promiscuity' as a serious problem requiring intervention (Hancock, 1980:10).

Historically, the sexuality of young women has been of concern to the justice system (Schlossman and Wallach, 1978). In her study of juvenile justice and child welfare legislation in Victoria, Jaggs notes that in the 1870s and 1880s there were roughly three categories of young offenders: 'larrikins, thieves, and unmanageable, sexually promiscuous girls' (Jaggs, 1986:60). Jaggs notes that while girls' larceny and other offences were of concern, 'wildness' and sexual misbehaviour were of greater concern: 'Passionate and wilful, they posed problems for administrators and socially concerned citizens alike' (Jaggs, 1986:62).

As often today, in these earlier times concerns regarding a young woman's sexual behaviour were not necessarily determined on the basis of evidence of actual sexual behaviour. As Schlossman and Wallach (1978) illustrate in their study of the early juvenile court in the United States, immoral conduct of girls was determined on the basis of a very broad range of behaviours including:

> staying away from home, associating with persons of dubious character, going to dance houses, fornicating, coming home late, masturbating, using obscene language, riding at night in automobiles without a chaperon, strutting about in a lascivious manner and so forth. To the courts, being 'on the road to ruin' was but one short step from being 'ruined'. (Schlossman and Wallach, 1978)

More recently in Australia, Hancock has similarly noted that in the case of young women, sexual history 'was related to a wider range of variables, including a girl's attitude towards authority, co-operation with police, her credibility, home situation and moral reputation' (Hancock, 1980:10). This sexualisation of young women's 'deviant' behaviour is a common form of sanctioning girls and is a key aspect of the 'informal' control mechanisms which are used by others to police girls' behaviour. Even a young woman's peers may call her a 'slut' in response to behaviour, which, while not necessarily sexual, is deemed by them to be unacceptable (Lees, 1986; Carrington, 1989).

In the juvenile justice system, the argument that a young woman is on 'the road to ruin' is most often supported in part by evidence that she is out of parental control: in most instances, it is her mother who is held most accountable for this situation. Assessments of the adequacy of parental arrangements and the home environment are culturally informed. This has been illustrated most explicitly in the history of 'welfare' interventions in the lives of young Aboriginal women.

> Thus different kinds of living arrangements, family cultures and parenting practices, particularly those circumscribed by poverty and welfare dependence, represent the 'other' – those failing families who need 'welfare assistance' ... within such a discourse Aboriginal families become constructed as obvious, or almost natural or inevitable, candidates for 'welfare assistance', rationalising unnecessary and often punitive kinds of welfare intervention. (Carrington, 1990:11)

In Carrington's study (1990) of young Aboriginal women who had been to court, all were considered to come from a 'bad home environment' and four of the six were made the subject of wardship proceedings.

In making a case that a young woman is 'in need of care', the police are often responding to a parental complaint, although Carrington's (1990) study indicates that this is probably not the case for Aboriginal young women (see also chapter 6). On the other hand, in a study regarding predominantly non-Aboriginal young people, Hancock (1980) found that parents are responsible for bringing their child to the attention of police in a far higher proportion of female than male cases (21% compared with 1% of boys). Similarly, in England, Gelsthorpe (1986:139) observed that police were 'inundated with requests from parents for officers to go and speak to their "difficult" children. The majority of these requests ... came from parents who were concerned about the difficult behaviour of their daughters'. In developing their case, police will also draw upon the reports of other people who have had contact with the young women such as teachers, welfare workers, doctors. Carrington (1992) has argued that the policing of young women is not only a function of police officers, but is also the responsibility of a range of other people in their environment.

Gelsthorpe (1986) found that in preparing their reports, police took into consideration their understanding of the expectations of court officials. Police often added material regarding the moral danger to the young women in order to impress magistrates, that is, it was added 'to meet the administrative and judicial need to present substantial evidence' (Gelsthorpe, 1986:139). In a similar vein, Hancock found that the offender's sexual history was less likely to be mentioned in cases which were simply warned by police. Hancock surmises that the finding that sexual history was mentioned only in cases resulting in court appearances indicates either that 'such behaviour is seen to be of a more serious nature and therefore warrants court attention', or, that it is included to 'justify the more serious police decision' (1980:10) to take the case to court.

In preparing their case against young women, the police take into consideration their understanding of what others in the juvenile justice process (magistrates, lawyers, youth workers) believe constitutes behaviour on the part of young women which warrants 'serious' concern. These data indicate that the preparation of care applications by police both reflects and reproduces broader social understandings of what constitutes a 'troublesome girl'.

YOUNG WOMEN AT THE POLICE STATION

From a young woman's perspective, a key aspect of the nature of policing is how she is treated by police officers. In the findings of a national study of police–youth relations, Alder (1992) found that in a group of young people from a mix of economic, educational and racial backgrounds, girls in general reported a lower level than boys of contact with police when it comes to being stopped and spoken to on the street or being taken to a police station. In part, this is probably a consequence of the less frequent use of street space by girls. Boys were also found to be more likely to report being yelled at, hit, pushed around, or 'roughed up' by the police, while girls were more likely to report that when at a police station they were 'spoken to nicely' and were 'overall treated fairly'.

The same study found that marginal (not in full-time school or work) and Aboriginal young people were more likely than others to be dealt with heavy-handedly by police. Consistent with this finding, other studies which have focused on marginal young women have found that their experiences have not been as even-handed as might be interpreted from the Alder (1992) study which involved a wider range of young women. In a study of homeless young people, Alder and Sandor (1990) found that 58 percent of young homeless men and 47 percent of young homeless women reported at least one incident of 'assault' by police. In a similar sample of young, homeless people, Hirst (1989:61) found that of those young women charged with criminal offences, 47 percent claimed to have been physically assaulted by the police compared to 68 percent of the male sample. The observation that girls were less likely to report physical violence by police was confirmed in the Alder and Sandor (1990) research by the youths themselves, who frequently referred to this as one of the differences in the experiences of young men and women who were living on the street. The reported level of physical violence experienced by girls appears to be somewhat less than that experienced by boys. Nevertheless, it is unacceptably high and needs to be considered in the context of reports of sexual assault and intimidation experienced by young women.

Both the young men and young women in the Alder and Sandor (1990) study felt that girls were more often 'hassled' by police. Consistent with this finding, Hirst found that 61 percent of girls reported being psychologically intimidated compared to 40 percent of the boys, and 13 percent of the girls reported being sexually intimidated compared to none of the boys (Hirst, 1989:61). As one lawyer has observed, 'in police custody, women are almost inevitably subject to abuse of a sexual nature. The very fact that the overwhelming majority of police officers are male puts women in a vulnerable position when they enter police custody' (McCulloch, 1991:7).

Many young women in their accounts of their interactions with police tell of sexual harassment in the form of verbal abuse including snide remarks, innuendos and the use of such terms as 'whore'. Young women have reported feeling as though they had been 'treated like a prostitute' (Robson, 1992:58). The Youth Justice Coalition noted that in the case of young women, 'The allegations of strip or body searches have been most serious' (Youth Justice Coalition, 1990:254).

A recent study of young homeless women's experience of the legal system reports 'some serious allegations of police violence', including allegations of sexual assault (Robson, 1992:59). Such allegations about the treatment of young women were also made by some service providers. The report notes that one social worker commented that:

> I can't count the number of women who work on the streets who are picked up by police and are taken out in the back room and asked for sex. It's like 'you do me a favour, I'll do you a favour'. (Robson 1992:60)

Unfortunately for some young women, most notably the homeless and young sex workers, it appears that concern for their moral well-being ends at the door to the police station.

Aboriginal young women

If non-Aboriginal young women are less likely than non-Aboriginal young men to report being bashed by police, the story is not the same for Aboriginal young women. In his study of Aboriginal juveniles and their experiences with police, Cunneen (1990) reports that the allegations of police violence made by Aboriginal girls were similar to those made by boys. This included reports of being 'punched in the head', 'ramming my head into the wall' and being 'hit by a baton'.

Along with the reports of sexual assault and other forms of sexual harassment, Aboriginal young women reported that police 'talked dirty' and that such talk included references to their Aboriginality. Police used terms with these young women such as 'black sluts', 'black bitches' and 'black moles' (Cunneen, 1990:41).

Their gender and their Aboriginality, as constructed in a discourse of sexuality, also have consequences for the policing of young Aboriginal women in public spaces. While in general, young women's access to and use of public spaces is regulated by parents and others, Carrington (1990:8) argues that Aboriginal young women's use of public space is subject to additional forms of regulation and surveillance:

> It is my impression from a reading of court documents, that popularised male discourses, mythologies and fantasies about the black female body underscore the hysterical fears expressed by extra-judicial agencies that the publicly visible presence of Aboriginal girls is somehow 'harmful to the local community' (an oft quoted phrase in court records). (Carrington, 1990:8)

It is in the context of such 'white male discourse about black female bodies', Carrington (1990:8) argues, that Aboriginal girls are more vulnerable to policing than non-Aboriginal girls. However, for Carrington, this discourse of sexuality is but one aspect of a complex process of 'criminalising otherness' that legitimises punitive intervention in the lives of Aboriginal young women. According to Carrington (1990), judicial and non-judicial agencies, drawing upon the 'deficit discourses' of psychology and social work, and social and cultural assumptions, also define other aspects of the young Aboriginal woman's life (her home environment, her assertive behaviour, her school attendance) as constituting grounds for intervention.

While the development of our knowledge of the process of criminalisation of young Aboriginal people is still in its infancy, it is patently clear that they are overrepresented in the juvenile justice system (see e.g. Freiberg, Fox and Hogan, 1988; Carrington, 1990; Gale et al., 1990). In regard to the policing of young women, Carrington points out that 'the highest rates of detection for female delinquency in the state of NSW occur, outside the metropolitan area, in regions with proportionately large aboriginal communities' (Carrington, 1990:2).

This finding in regard to young Aboriginal women is consistent with research in the United States. It is apparent that not all women are subject to the same scrutiny by police, or the same expectations, or are responded to in the same way. Horowitz and Pottieger (1991:76) note that 'several studies have found that White women are treated more leniently than Black Women' (e.g. Pawlak, 1977; Visher, 1983). Visher (1983:17) comments: 'Indeed, in these data chivalrous attitudes that may exist among police officers are apparently directed towards white females and withdrawn from their black sisters, resulting in more frequent arrests for black female suspects.' In fact, Visher found that the influence of demographic characteristics, such as race and age, on arrest decisions appears to be greater for female suspects than for male suspects (Visher, 1983:15). She notes also that, consistently, one study of juvenile court decisions found that black females relative to white females were given more severe dispositions than black males relative to white males (Datesman and Scarpitti, 1980).

SEEKING POLICE HELP

Young women are frequently the victims of violence both in their parents' home and if they have left home, in other living arrangements (Alder 1991). Yet few of these incidents are reported to police. There are numerous explanations for this (Stanko, 1985; Kelly, 1988), but among these is probably their expectation that the police would do very little to help and that potentially they would be placing themselves in a difficult situation. For example, in commenting on the situation of young women sex workers in the United States, Chesney-Lind and Shelden observed that:

> Even when girls experience terrible victimization on the streets, they tend to avoid reporting to police. Cases of girls who report rapes or physical abuse at the hands of male intimates only to be locked up themselves

as runaways or incorrigibles are unfortunately all too common. (Chesney-Lind and Shelden, 1992:132)

Feminist research in recent years has documented the inadequate protection afforded women who are victims of violence and demonstrated that, in general, women's interests are underrepresented in policing (e.g. Edwards, 1989; Hanmer, Radford and Stanko, 1989; Scutt, 1982). For example, from her analysis of the policing of domestic violence in England, Edwards notes:

> It is also the case that the police treatment of rape victims and prostitute women and their response to the sale and distribution of pornography, all of which involve violence against women or exploitation of women, are matters accorded low priority and sometimes are insensitively handled. (Edwards, 1989:31)

In Australia, feminists have observed that victims/survivors of rape cannot depend on police assistance or sympathy (McCulloch, 1991:5). One report notes that 'anywhere from $\frac{1}{3}$ to $\frac{1}{2}$ of rape complaints will be disbelieved by police' (Independent Police Complaints Authority, 1988:29, quoted in Robson, 1992). Many of these cases involve young women: drawing upon police information, Robson (1992:58) notes that of the 1473 rapes reported to police in Victoria from 1987–90, 70 percent were young women aged 25 and under. The failure to respond or to take seriously the violent victimisation of women suggests that the policing of women's behaviour occurs not only in regard to their offending behaviour, but also in terms of the form of the response to their victimisation.

CONCLUSION

Much of the past work on police responses to young women focused on the question of whether or not young women were treated with chivalry, that is, whether they were treated more leniently than young men. It is now apparent that the complexity of the issues involved in police decision making makes it difficult to determine, on the basis of different arrest rates alone, the ways in which that decision making is informed by gender. Certainly far fewer young women than young men are arrested by police. It is now clear that such figures are not simply a consequence of women in general being treated more leniently: a young woman's class, race, age and demeanour are some of the factors that have an effect on the way in which her behaviour is responded to.

Often implicit throughout the limited research on young women's experiences with police is support for Edwards' (1989:26) conclusion that: 'The policing of women, whether in public or private matters, whether as victims or offenders, protesters or campaigners, has been influenced by police stereotypes of appropriate female behavior.'

But police do not work in a vacuum, especially in matters relating to young women in care: they are frequently responding to the complaints of others, including parents; in developing their case, they will draw upon material provided by other professionals; and in preparing their case for court, they will draw upon the expectations of others in the legal system. This argument is not by way of absolving police of their responsibilities. In fact, in some aspects of their behaviour, particularly the harassment and physical abuse of young women, they need to be held directly accountable. However, it is also apparent that simply attempting to change police attitudes through education (the policy most frequently recommended) will not be sufficient to alter young women's experiences of policing. As Reiner is cited as arguing, 'cop culture ... both reflects and perpetuates the power differences within the social structure it polices. The police officer is a microcosmic mediator for the relations of power in a society' (Reiner, 1985; quoted in Edwards, 1989:26).

Thus, in examining police treatment of young women we probably learn as much about such things in our society as the status of young women, the range of behaviour considered acceptable, the blending of formal and informal controls and the centrality of sexuality to their control, as we do about policing.

REFERENCES

Alder, Christine (1991) 'Victims of Violence: The case of homeless youth', *Australian and New Zealand Journal of Criminology*, 24(1):1-14.

Alder, Christine (1992). 'The Young People' in C. Alder, I. O'Connor, K. Warner and R. White, *Perceptions of the Treatment of Juveniles in the Legal System* (pp.18-29). Report for the National Youth Affairs Research Scheme. Hobart: National Clearinghouse for Youth Studies.

Alder, Christine and Sandor, Danny (1990) *Homeless Youth as Victims of Violence*. Research Report for the Criminology Research Council. Canberra: Australian Institute of Criminology.

Carrington, Kerry (1989) 'Girls and graffiti', *Cultural Studies*, 3:89-100.

Carrington, Kerry (1990) 'Aboriginal girls and juvenile justice: What justice? White justice', *Journal for Social Justice Studies*, 3:1-18.

Carrington, Kerry (1992) Youth culture and delinquency. Paper presented at the 8th Annual Conference of the Australian and New Zealand Society of Criminology, October, Melbourne.

Chesney-Lind, Meda (1974) 'Juvenile delinquency: The sexualization of female crime', *Psychology Today* (July):43–46.

Chesney-Lind, Meda (1977) 'Judicial paternalism and the female status offender: training women to know their place', *Crime and Delinquency*, 23:121–30.

Chesney-Lind, Meda (1978) 'Young women in the arms of the law', in L. Bowker (ed.), *Women, Crime and the Criminal Justice System*. Lexington, Mass.: Lexington Books.

Chesney-Lind, Meda and Shelden, Randall, G. (1992) *Girls, Delinquency and Juvenile Justice*. Pacific Grove, California: Brooks/Cole Publishing Company.

Cunneen, Chris (1990) *A Study of Aboriginal Juveniles and Police Violence*. Report Commissioned by the National Inquiry into Racist Violence. Sydney: Human Rights and Equal Opportunity Commission.

Datesman, S. and Scarpitti, F. (1980) 'Unequal protection for males and females in the juvenile court', in S. Datesman and F. Scarpitti (eds), *Women, Crime and Justice* (pp.300–19). New York: Oxford.

DeFleur, Lois (1975) 'Biasing influences on drug arrest records: implications for deviance research', *American Sociological Review*, 40:1–103.

Edwards, Susan S.M. (1989) *Policing 'Domestic' Violence: Women, the Law and the State*. London: Sage Publications.

Elliott, D. and Voss, H.L. (1974) *Delinquency and Dropout*. Lexington, Mass.: Lexington Books.

Freiberg, A., Fox, R. and Hogan, M. (1988) *Sentencing Young Offenders*. Sentencing Research Paper No. 11. Australian Law Reform Commission and Commonwealth Youth Bureau.

Gale, Fay, Bailey-Harris, Rebecca and Wundersitz, Fay (1990) *Aboriginal Youth and the Criminal Justice System: The Injustice of Justice?* Cambridge: Cambridge University Press.

Gelsthorpe, Lorraine (1986) 'Towards a sceptical look at sexism', *International Journal of the Sociology of Law*, 14:125–53.

Hancock, Linda (1980) 'The Myth that Females are Treated More Leniently than Males in the Juvenile Justice System', *The Australian and New Zealand Journal of Sociology*, 16:4–13.

Hanmer, Jalna, Radford, Jill and Stanko, Elizabeth (1989) *Women, Policing and Male Violence*. London: Routledge.

Hirst, Claudia (1989) *Forced Exit: A Profile of the young and homeless in inner urban Melbourne*. Melbourne: Salvation Army.

Horowitz, Ruth and Pottieger, Anne E. (1991) 'Gender Bias in Juvenile Justice Handling of Seriously Crime-involved Youths', *Journal of Research in Crime and Delinquency*, 28:75–100.

Jaggs, Donella (1986) *Neglected and Criminal: Foundation of child welfare legislation in Victoria*. Melbourne: Phillip Institute of Technology.

James, Stephen and Polk, Kenneth (1989) 'Policing Youth: Themes and directions', in Duncan Chappell and Paul Wilson (eds), *Australian Policing: Contemporary Issues* (pp.41–61). Sydney: Butterworths.

Kelly, L.Z. (1988) *Surviving Sexual Violence*. Cambridge: Polity Press.

Krohn, Marvin D., Curry, James P. and Nelson-Kilger, Shirley (1983) 'Is Chivalry Dead? An analysis of changes in police dispositions of males and females', *Criminology*, 21:417–37.

Lees, Sue (1986) *Losing Out. Sexuality and adolescent girls*. London: Hutchinson.

McCulloch, Jude (1991) All's Fair in Love and War: Policing women. Paper presented at the Women and the Law Conference, sponsored by the Australian Institute of Criminology. September, Sydney.

Pawlak, E. (1977) 'Differential Selection of Juveniles for Detention', *Journal of Research of Crime and Delinquency*, 14:152–65.

Piliavin, Ivan and Briar, Scott (1964) 'Police Encounters with Juveniles', *American Journal of Sociology*, 70:206–14.

Robson, Belinda (1992) *Rough Justice: A report on sexual assault, homelessness and the law*. Victoria: Northeast Centre Against Sexual Assault.

Schlossman, S. and Wallach, S. (1978) 'The Crime of Precocious Sexuality; Female delinquency in the progressive era', *Harvard Educational Review*, 48:65–94.

Scutt, Jocelyn A. (1982) 'Domestic Violence and the Police Response', in C. O'Donnell and J. Craney (eds), *Family Violence in Australia* (pp.110–20). Melbourne: Longman Cheshire.

Smith, Douglas A. and Visher, Christy, A. (1981) 'Street-level Justice: Situational determinants of police arrest decisions', *Social Problems*, 167–79.

Smith, L.S. (1978) 'Sexist Assumptions and Female Delinquency', in C. Smart and B. Smart (eds), *Women, Sexuality and Social Control*. London: Routledge and Kegan Paul.

Stanko, B. (1985) *Intimate Intrusions: Women's experience of male violence*. London: Routledge and Kegan Paul.

Visher, Christy A. (1983) 'Gender, Police Arrest Decisions and Notions of Chivalry', *Criminology*, 21:5–28.

White, Rob (1990) *No Space of Their Own: Young people and social control in Australia*. Cambridge: Cambridge University Press.

White, Rob (1992) 'The Police' in C. Alder, I. O'Connor, K. Warner and R. White, *Perceptions of the Treatment of Juveniles in the Legal System* (pp.29–37). Report for the National Youth Affairs Research Scheme. Hobart: National Clearinghouse for Youth Studies.

Worrall, Anne (1990) *Offending Women: Female lawbreakers and the criminal justice system*. London: Routledge.

Youth Justice Coalition (NSW) (1990) *Kids in Justice: A blueprint for the 90s*. Sydney: Youth Justice Coalition.

CHAPTER 8

Policing Youth in 'Ethnic' Communities: Is Community Policing the Answer?

Janet Chan

POLICE AND ETHNIC YOUTH

This chapter is concerned with relations between police and young people from minority ethnic communities. The term 'ethnic' is used here as a shorthand for describing people of non-English-speaking background, although it is recognised that ethnicity is a matter of individual choice (self-identification) and the concept is not restricted to non-English-speaking groups (see, for example, Bell, 1987: chapter 1).

Since the late 1940s, Australia's population has become increasingly culturally diverse through immigration. By the late 1980s, about 25 percent of the population were from non-Anglo-Celtic origins. A report on ethnic youth estimated that in 1985, about one in five young people (15 to 24-years-old) in Australia was either born in non-English-speaking countries, or born in Australia with one or both parents born in non-English-speaking countries (Federation of Ethnic Communities' Councils of Australia, 1991:3). From 1976 to 1986 the percentage of overseas-born population from Asia has doubled (Human Rights and Equal Opportunity Commission, 1991:60–1). A shift in immigration pattern, especially the introduction of refugees from Indo-China and South East Asia in recent years, has resulted in a major change in the composition of ethnic youth (FECCA, 1991:4).

Concerns regarding the volume and composition of immigrants have been a recurring theme carried by the Australian media since the 1980s, through the so-called 'immigration debate', which has focused on the cultural, economic and, more recently, environmental consequences of continuing and increasing levels of immigration. In particular, the pace of Asian immigration was seen to be detrimental to the interest of 'national cohesion' by some commentators. While Australians remain divided on the issue, the National Inquiry into Racist Violence found that among reported cases of victimisation, Asian and Arab Australians were most likely to be subjected to intimidation, harassment and violence (Human Rights and Equal Opportunity Commission, 1991:172-5). Consultations with ethnic youth confirmed that Asians, particularly the Vietnamese, were increasingly the targets of racist comments and discrimination in the school setting and in the workplace (Cahill and Ewen, 1987; FECCA, 1991). Policing of ethnic youth must be seen against this context of mixed community reactions to the increasing numbers of culturally different and often visibly distinct groups in Australian society.

Tension and conflict between police and ethnic minorities overseas have been dramatically brought to Australian attention through media images such as the 1992 Los Angeles riots following the verdict in the Rodney King case and the 1981 Brixton riots in Britain. Researchers have also documented evidence of adversarial or hostile relations between police forces and minority groups, especially black youths, in specific communities (e.g. Bayley and Mendelsohn, 1969; Smith, 1987; Short, 1983). In Australia, the majority of work on police/minority relations has been focused on Aborigines (e.g. Gale and Wundersitz, 1987; Cunneen, 1990; Cunneen and Robb, 1987). The treatment of Aboriginal juveniles by police was also identified as a major concern following the findings of the National Inquiry into Racist Violence (Human Rights and Equal Opportunity Commission, 1991).

In spite of the paucity of Australian research specifically on police–ethnic youth relations, a negative portrait, based predominantly on accounts by community youth workers and solicitors, is already emerging. It is a portrait replete with many of the images already familiar to students of police–youth relations: unfair or unwarranted targeting of certain youth by the police; police abuse or harassment of young people; as well as their lack of concern for young people's legal rights. The picture is, however, more complicated in the case of ethnic youths, when issues of police stereotyping and prejudice are raised, along with language and cultural barriers.

Language and cultural barriers

A major problem encountered by recent immigrants and refugees to Australia is their lack of ability or confidence to communicate in English. An unpublished survey of fifty-five community organisations conducted by the New South Wales Ethnic Affairs Commission (NSWEAC, 1991) found widespread concern that police did not always use interpreters when needed and that unqualified or inappropriate persons were often used as interpreters. A 1991 survey of 332 New South Wales police officers found that professional interpreters were used on average less than ten times during the past year, even though officers estimated that they encountered language problems an average of fifty-two times during that year (Chan, 1992:13–15). A 1987 survey of sixty Vietnamese migrants in Victoria came to a similar conclusion about the low usage of interpreters by the Victorian police (Wilson and Storey, 1991:18).

While administrative costs – both financial and in terms of delay – have often been cited as reasons for police not to use professional interpreters, a crucial issue concerns the extent to which police discretion is appropriately exercised in these situations. When dealing with ethnic youth, there were complaints that police had a tendency not to accept that interpreters were needed – 'it was commonly presumed that the youth concerned went to school hence would understand English' (NSWEAC, 1991: Section 2B). The assumption that someone with a reasonable grasp of conversational English would be competent to give legal evidence or answer questions in a police interrogation has already been challenged by linguistic specialists and lawyers (see Commonwealth Attorney-General's Department, 1990:42; Roberts-Smith, 1989:76). When interpreters are not used in criminal investigations, the disadvantages suffered by a person of non-English-speaking background may be compounded by their cultural fears and inhibitions:

> The intrinsic nature and potential consequences of criminal investigation make it perhaps the most stressful of all legal situations. This stress may be greatly increased by cultural and language difficulties. The relationship of citizens to police in their native country will be reflected in behaviour and attitudes shown by migrants to Australian police. Those migrants who come from a police state are likely to have a very different perception of the role and the function of police. Any encounter with the police, for whatever reason, may be a frightening experience. (Commonwealth Attorney-General's Department, 1990:60)

The right to an interpreter has not been uniformly established in legislation throughout Australia; some states still rely on police and judicial discretion in establishing the need for an interpreter.

NEGATIVE STEREOTYPING AND HARASSMENT

One common complaint from workers in ethnic communities has been that police form stereotypical images of particular ethnic groups and have a tendency to harass members of these groups, especially the young people. A report on juvenile justice in New South Wales suggests that this is a fairly common complaint among young people:

> The most common reaction of young people to the police is the objection that they are picked on, that once the police know them they keep them under surveillance, that they investigate them first in connection with offences occurring in their vicinity, or with those in the style of that young person's previous offence. While such attention may be regarded by officers as rational and efficient, it is often unjustified and consequently may damage police–youth relations . . . The concern that they are picked on usually derives from their record: they are picked on *because* they are known to the police. This can also interact with police racism, according to the young people. Racism against Aboriginal and Asian young people was often mentioned by young people and their families: this was seen to result in unfair suspicion, 'picking on' them, and racist remarks. (Youth Justice Coalition, 1990:232)

The Australian Law Reform Commission in its report *Multiculturalism and the Law* describes a similar problem raised by bodies such as the Ethnic Affairs Commission of New South Wales, the Marrickville Legal Centre and Children's Legal Services, and the Federation of Ethnic Communities' Councils of Australia:

> The Commission's consultations reveal concern about negative ethnic stereotyping resulting in whole communities being put on trial and stigmatised for the real and imagined activities of some members of those groups. The experience of the Greek community in the 'Greek social security conspiracy' case, and the continuing problems for the Italian and Asian communities of being popularly associated with organised crime, are cited as examples. There is concern about a perceived tendency to cast young people of particular ethnic backgrounds as delinquent. This may result in a young person being at a disadvantage in dealings with the police and at court. Young people who gather together because they are related, are family friends, go to school together or live near each other, may be assumed by the police to be involved in illegal gang activities simply due to their appearance. (Australian Law Reform Commission, 1992:201)

The unpublished NSW Ethnic Affairs Commission survey of community organisations also identifies stereotyping and harassment of youth from non-English-speaking background as a common complaint:

> Stereotyping was frequently identified as a problem in police work with youth of non-English-speaking background. The stereotypes that were observed as being part of police attitudes included the following:
> - Youth of non-English-speaking background as trouble makers.
> - Youth of non-English-speaking background constitute themselves as gangs and not as groups. An example referred to in this case was of groups which dressed in tracksuits, Reebok shoes, and were identified as colour gangs instead of groups of kids.
> - Police tend to judge people by the way they dress. This is especially important for young people who are often on the street. This can lead to unwarranted attention and harassment. (NSWEAC 1991: Section 2B4)

Police harassment reported includes

> racist taunts on the part of the police, lack of attention to requests for assistance from youth of non-English speaking background, occasional physical abuse by police, victimisation by police through the selective use of police powers, police brutality whilst youth are being detained or questioned by police. (NSWEAC 1991)

Similar complaints against the Victorian police have been documented by Wilson and Storey (1991). Among eighteen Vietnamese respondents who had had some contact with the police, eight were the subject of criminal investigation or surveillance. Six of these eight people complained of poor treatment by the police, including 'rudeness, use of abusive language, acting in a menacing fashion, verballing and beatings' (Wilson and Storey, 1991:15). Seven respondents who sought general police assistance found the police unhelpful, rude, and in two cases the respondents requesting assistance were victimised by the police (Wilson and Storey, 1991:16). The only group who reported that they were well treated by the police were the six respondents who were victims of crime. Allegations of beatings in custody, property searches without warrants, harassment and abuse of individuals were reported by nine community workers (75 percent of those interviewed) and six solicitors (one-fifth of those interviewed). The authors argued that things were no better in 1991, in spite of recent police initiatives to mediate and resolve conflict with that community:

The Vietnamese continue to complain about harsh treatment by police. In 1991 Footscray Community Legal Centre received complaints from a group of young men who alleged that they had been continually harassed and questioned about their activities by police in the main shopping area of Footscray. The local Vietnamese community association claimed that this was a regular problem for Vietnamese youth in the area. In a number of other cases the legal centre received complaints from individuals seeking assistance from police who said that they were treated in a rude and unhelpful manner. (Wilson and Storey, 1991:28)

It is significant to note that the Victorian and the Western Australian police, in their submissions to the Australian Law Reform Commission, had denied that this type of stereotyping influenced police behaviour (ALRC, 1992:201). When accused of irregular, unfair or discriminatory practices, police organisations have tended to deny their existence or prevalence, to discredit the critics, to scapegoat a small number of officers, and to point to a host of progressive initiatives already planned or implemented to address the problem. This can be frustrating for those who are genuinely interested in improving the situation. They feel that no matter how real these problems appear to be, and no matter how sincere they have been about working with the police to find a solution, their complaints are never taken seriously. Critics see the police as defensive, close-minded, and unwilling to change. On the other hand, police executives may feel that no matter how hard they have tried to implement reforms within the police organisation, and no matter how sincere they have been about working with the community to solve the problem, they are constantly under attack for not doing enough. Police believe the critics are being unfair, politically motivated and disruptive. Often, advocates for police reform within the organisation find their positions weakened and fundamental reforms abandoned in favour of short-term cosmetic initiatives to appease public outrage. At times, they are able to turn outside criticisms to their advantage by using the critics' voice to reinforce their own call for reform. In other instances, however, each allegation of police racism results in the critics and the police moving further apart.

It has been suggested recently that the development of community policing strategies and a more 'service-oriented' style of policing may go some way towards improving relations between ethnic youth and the police (FECCA, 1991:31–2). Police forces in Australia have in fact begun to implement a large number of strategies aimed at addressing the needs of ethnic communities (see *Report* of the National Conference on Police Services in a Multicultural Australia, 1990). The aim of this chapter is to explore some of the reasons why these initiatives may not have made a great deal of difference to the problems cited earlier. Using community policing as an example of such initiatives, I will describe why this policing strategy is considered to be a solution to problems of police–ethnic relations, what it is supposed to achieve, and why it may not produce the outcomes intended. It will be argued that the problems reportedly faced by ethnic youths have more to do with their *youthfulness* than their ethnicity (see White et al., 1991). Consequently, many of the initiatives taken by police to ensure 'access and equity' with regard to people from non-English-speaking background are largely irrelevant to these young people.

COMMUNITY POLICING

Advocates of police reform believe community policing is the answer to many policing problems, including those between police and ethnic minority groups (see Alderson, 1983). The idea is that if the police establish a partnership with the local community (which may consist of Anglo, Aboriginal, European, Middle Eastern, Asian, or other ethnic groups), then the problem of police–minority relations can be solved. The reasoning behind this is that the police cannot serve the needs of the local community satisfactorily unless they abandon any prejudice they have against sections of the community, reach out to its members, establish a sense of trust and co-operation among them, and involve them in the policing of their community.

Although students of criminal justice reforms are justifiably sceptical about any reform package which bears the label of 'community', given the disillusionment brought about by many aspects of 'community corrections' (see, for example, Cohen, 1985), it would be presumptuous to simply dismiss community policing as yet another police public-relations exercise to convince citizens that something is being done. Just as the ideals of community corrections are appealing to penal reformers, the conceptual basis of community policing is, even to the most scathing critics, remarkably soundly based, convincingly argued, and, in some instances, expertly and carefully worked out. This is not to detract from the observation that there are, as will be pointed out in this chapter, some serious pitfalls in what appears to be the perfect solution. As a general reform blueprint, however, community policing deserves a great deal of serious consideration.

Advocates of community policing recognise that the existence of large, urban police forces is a relatively recent phenomenon. Until the passage of the Metropolitan Police Act in England in 1829, the tasks of surveillance and order maintenance were largely left to private citizens. The evolution of the English police model to the present-day organisation of police can be traced to the progressive movement in the late nineteenth century in the United States, where political control of the police became a major issue. As a result of a movement to rid police of corruption, police departments in the United States became committed to crime control as their primary function; developed a paramilitary organisational structure, with central command and functional specialisation; and gained independence from the political system. This trend accelerated in the 1940s to 1960s, when technological advances and statistical reporting pushed policing practices towards the achievement of rapid responses to alarms, the allocation of patrol resources to optimise response time, and the use of serious crime statistics as performance indicators. Doubts about the appropriateness of this style of policing were raised in the United States amid the civil rights movement, which brought out the conflict between the crime-fighting role of the police and individual political rights and freedoms. At the same time, research on police work was raising new questions about the effectiveness of random patrol, rapid response and detectives' investigation procedures (Kelling and Moore, 1982).

Although there are important gains to be achieved by enhancing the protection of individual citizens' civil rights through legislation, and by strengthening the structure of police accountability and improving accessibility to a complaints mechanism, advocates of community policing see a fundamental overhaul of the ideological and organisational basis of policing as a far more effective and necessary step towards greater police accountability. The gentleness of the label 'community policing' in fact disguises some extremely harsh and drastic measures which turn traditional policing upside down. A full embrace of the community-policing model involves the following major shifts in emphasis in policing style (Sparrow et al., 1990).

Pro-active rather than reactive policing

Acknowledging the limited utility of motorised patrol, of rapid response to calls for service and of retrospective investigation of crime, community policing advocates emphasise the 'problem-solving' approach to policing (Goldstein, 1979). This approach releases expensive police resources traditionally consumed by reactive policing and puts these resources into removing conditions and opportunities which are conducive to the occurrence of offences. Instead of rushing around from call to call and never stopping long enough to get to know the victims and their communities, police are now encouraged to become familiar with neighbourhoods and the people within these communities so that they are in a position to assist them in solving their problems, which may or may not be directly related to the occurrence of crime.

Fear reduction and order maintenance rather than crime fighting

Advocates of community policing point to the obvious disjunction between police self-perception that they are predominantly crime-fighters and the reality that police officers spend most of their patrol time dealing with non-criminal matters involving disputes or emergencies. For many years, these 'social service' calls were considered peripheral to real police work. Consequently, police resent these tasks and receive no training in handling disputes and maintaining order, relying instead on actual use or the threat of law enforcement or physical force to restore order. Community policing suggests that police may serve their community better by not denying the importance of their order-maintenance role and by addressing matters such as vandalism and disorder which may help to reduce the community's fear of crime.

Reliance on and accountability to the community rather than operational autonomy

The ideals of community policing place heavy emphasis on the involvement of members of the community in defining and assisting police work. Rather than asserting that police operational decisions are police matters, the new approach to policing makes it clear that the police must be accountable to the community they serve.

Accordingly, police must listen to and give credence to the wishes of the community, for ultimately the success of their work depends on the consent and support of the community.

That these principles constitute a radical departure from traditional policing philosophy and practices cannot be over-emphasised. In fact, community policing raises some 'fundamental questions about the proper limit to and scope of police activity' (Weatheritt, 1987:19). The adoption of community policing as official policy is often accompanied by drastic changes to police organisations, e.g. the decentralisation of authority, a move away from functional special-isation to geographical command, a flattening of the rank structure, and a thorough overhaul of the training curriculum (see Chan, 1992). In some police organisations, these structural changes are reinforced by the introduction of contract employment, merit-based promotion and changes to recruitment procedures. More important than the structural transformation of the organisation is the necessity to change the culture or value structure of the police force. Often this involves a new openness, a commitment to professional integrity and the upholding of civil rights and the rule of law, necessitating the abandonment of dubious police practices which are often the target of criticisms.

Flowing from the principles of community policing are concrete initiatives which police organisations may decide to implement: the establishment of programs such as neighbourhood watch and safety house, the setting up of community consultative committees, the increased use of foot patrol (beat police), and putting additional resources into community liaison activities (see chapter 9). With minority ethnic communities, there may be additional initiatives such as: group-specific or language-specific community consul-tative committees, the recruitment of police officers from ethnic groups, the appointment of special ethnic liaison officers, the institution of cross-cultural training courses for police officers, and offering incentives for police officers to acquire ethnic language skills and understanding of multicultural issues (see FECCA, 1991; Chan, 1992).

Given the appeal of mobilising the community in policing, the enthusiastic adoption of community policing principles by many police organisations is not surprising. But as a blanket strategy to reform policing, community policing carries an obvious weakness:

the question of who constitutes the community. This weakness is especially relevant to the problems apparent in the relationship between the police and young people in ethnic communities.

WHOSE COMMUNITY

The reason why the adoption of community policing as a policy does not immediately solve problems between ethnic youth and the police is quite simple: the 'community' being served by the police in community-policing strategies does not include young people, especially those who are judged to be 'not from good homes'. If the aim of policing is to maintain order in the community, then it usually means the removal of nuisance and troublesome elements such as 'youth gangs'. After all, the community being served is predominantly made up of law-abiding citizens and respectable business interests, not the beleaguered community of street kids.

Likewise, community-policing initiatives being actively pursued by police forces are largely irrelevant to ethnic youth.* The employment of ethnic community liaison officers aims at the improvement of police–minority relations, but street kids do not see ethnic liaison officers as their friends and advisers. More likely these officers are seen to be interpreters, or as spies, for the police. The regular community consultative meetings are not likely to be attended by young people either. The purpose of these meetings, as far as these young people are concerned, may well be to legitimise law enforcement activities directed at them. Young people do not find the presence of beat police reassuring; rather, beat officers symbolise the ubiquitous arm of the law which constantly watches, threatens and hassles them in their activities. Because many young people from ethnic communities are born or brought up in Australia and can speak English reasonably well, police do not consider it necessary to use interpreters when questioning them. In fact, police often claim that some ethnic kids feign ignorance of English as a stalling tactic when interrogated. It may be very nice of the police to disseminate information about police services in twenty different community languages, but few of these youngsters would recognise their native language in writing. What they feel they need – but what

* The views described in this section were expressed to me by migrant resource centre workers, youth workers and a group of Asian youth in New South Wales. Also see Chan, 1992.

is not included among the glossy brochures – is information about their legal rights and the names of lawyers to contact when they are in trouble (see FECCA, 1991:25).

The implementation of community policing requires that police commanders take a genuine interest in the wishes and needs of the community. It is not sufficient that structures like community consultative committees are established; that is only the first step. In patrols where a large ethnic community resides, there may be the necessity to establish ethno-specific consultative committees, so that people with language difficulties feel free to attend. Yet, even in these committees, the general problem of representation cannot be ignored:

> The case of consultative committees is illustrative: their membership is largely representative of other bodies – neighbourhood watch committees, local business interests, adult community groups, and the churches. Young people are more likely to be seen as the problem or the subject of the committee's attention, rather than as an appropriate constituent of it. (Youth Justice Coalition, 1990:220)

In Britain, where community consultative committees have been set up to satisfy the requirement of the *Police and Criminal Evidence Act* 1984, there is a divergence of views about the purpose of these committees:

> There is a fundamental difference between left and right on this question however. Whereas the government has introduced consultation as an adjunct to the existing framework of constabulary independence – consultation without power and formal political accountability – those on the left seek consultation within a system of elected local authority control over police policy. Indeed many left-wing critics dismiss the current consultative arrangements as a public relations charade ... (Morgan, 1987:32)

Morgan's account of the nature and composition of British community consultative committees is illustrative of the problems inherent in this strategy.

> Committee members are seldom under 30 years of age and typically are active 'respectable' members of the community. They *represent* one organisation and are usually involved in others. Generally speaking, they are *not* the sort of people who have previously had much contact with the police (except possibly socially) and, though they know little of the police, are invariably well-disposed towards them. They are not generally people who have been in conflict with the police or have

adverse personal experience of them. Groups hostile to the police typically dismiss consultative committees as a meaningless charade on the grounds that they lack power and are merely for public relations; such groups often refuse to be involved. (Morgan, 1987:33)

The establishment of community consultative committees was originally intended also to involve members of the community in the planning of police operational strategies. However, operational policy is rarely a topic for discussion in British committees partly because most committee members prefer to leave operational matters to the police, and partly because of the sensitivity of such matters when police discretion is exercised. Consequently,

> those members who seek information about operational policy are unusual and tend to be marginalised by their fellow politicians, the media and the police. They are referred to as trouble makers. They are described, quite meaninglessly, as 'politically motivated', as if the decision *not* to call the police to account amounted to political impartiality or squared better with democracy, whereas of course it does neither. It follows that the perception of these members and committees as 'troublesome' both feeds police fears about the motives behind operational questions and makes it easier for them to resist providing answers. The consequence . . . is to encourage conservatism and paranoia on the part of the police. (Morgan, 1987:39)

The problem, as Smith (1987:63) points out, is that there is not going to be a consensus about the kind of policing the community wants. There is not one, but many publics and policing is about dealing with conflicts, often between some of these publics:

> The idea of community does not seem to provide us with a model for dealing with these conflicts. It is an idea that is best adapted to mobilising the support of the respectable majority for tough law enforcement and order maintenance. This may be useful for a time, but the problem for the police is that they have to live with the groups who bear the brunt of law enforcement and order maintenance. The idea of community cannot be successfully applied to policing if it is used to avoid finding the forms and institutions needed to strike a balance between conflicting demands. (Smith, 1987:63)

In Australia, there has not been a systematic examination of community consultative committees, although committees of this type which liaise with ethnic communities have been set up in virtually every state (National Conference on Police Services in a

Multicultural Australia, 1990). A Victorian report found 'a great deal of scepticism on behalf of all involved that any concrete changes would be made' as a result of these committees (FECCA, 1991:32). The assessment of the Youth Justice Coalition of the committees in New South Wales again raises the issue of representation:

> In NSW, Community Consultative Committees have been established along similar lines [to UK committees] in patrol areas. In some regions such as Fairfield/Cabramatta, committees have been established with a specific focus on youth issues, while in South Sydney consultation networks have been formed between Aboriginal people and the police. As an effective exercise of consultation with the community, it seems that there is distinct room for improvement. There needs to be a broader representation of the local population to ensure that those groups who are marginalised from decision-making procedures (such as young people and people from non-Anglo backgrounds) are included. In addition, procedures need to be established so that representatives have more influence in the determination and review of operational policy to ensure that it suits local needs and the needs of different groups within the locality. (Youth Justice Coalition, 1990:223)

The coalition reports that where youth workers are represented on the committees, 'issues which are raised in the spirit of "cracking down on delinquents" can be diverted into more constructive approaches' (Youth Justice Coalition, 1990:221).

In summary, community policing will not solve the problem between police and ethnic youth unless police organisations consider young people, even those in the margins of social respectability, as a legitimate and important constituent of the community. Consequently, when providing service or consulting with ethnic communities, it is important for the police not to equate the interests of community 'leaders' with the interests of young people. Community policing strategies cannot succeed in building bridges between the police and young people in the ethnic communities unless young people are trusted to have a voice in deciding how the community should be policed.

CRIME FIGHTING AND ORDER MAINTENANCE

No matter how much the new ideals of community policing stress the importance of the service functions of police work, the 'bottom line' for traditional policing remains that of catching criminals and solving crimes. But even if order maintenance rather than crime fighting is given more priority in the new style of police work, it makes little difference to the policing of ethnic youths. Much of order maintenance is done on behalf of the propertied, the law-abiding and the respectable citizens. If the role of the police is to maintain order in the community, then it is precisely the marginal, loitering, and often suspicious-looking youths who need to be controlled and removed from the streets. The nature of patrol work is such that officers develop indices of respectability for different categories of people in the community, as a Canadian study of a suburban police force shows:

> This identification with middle-class respectability makes some officers react negatively to any groups whom they cannot place within it. Thus, in discussion among themselves, there is derision of certain racial and ethnic minorities, as well as citizens at the bottom end of society's 'scheme of things' who do not appear to be seeking upward mobility in a way that would indicate an identification with the values of middle-class respectability. Indeed in this latter group are persons identified by patrol officers as 'Coasters' (people from the Maritime region of Canada) and 'pukers' (apparently hedonistic young people whose activity, dress, and demeanour indicate a departure from middle-class respectability). There is constant talk about these types being 'the scum of the earth,' 'the source of all police problems,' and so on. For example, an officer came into the lunchroom stating, 'I got my spook for the day,' followed by a statement that he almost ran over a 'fucking Paki' who was hitchhiking (actually the hitchhiker was Chinese). This type of talk is common. (Ericson, 1982:66–7)

Ethnic stereotyping works to reinforce police perception of respectability. For example, the 'brainy' Asian kids attending private schools in good neighbourhoods are going to be left alone, but the Vietnamese street kids loitering around bowling alleys fit the stereotype of the tough, trouble-making members of youth gangs. If they have been in trouble with the law before, they become prime targets for regular questioning and surveillance.

The shift to pro-active policing, ostensibly as part of the problem-solving approach to police work, may also work against marginal young people from ethnic communities:

> Patrol officers themselves develop their own criteria for deciding what is worthy of proactive activity. Most of these are developed collectively as 'shared-recipe' knowledge about whom to stop for what purpose in particular circumstances. In general, patrol officers develop and use

cues concerning 1) individuals out of place, 2) individuals in particular places, 3) individuals of particular types regardless of place, and 4) unusual circumstances regarding property. (Ericson, 1982:86)

Following these 'cues' may be routine police work, but the effect may be serious for minorities:

What is important to realise is that measuring people against their surrounding is an essential part of police activity. A policeman [*sic*] is chronically suspicious and he [*sic*] is forced, by the nature of the duty with which he is entrusted, to make snap decisions about the appropriateness of what people are doing. Since he is looking for the unusual, his decisions are environment-specific; what action he takes depends upon what is perceived to be common for that area. The fact that policemen are alert for incongruity probably does militate against minority persons. (Bayley and Mendelsohn, 1969:93)

In Redfern, Sydney, for example, an individual 'out of place' is an Aborigine driving a red Laser (as mentioned in the television documentary *Cop it Sweet*). Young people congregating in parks, shopping malls, pinball parlours, etc., are obvious targets for pro-active stops. A recent report highlights this conflict regarding the use of public space:

Young people who are unemployed, who have little money to pay for entertainment, who may be geographically isolated and have little access to public transport, and who may not have a home in which to socialise with friends are very limited in where they can spend their time. Public spaces like shopping centres may be the only free, dry, warm (or cool) and accessible places where they can amuse themselves in the hours of boredom without employment, educational or family commitments. However police often see it as their role to 'move them on', and remove these 'non-paying' customers from areas legitimately inhabited by shoppers and shopkeepers. The police see them as 'detached' and 'disreputable', the 'rabble' to be watched and arrested, although they have committed no crime, and they frequently respond with hostility, if not physical violence ... Reports of young Indo-Chinese men being photographed, finger printed and manhandled without any formal charges for just 'hanging around' have come to the attention of youth workers. (FECCA, 1991:33)

Young people known to have criminal records, or thought to be members of a 'gang', are regularly checked, questioned or even searched. Young people who insist on their rights are resented by the police, who see the refusal to co-operate as additional reason for suspicion (see chapter 4). The Youth Justice Coalition report gives an example of a male juvenile whose invocation of rights led to his being taken to a police station:

> the police officer wanted to check out someone whose behaviour ... made him suspicious. Officers routinely stop young people in such circumstances, ask for names and addresses, and often search. Existence of reasonable suspicion on which exercise of the specified power depends was doubtful in this case: most incidents of stopping and questioning do not have even this narrow evidential base ... [T]he officers regarded [the juvenile's] invocation of 'rights' as being simply inappropriate in the circumstances: for such a person to assert his rights is 'buggering about' and/or additionally suspicious. In this situation, knowledge of rights may itself be regarded as an indication of previous contact with police, and therefore as worth further investigation. (Youth Justice Coalition, 1990:235)

The introduction of beat police officers on foot patrol may make the respectable members of the community feel safer, but to the street kids who are the object of pro-active policing, this is merely further evidence that the police are out to hassle them.

The problems raised with respect to community policing are not meant to give the impression that 'nothing works'. Obviously, if police were to see young people from minority ethnic groups as legitimate members of the community, even though they may have committed minor offences, or appear not to be following middle-class norms of respectability, chances are that many of the problems can be dealt with in a fair and appropriate manner. Young people apparently do respect authority when it is exercised even-handedly and not disproportionate to the seriousness of the matter:

> A number of young people complained of the negative attitudes that police had towards them, often related to their sense of the proportion of their crimes. They thought that police treated them in ways which should be reserved for more serious offenders ... Many of the young people who spoke about the police said there were 'some good ones', characterised by being fair, offering smokes in the cells, overlooking offences because they don't want a young person on a bond to be breached, etc. 'Good ones' are also those who will have contact with young people through social and sporting events, or who simply will pass a friendly remark to them on the street. (Youth Justice Coalition, 1990:232–3)

Similar feelings are found among street kids in ethnic communities. For some of these young people, their fear or suspicion of the police came from their own experience or the experience of their parents in dictatorial political regimes with corrupt and arbitrary police authorities. They have learnt not to trust the police, and any negative experience with Australian police merely serves to reinforce their conviction. In fact, as the NSW report indicates, young people's negative attitudes towards the police are developed, and further aggravated, through increasing contact with the police. This suggests that the situation could be turned around by making police–youth contacts a positive experience, instead of having 'a stock of potential goodwill ... dissipated by activities which could be changed without reducing police effectiveness' (Youth Justice Coalition, 1990:236).

OBSTACLES TO CHANGE

The crucial point to recognise is that community policing is not the same as, and cannot be reduced to, the ritual of setting up a few community consultative committees and having officers walk the beat, so that police are seen to be closer to the people. The ideals of community policing require a fundamental change in police values and police practices which have been galvanised by years of isolation and alienation from the community. Critics of police racism are merely addressing a symptom: police may be prejudiced against minority groups, but they are probably only slightly more so than the general population (Bayley and Mendelsohn, 1969:144). The problems marginal ethnic youth encounter with police have something to do with ethnicity, but a lot more to do with marginality or criminality. The most important change required is not that the police suddenly become friendly and tolerant towards ethnic youth, although that may be a start, but that police, as professional law enforcement workers, *have genuine regard for the due process of the law*. This is not asking for much, but as Sparrow et al. (1990) noted, there appears to be, in many police jurisdictions, an implicit 'deal' between police and citizens:

> The deal between the citizens and the police appeared to be that if the police did a good job of fighting crime and responding to calls for service, they could be indulged a little in other ways ... for the police force to be willing to do the job of 'shoveling shit', they had to be allowed to sleep on the job, be rude, harass defendants, and extort bribes. We suspect that this deal – trading the appearance of crime-fighting effectiveness for the indulgence of a certain amount of misconduct – is

often implicitly made between the police and their communities ... It is what allows the police to cut corners in crime-control efforts, as often for self-expression as for effectiveness. (Sparrow et al., 1990:133–4)

This implicit deal, which, as Sparrow et al. suggest, will always be denied when revealed, explains the silence of the law-abiding citizens when police misconduct is alleged by marginal groups. Yet, even to critics of the police, a new vision of the police as 'guardians of civil liberties of ordinary citizens' may seem too far-fetched for words. Traditionally, society assumed and accepted the stereotype that police officers were not very bright, not very well educated, from working-class backgrounds and conservative in outlook. In effect, we never trusted the police with such important matters as being the champion of civil liberties:

Restraint, respect, decency, and so on were upper-class values. They were the sort of things best left to judges and lawyers, not the blue-collar people who became police officers. From the reformers' perspective, the problem was usually how the people with the proper values could control the police, not how they could elevate the rank and file to a position of similar virtue. (Sparrow et al., 1990:136–7)

Perhaps it is this mental threshold that has prevented police and critics of the police alike from taking the logical next step: more important than getting police to learn another language or take compulsory courses on cross-cultural issues, train them to be fair and professional in carrying out their work.

There are, of course, many obstacles that stand in the way of bringing about such a drastic change in police values. The organisational structure and culture of police work both militate against change. For example, the reality of shift work means that police officers are often not able to socialise with people outside police circles. As well, the perceived dangers of police work contribute to police officers' feeling that the outside world is unpredictable, hostile and 'out to get them'. This kind of 'siege mentality' reinforces solidarity around police values that are now found to be badly in need of review. In addition, the rank structure and hierarchy of police organisation ensure that changes initiated at the top, unless they involve straightforward revisions of operational procedures, are not always picked up by officers at the bottom. A familiar scenario in police organisations is one in which police executives are enthusiastic and optimistic about change, but for patrol officers at the 'coalface', it is business as usual. Yet, it is precisely on the street and on the beat that the police interact with citizens, especially victims of crime and suspected offenders. Change, if it has any meaning at all, has to be demonstrated when police officers stop a motorist, interview a victim, question a juvenile, carry out an investigation, and arrest a suspect. However, change coming from the top is bad news for the line officers:

> The legacy of militaristic management ... poses problems as [police] chiefs work toward change. They have to grapple with the fact that patrol officers are deeply resentful of virtually anything new that comes out of headquarters. Patrol officers feel that nothing from headquarters ever made their job easier, and rarely failed to make it more difficult ... It all comes from headquarters; it is all imposed; it is all thought up by somebody else – probably somebody with a carpeted office who has time to sit and think these things up. We are too busy already; too busy doing 'real police work' to pay serious attention to any more of their fanciful schemes. We already have more rules and procedures than we can possibly remember. There is no time for trying new schemes out – it takes all day just to avoid making mistakes. (Sparrow et al., 1990:147–9)

The difficulty of implementing police reforms, however, does not mean that change is impossible. It simply means that reform will be slow in coming. It also means that the forces against change will be enormous and victories are never permanently secured.

CONCLUSION: ACHIEVING OPENNESS AND ACCOUNTABILITY

In their critique of American policing since the 'reform period', Sparrow et al. (1990:51) isolate several powerful beliefs among police officers. These beliefs form the 'building blocks' of current police culture. They are responsible for setting police officers against young people, against people from different cultural backgrounds, and even against the public. They constitute the most formidable obstacles to positive change:

> The police's strong self-image as the only true crime fighters inhibits them from talking about their inability to control crime and from consciously or explicitly accepting any limitations in that regard. Thus, it denies access to one of the strongest justifications for experimenting: a consensus that existing methodologies are inadequate. The police's belief that no one else understands their job prevents open discussion with the community about what police do well, do badly, could do

differently, or don't need to do at all. Their steadfast fraternal loyalty fosters mutual protectiveness, which can include defense of the status quo precisely because it threatens one's colleagues least. The police's belief that crime fighting requires breaking the rules ... shifts attention first to the other parts of the criminal justice system (inadequate sentencing, incompetent juries, insufficient prison space) and subsequently to politicians, city management, housing planners, and the like ... There is no incentive for innovation in policing where everybody agrees that what needs to change is the rest of the world. Officers' belief that the public is basically unsupportive and unreasonable disinclines them to acknowledge the seriousness of problems that members of the community face. Those who complain are complainers; those who call repeatedly are nuisances; those who write to senior officers are treacherous and untrustworthy. It is difficult with such beliefs to pay close attention to clients' problems or even to be sure who to regard as the client. (Sparrow et al., 1990:202–5)

These beliefs figure prominently in police practices in relation to marginal, troublesome youth from ethnic communities. The crime-fighting mandate is used to justify targeting certain youth for checking, questioning or search, a practice much resented by young people. Loyalty to colleagues and a 'siege mentality' mean that when excessive force or irregular procedures are used against young people, these instances are covered up, denied, or justified by deliberate lying, bending the truth, or laying counter-charges against those who complain.

The fatal error in police organisations' defensive or sometimes even aggressive stance towards criticisms from marginal groups is that they have mistaken community policing as a public-relations exercise, the 'smiley face' of the iron fist. As Sparrow et al. (1990: chapter 6) point out, 'community relations' and 'complaints and discipline' functions must not be seen as separate and incompatible functions within the police organisation. Complaints – both serious and minor ones – are the 'ink blot' tests of community feelings towards the police. They should not invariably be seen as politically motivated attacks by interest groups, or a source of constant annoyance. Police officers investigating complaints should not be motivated to maximise the number of withdrawals by complainants to make the organisation look good. Complaints are a valuable source of information about areas of community discontent, unprofessional practices, administrative deficiencies, training or recruitment inadequacies, and communication failures. Complaints supply views from dissatisfied members of the public, people whose voices are not likely to be included in community consultative committees. Instead of discouraging complaints and discrediting complainants, police organisations would do better to pursue the opposite goal: to make police organisations more open and accountable. Such a change, however, takes courage and a strong sense of conviction that public accountability is not incompatible with effective policing.

This chapter has focused on the relations between police and marginal ethnic youth, predominantly those labelled as 'street kids', 'youth gangs', or 'known criminals'. The reason for this focus is that complaints against police rarely emanate from respectable, middle-class youth from ethnic communities. I have argued that while racial prejudice and stereotyping may be a factor, the more problematic area is the police's perception of their work, particularly in relation to juveniles. There may be, in addition, cultural and language impediments in the case of ethnic youth – impediments which further disadvantage them in front of the law. Nevertheless, the tension and problems between police and marginal ethnic youth cannot be solved simply by initiatives such as the use of interpreters, the recruitment of ethnic officers, cross-cultural training of police officers and improved community relations. Community policing, with its emphasis on community consultation, local accountability, and problem-solving orientation, is often seen as an effective remedy to most police–community relations problems. It has been argued in this chapter, however, that unless young people, including the troublesome ones, are included in the police's definition of 'community', unless police are prepared to see the upholding of due process as beneficial rather than damaging to their work, and unless changes in police values permeate throughout the organisation, community policing is but an empty slogan. It is suggested that, like other ideals in criminal justice reform, the official adoption of community policing must be seen as the beginning of a long and uncertain process towards positive change.

REFERENCES

Alderson, J. (1983) 'Community Policing', in T. Bennett (ed.), *The Future of Policing*. Cambridge: Institute of Criminology, University of Cambridge.

Australian Law Reform Commission (ALRC) (1992) *Multiculturalism and the Law*, Report No. 57. Canberra: AGPS.

Bayley, D.H. and Mendelsohn, H. (1969) *Minorities and the Police: Confrontation in America*. New York: The Free Press.

Bell, R. (ed.) (1987) *Multicultural Societies: A comparative reader*. Sydney: Sable Publishing.

Bennett, T. (ed.) (1983) *The Future of Policing*. Cambridge: Institute of Criminology, University of Cambridge.

Cahill, D. and Ewen, J. (1987) *Ethnic Youth: Their assets and aspirations*. Report of the Department of Prime Minister and Cabinet (quoted in FECCA 1991). Canberra: AGPS.

Chan, J. (1992) Policing in a Multicultural Society: A study of the New South Wales Police. Final Report to the NSW Police Service (unpublished).

Cohen, S. (1985) *Visions of Social Control*. Cambridge: Polity Press.

Commonwealth Attorney-General's Department (1990) *Access to Interpreters in the Australian Legal System. Draft Report*. Canberra: AGPS.

Cunneen, C. (1990) *Aboriginal–Police Relations in Redfern*. Sydney: Human Rights and Equal Opportunity Commission.

Cunneen, C. and Robb, T. (1987) *Criminal Justice in North-East New South Wales*. Sydney: Bureau of Crime Statistics and Research.

Ericson, R. (1982) *Reproducing Order: A study of police patrol*. Toronto: University of Toronto Press.

Federation of Ethnic Communities' Councils of Australia (1991) *Background Paper on Ethnic Youth Prepared for FECCA's Multicultural Youth Conference*. Sydney: FECCA.

Gale, F. and Wundersitz, J. (1987) 'Aboriginal Youth and the Criminal Justice System in South Australia', in K. Hazlehurst (ed.), *Ivory Scales: Black Australians and the law*. Sydney: NSW University Press.

Goldstein, H. (1979) 'Improving Policing: A problem-oriented approach', *Crime and Delinquency*, April:236–58.

Human Rights and Equal Opportunity Commission (1991) *Racist Violence*. Report of the National Inquiry into Racist Violence in Australia. Canberra: AGPS.

Kelling, G. and Moore, M. (1982) 'Observations on the Policing Industry', Program in Criminal Justice Policy and Management, Kennedy School of Government, Harvard University, Working Paper, 1982 (reprinted in New South Wales Police, *Commmunity Based Policing*, Paper 1).

Morgan, R. (1987) 'The Local Determinants of Policing Policy', in P. Wilmott (ed.), *Policing and the Community*. London: Policy Studies Institute.

National Conference on Police Services in a Multicultural Australia (1990) *Report*. Victoria Police and the Australian Bicentennial Multicultural Foundation.

New South Wales Ethnic Affairs Commission (1991) Policing and Ethnicity in NSW (unpublished report).

New South Wales Police (n.d.) *Community Based Policing*, Papers 1-8.

Roberts-Smith, L.W. (1989) 'Communication breakdown', *Legal Service Bulletin*, 14(2):75-8.

Scarman, Rt Hon. (1981) *The Brixton Disorders 10-12 April 1981*. Report of an Inquiry by the Right Honourable the Lord Scarman, OBE. Harmondsworth, Middlesex: Penguin Books.

Short, C. (1983) 'Community Policing – Beyond Slogans' in T. Bennett (ed.) *The Future of Policing*. Cambridge: Institute of Criminology, University of Cambridge.

Smith, D. (1987) 'Research, the Community and the Police', in P. Wilmott (ed.) *Policing and the Community*. London: Policy Studies Institute.

Sparrow, M.K., Moore, M.H. and Kennedy, D.M. (1990) *Beyond 911: A new era for policing*. New York: Basic Books.

Weatheritt, M. (1987) 'Community Policing Now', in P. Wilmott (ed.) *Policing and the Community*. London: Policy Studies Institute.

White, R., Underwood, R. and Omelczuk, S. (1991) 'Victims of Violence: The view from the youth services', *Australian and New Zealand Journal of Criminology*, 24(1):25-39.

Wilmott, P. (ed.) (1987) *Policing and the Community*. London: Policy Studies Institute.

Wilson, P.L. and Storey, L. (1991) *Migrants and the Law – The Vietnamese: A case study*. Footscray, Vic: Footscray Community Centre.

Youth Justice Coalition (NSW) (1990) *Kids in Justice: A blueprint for the 90s*. Sydney: Youth Justice Coalition.

CHAPTER 9

Contemporary Programs with Young People: Beyond Traditional Law Enforcement?

Stephen P. James

INTRODUCTION

Formal processing of young offenders represents an important but statistically small portion of the contact that police have with young people. Much of police contact takes place through the routine operational work of police, and a (generally unknown) proportion of that work involves informal law enforcement processes. The present chapter is concerned with another prevalent form of police contact with young people: the engagement of police in programs, purportedly removed from routine law enforcement, designed to prevent young people getting into trouble, or to assist them to get out of trouble. Such programs have a bewildering nomenclature, and they are variously anchored in a range of current 'buzz' concepts in contemporary policing – pro-active policing, community policing, problem-oriented policing, partnership policing and so forth. But they are all united by a number of shared themes. They reflect an assumption that traditional law enforcement responses to juvenile delinquency and crime are ineffective. They reflect an acknowledgment that relations between police and young people are typically poor and need to be improved. They represent a belief that police are in a very good, if not the best, position both to understand the causes of juvenile crime and to design, implement or co-ordinate programs to prevent such crime.

There is nothing particularly novel about recent police attempts to prevent juvenile crime through a range of programs and activities beyond traditional law enforcement, nor are the rationales that give those programs impetus new. The logic of primary crime prevention was formally articulated by Robert Peel over 150 years ago (Critchley, 1967), and programs such as the New South Wales Police Youth Clubs emerged in Australia over fifty years ago (Carter, 1991).

199

As Challinger (1985a) reminds us, there is nothing new about community (and police) fears that our youth are increasingly lawless, or about the lack of cordial relations between police and young people, especially working-class young people (Chappell and Wilson, 1969; Cohen, 1979). Nor have police only recently begun to have doubts about the utility of law enforcement endeavours with young people; in the American context, Sanders (1981) argues that police have for many years had a rather jaundiced view of the effectiveness of legal processing of young people. In a recent survey of Australian police, 31 percent of police respondents reported that they take informal action against young offenders because of dissatisfaction with court processes (White, 1992; see also Muir, 1977).

But there appears to be a new breadth, a new sophistication, and a new commitment in current developments in police-driven crime-prevention programs for the young which set them apart from older forms. The sweat-stained boxing-ring of the old Police Youth Club has been replaced by a complex and expensive multi-program enterprise. The reluctant constable dragooned into giving an occasional talk at the local primary school as a punishment posting has been replaced by a phalanx of young officers trained and deployed to service the needs of schools, their teachers and their students. And it is the rare police annual report that does not proudly exhibit a list of crime-prevention initiatives, and the rare crime-prevention conference that does not feature a specialist police officer or two describing recent innovations in youth crime prevention.

The emergence over the last decade or so of a concerted drive by Australian police to develop their youth crime-prevention activities raises a number of intriguing questions. What has changed in the youth–police arena to warrant the attempt to bring into the 'mainstream of policing' what, despite its historical existence, has always been a somewhat marginalised police activity? Does the emergence reflect an objective escalation in the lawlessness of the young, coupled with a more pervasive belief by police in the ineffectiveness of traditional law enforcement? Or have there been more fundamental changes to police organisations, attitudes, and priorities? These questions, and their answers, need to be placed alongside what appear to be several quite marked paradoxes. For instance, at a time when crime-prevention rhetoric and practice is pulling us away from reliance upon the traditional agencies of criminal justice (Bottoms, 1990), police are assuming an even higher profile in youth crime prevention. At a time when police administrators are feeling the fiscal pinch of static or declining budget allocations, and when the call is for rationalisation and contraction of services and activities (Vernon and Bracey, 1989), they are expanding their youth crime-prevention programs. During a period in which police departments have devoted considerable resources and energy towards expanding their youth crime-prevention programs, they have continued to be accused of mistreating young people (Alder, 1991; Federation of Community Legal Centres, 1991). Despite the public emphasis by police departments on the necessity for and utility of their programs, there are clear schisms concerning this emphasis within police organisations among both rank-and-file and managers (Beyer, 1991; Freeman-Greene, 1991). And there are the criticisms levelled at some police youth crime-prevention programs under the rubric of community policing which argue that many of these activities are barely disguised perpetuations of historical discriminatory law enforcement against groups of young people (Cunneen, 1991; White, 1991). These are, of course, not really paradoxes; rather they are problematic features of the police role in crime prevention which considerably complicate our understanding of the development and effectiveness of programs.

In their rationales for and development of crime-prevention programs, police organisations reveal much about their comprehension of the problems of youthful crime and the breadth of their solutions to those problems. In turn, police comprehension of the problems and their solutions have much to tell us about the nature of organisational responses to contemporary challenges to policing: challenges posed by questions of its effectiveness, the appropriateness of their role in the community and in general crime prevention.

The purpose of the present chapter is to outline the kinds of crime-prevention programs with young people currently undertaken by Australian police, and to examine them critically by addressing the questions and issues raised above. I am concerned particularly with the organisational characteristics of police youth crime prevention.

The chapter proceeds by describing a number of key youth crime-prevention strategies adopted by Australian police, and then examines these for their stated aims, processes and, when available, their outcomes. The chapter concludes by examining the broader policing and crime-prevention contexts within which youth crime prevention by police takes place.

Three immediate caveats need to be made clear. First, there is a considerable diversity in police approaches to young people in Australia, both within and between the separate police departments. Given the relative autonomy of many aspects of police decision making and action, significant variations can be expected to exist both in the formalisation of policy and in the translation of those policies into programs and action within the one department. Between the states, variations exist between police departments in organisational ideologies, resources, structures, leadership and so forth (for example, the extent of the use of formal police cautions with young offenders differs dramatically between New South Wales and other states; see Youth Justice Coalition, 1990). Thus, it is extraordinarily difficult to generalise simply across the country in terms of any modal approaches and their anchoring philosophies.

Second, despite several enduring characteristics of the policing of young people, the rate of change in the development, implementation and abandonment of police–youth policies and programs is at times breathtaking (for example, school-based community policing was introduced in NSW in 1988, abandoned later following a change in government, and has been reintroduced in a different guise under the General Duties Youth Officer scheme; see Smith, 1991). The policing of young people, like most other aspects of police organisational and occupational activity, is a profoundly socio-political endeavour. As such, flux in the social and political environments within which policing takes place directly or indirectly influences policies and programs directed at the policing of young people.

Third, in common with many police endeavours, levels of systematic evaluation of police programs with young people can be described charitably as poor. Police organisations have only relatively recently recognised the need for comprehensive assessment of the effectiveness and efficiency of their programs, and few have the necessary structures and personnel to conduct other than superficial accounts of programs. While external and often critical assessments have been made of police programs, police organisations themselves have not been prominent in public debate and discussion about their youth programs in other than general rhetorical and defensive terms. A particular consequence of this lack of evaluation is that the formal statements of policies and descriptions of programs by no means guarantee that operational practice conforms to those policy and program objectives. As a consequence, it is difficult to provide a balanced assessment of 'what works' or even 'what is going on' in the youth–police arena.

The caveats above need to be taken into account in the reading of this chapter. Their consequence is that the chapter seeks to identify general themes in the development of police programs among young people wherever possible, and to relate these themes to a broader understanding of policing developments. While there can be no certainty that those programs are operationalised as intended, they reflect important aspects of organisational thinking and conceptualisation about the appropriate police approach to young people.

POLICE PROGRAMS WITH YOUNG PEOPLE

There is a remarkable variety of police approaches to crime prevention among young people. Many approaches are embedded in relatively long-standing police practices such as police cautioning, which is designed to prevent further offending by detected young offenders (Challinger, 1985b; James and Polk, 1989; O'Connell, 1992a). Others represent a reorientation of existing routine police work, such as the New South Wales General Duties Youth Officers (McDonald, 1991b), where patrol officers are trained and deployed to operate upon a 'problem-solving' rather than a reactive model with young people. Still others remove police from routine operational work, and deploy them in specialised positions or programs designed explicitly as crime-prevention activities, such as Police Youth Clubs (Carter, 1991) and Police in Schools programs (Shaw, 1991). In general, the present chapter is concerned with forms of specialised crime-prevention activities rather than with activities that serve traditional and explicit law enforcement purposes such as cautioning. At the same time, it is not the intention here to provide an exhaustive account of all of the relevant programs across the country; rather, by examining in some detail a number of the most prominent programs, it is possible to capture the major issues and themes. Thus, we will concentrate here upon the essentials of the development of Police Youth Clubs, Police in Schools programs, and the general duties youth officer strategy. Other programs will be addressed where relevant.

Police Youth Clubs

A useful place to begin a review of police programs with young people is to examine the earliest of such programs: the Police Youth Club (PYC). There is an Australian Association of Police–Citizens Youth Clubs, with some 129 clubs throughout the country, fifty-one of which are in New South Wales (Carter, 1991). The development of PYCs from their early beginnings has been broadly illustrative of the traditional conceptions and processes of police crime-prevention approaches to young people: they have been underpinned by simplistic conceptions of the causes of youth crime, they have been narrowly focused both in the groups they target and in their activities, and they have been executed by police divorced and indeed isolated from the mainstream of operational thinking and work. Recent developments in PYCs, however, appear to illustrate a more sophisticated understanding of the dilemmas facing young people, and reflect a considerably broader range of crime-prevention initiatives.

Perhaps the most prominent system of PYCs operates in New South Wales, where the Federation of NSW Police Boys Clubs (later the Federation of New South Wales Police–Citizen Boys Clubs) was incorporated as a company and registered as a charity in 1938. The first club house was established in Woolloomooloo, chosen according to Carter (1991:45) because 'it was one of Sydney's most difficult areas to police. Crime and antisocial behaviour in the area involving young people was rampant and there existed a rising incidence of substance abuse.' For many years, the essential pursuit of the clubs was sporting success, particularly in the arenas of boxing, wrestling and weightlifting. This entailed a specific gender focus, of course, and represented an appeal to the 'aggressive masculinity' of the predominantly working-class boys who attended the clubs, fostering the myth that such lads could 'make it' through life as sporting heroes. The assumptions behind this club focus are not difficult to identify. They capture the enduring belief that boredom and lack of appropriate recreation provides the essential stimulus for delinquency, and that young people at risk will benefit from the kinds of sporting activities that characterise 'manliness'. In this regard, it is interesting to note Challinger's (1985b:298) comment that the Queensland Police–Citizens Youth Welfare Organisation receives 'referrals of idle or bored young offenders from the Juvenile Aid Bureau who feel such youths should be involved in some activity'.

Organisationally, it appears that those police involved in the NSW clubs suffered the fate which is not uncommon for police removed from general operational policing who conduct 'welfare' work: they became marginalised. Carter (1991:46) reports that 'Mainstream operational police regarded the "Boys Clubs" as a backwater and police commanders took the opportunity to unload un-productive units to the "Boys Clubs".'

The NSW federation began to experience considerable criticism in the 1980s. The Lusher Report (1981) argued against the use of on-duty police for federation activities as an inappropriate deployment of personnel, while later (1983 and 1986), inter-departmental committees established by state cabinet proposed a number of significant reforms (Carter, 1991). The federation's name was changed to substitute 'youth' for 'boys' in 1985, in an acknowledgment of the gender bias of the old club orientation, and an extensive overhauling of both administrative structures and the range of programs offered has taken place since then in order to revitalise what had become a moribund institution. McDonald (1991a) reports that some 125 police officers in New South Wales are attached to the various clubs, with an annual cost in wages of $6.7 million (Carter (1991) notes that there are 225 police on full-time duties with youth clubs throughout Australia).

In order to capture the flavour of both the purposes and activities of PYCs, it is useful here to reproduce parts of the Memorandum of Association of the NSW federation:

a) to promote programs and activities directed to the personal, physical and cultural development of children and adolescents in New South Wales;
b) to awaken citizens and police to their responsibilities towards children and adolescents;
c) to nurture citizenship;
d) to provide an interface between the police force and the citizens of New South Wales, especially children and adolescents, which fosters mutual respect and understanding;
e) to provide cultural, recreational and sporting programs for indi-viduals, community groups, organisations and the underprivileged, regardless of sex, race, creed or ethnic background;
f) to provide educational programs pertaining to the maintenance of law and order, such programs to include but not be confined to such matters as: the role of the police, crime prevention, road safety, and drug abuse. (Carter, 1991:50)

It is instructive to examine the kinds of programs designed to give them effect. One of the most significant of the outcomes of the 're-vitalised' PYC appears to be that it now acts as an umbrella organisation for a complex array of both police and community-based crime-prevention initiatives. In the police arena, specific activities are directed at two broad target groups: young offenders, and the general youth population.

For young offenders, youth club police supervise young offenders placed on community service orders at Police–Citizens Youth Clubs; Carter notes:

> The police officers support these young offenders in a non-judgemental, non-moralistic and non-authoritarian manner. This helps to improve the young offenders' general relationship with the police. An additional benefit is improvement in self-esteem and an improvement in perception of 'the system'. The program also encourages young offenders to utilise the branch facilities during their leisure time. (Carter, 1991:51)

Youth club police also service the transport needs of young offenders undertaking drug and alcohol counselling from a number of children's courts; again, the explicit rationale is improved relationships with and perceptions of the police and the 'system' (Carter, 1991:52). Finally, the Federation of New South Wales Police–Citizens Youth Clubs is involved in broader programs for the rehabilitation of young offenders. Carter (1991:52) reports that young recidivists and first-time gaol servers who are believed to be likely to benefit from youth club activities are identified and referred by the Probation and Parole Service to the federation, which then 'involves the offender in a full range of activities'.

A range of programs and activities for the wider youth population is organised by the Police Youth Clubs. For instance, three-day crime-prevention workshops for year 9 students are arranged with the assistance of Family and Community Service Department officers, schoolteachers, State Rail workers and others, with the aim: '... to offer alternatives and set out the consequences and difficulties presented by peer group pressure, anger, boredom, frustration, desperation and aggression' (Carter, 1991:51). Federation branches transport year 11 and 12 students from the western areas of Sydney to a central Sydney 'Police Careers' program which involves talks and visits to operational police districts; in addition, wider careers 'markets' are set up in youth club premises during which prospective employers provide careers advice. The clubs also host end-of-school break-up parties in a 'safe environment with sufficient unobtrusive supervision . . . [shielded] from alcohol and drugs' (Carter, 1991:52). The federation hosts 'Drive to Survive', bicycle safety, protective behaviours and Alteens programs as well, besides opening up a range of passive recreational activities on club premises, such as pinball machines, videos and jukeboxes; Carter is positive about the aims and outcomes:

> The aim is to encourage young people to find entertainments off the streets and to prevent them becoming victims or offenders. In one particular area where this program has been running there has not been a single break and enter offence or act of malicious injury to property committed at the local primary school for over six months . . . The kids have reported that before going to the Club for the passive activities they used to 'give the school hell' and 'hate the cops'. These attitudes are now changing. (Carter, 1991:52)

Several of the above programs are clearly based on the 'partnership' conception that entails officers from relevant government agencies both from within and outside the criminal justice system working together on joint activities and strategies. In addition, the New South Wales federation is presently taking part in a pilot program with the National Association for the Prevention of Child Abuse and Neglect, designed to encourage isolated members of the community to form friendships as a protection against victimisation (Carter, 1991:51). Importantly, under the auspices of the head office of the federation, attempts are being made to forge 'coalitions' with private sector corporations in order to develop joint strategies 'to counter juvenile crime and antisocial behaviour by young people' (Carter, 1991:55). The aim is to encourage the private sector to contribute to or sponsor particular federation programs.

Several other Australian state and territory police departments have also established Police (and) Citizen Youth Clubs: Western Australia (Boyle, 1991), Tasmania (Vincent, 1991), Northern Territory (Langmair, 1991), and Queensland (Tansky, 1991). Vincent captures both the typical outline of youth club endeavours in other states and the levels of optimism which accompany those activities:

> There are 17 Police and Citizens Youth Clubs in operation around Tasmania which address the problems facing the young people in their respective areas by providing a wide range of leisure activities. The Clubs are becoming more community based and also give instructions in law, safety, and community and social responsibility. Evidence suggests that

very few of the members of the Clubs come before the courts for offences and experience has shown that members have a much improved attitude towards the police. The number of offences committed by young people are lessened where Police and Citizens Youth Clubs are operating. (Vincent, 1991:46)

Police In Schools Programs

The second of the major youth crime-prevention programs described here concerns the Police in Schools program, which has only recently been formalised into a concerted strategy across many of the Australian states. There is, of course, little new about the occasional visit to schools for the odd lecture, but the systematic deployment of trained personnel designated as school liaison or resource officers has arisen only in the last eight years or so. The first police department to establish a formal program was the Northern Territory Police Force, which placed a full-time constable in the Casuarina High School in 1984 (Maley, 1991). Smith (n.d.:1) reports that this first school placement arose following a request by the school council at a time when 'there had been an increasing community concern about the dual problems of school truancy and juvenile crime' in the Northern Territory. The placement was not entirely novel; previously a constable had serviced Darwin and close rural areas through the School Lecturing Program, and individual schools had been 'adopted' by individual CIB members, so that 'the member was able to develop a more personalised rapport with the school community and was better able to deal with criminal matters involving that school' (Smith, n.d.:1). However, the adoption scheme was seen to be limited, and the Casuarina placement heralded a more systematic approach to placing police in schools (Maley, 1991). Smith provides a nice illustration of the work of the first constable:

> the school principal ... consulted with Constable ... regarding the behavioural problems of some students, and he assisted with counselling and in other positive ways. One example was a 5th year student who had been achieving well, but had recently become difficult to manage with some fall-off in achievement levels. The problem was identified by (the constable) as one of excessive spare time and he involved the boy with supervising at the youth club. Very quickly the boy progressed from requiring help to becoming a helper ... (Smith, n.d.:2)

Positive reports about the placement encouraged the police force to expand the scheme, 'despite severe Government cut-backs throughout due to general economic constraints' (Smith, n.d.:2). Maley (1991:130) reports that the twenty high schools and secondary colleges and fifty-eight primary schools in the Northern Territory are now serviced by a sergeant co-ordinator and eighteen constables.

There was some initial resistance to the Northern Territory School Based Community Policing Scheme; Maley (1991:127) reports that other police viewed school placements as a 'kiddy cop' position divorced from real policing, while teachers thought that education should be left to teachers and policing to police. But '(o)nce these myths were dispelled by consultation and accurate information about the theory of school based community policing this new concept of policing was about to take a great leap forward'.

Maley describes the Position Profile for the Scheme, *inter alia*, as follows:

Section Objective

To reduce the incidence of juvenile crime in the community and improve community confidence in the police.

Job Description
- Be seen as a member of the school community.
- Liaise with school staff, parents and shopkeepers.
- Take any complaints or particulars of offences.
- Lecture within the schools on selected topics if requested.
- Advise on security.
- Observe the performance of monitors at school crossings.
- Advise on parking restrictions in the vicinity of the school.
- Monitor the activities of any undesirables in the area.
- Liaise with truancy officers and home liaison officers.
- Counsel students as required.
- Pass on information to other instrumentalities or elements of the police force as necessary.
- Liaise with relevant government departments regarding welfare of students, e.g. Health, Community Development.
- Attend appropriate school council meetings.
- Assist in organising approved after school activities.
- Be responsible for the teaching of the Drug Abuse Resistance Education (DARE) in feeder primary schools and preschools.
- Perform normal police duties as required. (Maley, 1991:128)

According to Maley, constables for the scheme are selected carefully, trained in classroom techniques and need to know relevant juvenile justice legislation. Their role, as he sees it, is complementary to regular school curricula:

> Whilst it is not in dispute that teachers are the best people to educate children in the three Rs, the police input adds the other two Rs (Rights and Responsibilities) to the school communities ... They have become a tremendous resource in assisting teachers with their curriculum. In the Northern Territory 'Youth and the Law' is a core subject at Year Ten level. They also assist in other subjects such as legal studies, forensic science, home economics (domestic violence), student driver education, and act as advisers and consultants in protective behaviours education. (Maley, 1991:129)

In common with virtually all other police youth crime-prevention strategies, Northern Territory police spokespeople for the scheme are very positive about its outcomes. Smith (n.d.:4) reports that following the appointment of the first constable to Casuarina, unlawful entries and damage to school property dropped dramatically. He goes on to write: 'More importantly there has been a perceptible change which has shown an improved attitude by the children towards law and order issues and the Police generally. This of course is the purpose of the scheme.' Further on, he reiterates his confidence in the scheme:

> The programme in the Northern Territory shows considerable promise as a pro-active Police initiative. At this stage it has attracted considerable support from the school communities, including teachers, parents and students. It is yet to be demonstrated if this scheme will have any long term benefits in terms of juvenile or young adult behaviour, although on present indications, this appears most likely. Certainly it has been an excellent image building exercise which should result in a better understanding in the wider community of the Police role. (Smith, n.d.:8)

Indeed, the lack of long-term data on the scheme appears to hold little fear for other commentators as well. Harvey (1987:3), a school principal, writes that while he is aware of the need for a longitudinal evaluation of outcomes, 'it is possible to look at how the scheme is developing now. In my opinion it shows that it is most effective and signs are good.' Later (page 6), he writes that 'I am convinced that the scheme is a success. It has not yet had any noticeable effect on the crime rate ... But short term the benefits are clear.' Maley (1991:131) concludes his outline of the scheme by describing it as a 'cornerstone to build strong foundations for the police and community', despite an earlier statement that: 'It will only be with longitudinal studies using many and varied performance indicators to know if proactive policing programs ... will in fact fulfil the community's desire to be policed in this manner'.

Victoria also has a school-based crime-prevention program which it calls the Police/Schools Involvement Program (PSIP), a title derived from the two Victoria Police Community Involvement Programs (PCIP) conducted in the early 1980s which prototypically introduced police into schools (Beyer, 1991). In a recent article, Shaw describes the formalisation of police engagement in schools, which began in 1988. Shaw (1991:74) begins by sketching in the need for such engagement. He argues that crime levels are unacceptably high, and that traditional law enforcement methods 'appear to be doing little to stem the rising tide of antisocial behaviour'. He goes on to quote Victorian Chief Commissioner Kel Glare, who stated in a press release: 'An anti-crime program which teaches basic rights, obligations and responsibilities, together with the consequences of breaching the criminal law, could and should be integrated with all other programs aimed at eliminating the causes of crime'. Besides the need to tackle the moral deficits which are seen to be a primary cause of crime, Shaw acknowledges that the police have grown apart from the community:

> What is needed is a means of getting the police interacting with the public to form a closer relationship. More positive contact will hopefully remedy this situation and this should commence at an early age. It is argued that if a child's first contact with police is positive, then it will take a great deal of negative influence to turn this perception around. The same applies in the opposite case.
>
> Children also need to be given information on how and why the police do their job and where they (the police) fit into society. Complaints have been lodged against members of the force which result directly from ignorance and lack of understanding of why particular actions are being taken. (Shaw, 1991:75)

Shaw reports that Glare developed his zeal for the school program following a visit to a Florida school-based program developed by a judge who had been concerned that a 16-year-old he had sentenced to death appeared to have had no moral education at school. The judge then examined the local schooling system, and found 'to his disgust' that Florida school children received no moral training, and indeed were taught only their legal rights and not their responsibilities (Shaw, 1991:75). Impressed with the program, Glare had the Victorian scheme developed.

The aims and objectives of the Victorian PSIP are rather more precise than those of the Northern Territory scheme:

Aims
- to reduce the incidence of crime in society;
- to develop a better relationship between police and youth in the community;
- to create in young people an understanding of the police role in the structure of society;
- to extend the concept of crime prevention into the Victorian school system;
- to equip young people with the necessary skills to avoid dangerous or threatening situations.

Objectives
(after the program) children will:
- demonstrate the values, responsibilities and obligations society currently deems valuable;
- state the consequences of a person's actions regarding unlawful behaviour;
- demonstrate sufficient self-esteem and skill to say no to drug abuse and other anti-social behaviour;
- engage in positive interactions and consultation with police members; and
- state the basic role of the police and the legal system in Victoria. (Shaw, 1991:76)

Victorian police deployed in schools are known as School Resource Officers (SROs), and, like their counterparts in the Northern Territory, they are selected and specifically trained (by the Institute of Early Education) and deployed to cover a range of schools across a geographical area. SROs were originally deployed only in primary schools, but the fifty SROs are now servicing an increasing number of secondary schools – twelve in 1990, in addition to the 500 primary schools serviced by the program (*Police Life*, 1990).

Like Maley, Shaw (1991:77) acknowledges that there has been some resistance to the program, particularly by other police, and he implies that the labels 'plastic police' and 'kiddy cops' have come from police conducting routine operational work. To overcome the prejudicial labels, SROs in Victoria are deployed from local police stations and encouraged to undertake occasional operational shifts so that they do not become distanced from their orthodox peers.

The Victorian police involved in the program express practically identical sentiments to those of their Northern Territory peers:

despite the lack of long-term data, the program has been declared a success. Within a year or so of its introduction, Ron Marshall, the civilian teacher responsible for the administration of the program, felt able to write in a brochure outlining PSIP: 'The success of the program has been outstanding so far and the demand for School Resource Officers exceeds our staffing allocation at this stage' (Victoria Police, n.d.:3). In a later interview in the Victoria police magazine, Marshall said: 'Requests from secondary schools have been overwhelming ... One principal said he could use a police officer in his school full-time five days a week! ... There are another 300 schools who want the program' (*Police Life*, 1990:12). In the same article, a school deputy principal is quoted as saying that the program 'is making measurable changes in kids' attitudes towards police'. And Shaw concludes his description of the program with a now familiar flourish:

> The results will not be felt overnight, and we must be prepared to wait for the harvest when it hopefully arrives in years to come. [But] we now have a chance to attack crime at the grass roots level and prevent it through education of the forthcoming generation. It is our responsibility to make sure that we take positive action to check the spread of crime. As Seneca, the Roman statesman and philosopher, said in 65 AD, 'he who does not prevent a crime when he can, condones it'. (Shaw, 1991:78)

Variations on school-based police crime-prevention programs exist in other Australian states. In New South Wales, General Duties Youth Officers have been allocated to school districts to act as resource officers for local school communities, where they conduct activities similar to those described above (McDonald, 1991a). In addition, the crime-prevention workshops described previously in the section on youth clubs are conducted through schools with significant police input (McDonald, 1991a). Western Australia deploys police in schools (Boyle, 1991; Wallace, 1988), while in South Australia, the Police Deputies Club (Cornish, 1991) and the School Watch program (Sobulis, 1991) appear to contain elements of a school-based police crime-prevention input.

The General Duties Youth Officer

The last of the major relatively recent initiatives in police youth crime prevention to be discussed here is the New South Wales program which has developed the General Duties Youth Officer

(GDYO). McDonald (1991b:116) describes the GDYO program as 'the major NSW Police Youth Crime Prevention initiative'. The program began in 1988 in one NSW country town, and has since expanded state-wide; by the end of 1990 the program involved 120 police patrols (McDonald, 1991b:118). The GDYO program differs somewhat from the other two programs described above in that it integrates the crime-prevention function into routine operational police work, rather than relocating it as a speciality within youth clubs or schools. In addition, it is geared primarily towards known young offenders or 'potential' offenders rather than the wider youth population. McDonald (1991a:1) notes that it costs the NSW police $1.5 million per annum.

The Charter of the General Duties Youth Officer Program is as follows:

- participating police act as protectors of, and advocates for young people;
- the officers act to divert young offenders away from the criminal justice system wherever possible;
- patrols adopt a multi-agency approach to youth crime prevention; and
- participation in the program be dependent on the GDYOs working to a performance-based work contract. (McDonald, 1991b:116)

Participating officers are trained through a four-day residential workshop, which covers the causes of youth crime, youth development, the use of public space, child abuse and the 'myths and realities of juvenile and youth crime' (McDonald, 1991b:116). Officers then return to their patrol deployments, and are required to draft strategic plans in keeping with the objectives above. The plan requires the identification of the specific policing problems with young people in the patrol district, through contacts with other operational police, youth workers, young people and so forth, followed by the drafting of a strategy to deal with the problems within a multi-agency framework. A key element of the GDYO initiative is the establishment by the individual officers of implementation time-frames and evaluation approaches for the strategies. According to McDonald (1991b:117), GDYOs are expected to establish both quantitative and qualitative performance indicators at the outset to monitor 'effectiveness, efficiency and appropriateness', particularly in terms of change in outcome variables. Importantly, GDYOs are given considerably more latitude in their work practices than traditional operational police:

GDYOs are given a great deal of professional freedom to solve policing problems with young people in their patrols; they can set their own roster and choose to work in plain clothes or uniform; they come and go as the situation or problem requires; they strive to keep young people out of the criminal justice system. (McDonald, 1991b:117)

Indeed, this degree of flexibility is somewhat greater than that of the school-based officers described in the last section; both the Northern Territory and Victorian schemes require officers to be dressed in uniform, and Victoria has made efforts to anchor school-based officers in their local patrol stations so that they do not become distanced from other police. The NSW approach appears to be one where district and regional support levels for GDYOs is emphasised so that middle-level management allows the desired flexibility.

In the following extract, McDonald describes the essence of the GDYO program:

Most of the GDYOs target those young people in the area known to police. They concentrate on establishing constructive relationships with these young people, working on the premise that many of them are in need of protection and assistance which it is impossible to offer to people who do not trust you and see you as the enemy. Once the officer is able to gain the trust of a young person, he/she is then in a position to assist and work with that young person to prevent further offending.

Police in the program have used a variety of techniques to establish contact with young offenders. Often they have only to take an interest in the young person who has come to notice, or approach him/her on the street and engage in conversation (without taking notes), ensuring that the young person is OK, has somewhere to stay, or has transport home. Having established contact, the officer then attempts to be constructive and supportive in the way that they relate to the young person. Police are, or should be, the major agents of protection in the community. Young people, and in particular young offenders, do not see the police as offering them protection. As many young people who are involved in offending are simultaneously victims, it is important that police recognise the needs of this group to assist them in seeking help if it is required and/or desired. (McDonald, 1991b:118)

Like other proponents of police youth crime-prevention approaches, McDonald (1991b:118) recognises the existence of resistance to them by both other police and, in the NSW case, people in the youth sector. He implies that the best way to deal with such resistance is to build into the program sophisticated evaluation techniques which offer the promise of a substantial demonstration of the program's efficacy. Indeed, on a reading of the accessible documentation of the various police youth crime-prevention schemes, the commitment to evaluation by the NSW Police appears to exceed that of the other programs described. Nevertheless, full evaluations across the state have not yet been documented, and McDonald (1991a:1) is left to argue that the program 'has been judged successful by those police involved'.

While other Australian states do not appear to have developed to any great extent a youth-targeted crime-prevention strategy along the lines of the NSW GDYOs, South Australia has recently trialled a general approach known as Problem Oriented Policing (POP) (West, 1991) which shares several similarities with the NSW program. POP involves the identification by police (in consultation with the community) of local problems and their causes, the drafting of a strategy plan in conjunction with members of the community, other government agencies and the private sector, and a multi-agency implementation of remedies. While the approach is not specifically directed at youth crime prevention, such prevention clearly falls within the broad embrace of the program.

Other programs

The programs described above capture the thrust of recent initiatives by police in systematic youth crime-prevention activities, and we will turn next to exploring their implications. But these three kinds of programs by no means exhaust the engagement by police in formal and informal youth crime-prevention programs.

Many of the 'community policing' initiatives which have emerged in the last ten years or so across the country, such as Neighbourhood Watch, involve police activities with young people (see Vernon and McKillop, 1991), or have absorbed earlier schemes such as Blue Light Discos designed specifically to offer non-law enforcement services to young people (Challinger, 1985b; Smith, 1991). Police have generated or take part in several of the 'outdoors' programs designed to expose young people to the allegedly character-building experiences and challenges of the Australian countryside (see Smith, 1991, for a description of the Northern Territory's 'Junior Police Ranger Program'; Pearson, 1991). Operational, school-based and youth club-based police are prominent in youth education programs designed to combat substance abuse and graffiti (O'Doherty, 1991; Williams, 1991). And police are variously engaged in community programs generated beyond the respective police departments designed to tackle the causes and effects of crime, including youth crime, such as Victoria's Good Neighbourhood Program (Vicsafe, 1992). Other more diffuse attempts to 'reach' young people with a police message include the introduction of icons and marketing strategies such as 'Constable Care', a comic book character around which activities like drawing and essay competitions are designed in order to fix in the minds of children the image of police benevolence (see White, 1989).

One further program can usefully be mentioned here. Juvenile cautioning programs have been in place around Australia for many years now, and they can in general be considered part of the routine processing of young offenders (although the extent to which the cautioning procedure is used in preference to a court appearance differs quite significantly across state police departments: see Youth Justice Coalition, 1990), and therefore beyond the scope of this chapter. But a modified cautioning program which has been implemented in Wagga Wagga in New South Wales generated considerable interest at a National Conference on Juvenile Justice in Adelaide in 1992 (O'Connell, 1992b). The Wagga Wagga approach brings together offenders, their families and supporters, and victims as part of a general integrated community-based policing strategy. Grounded in principles drawn from the contemporary family group conference procedure in New Zealand (McDonald and Ireland, 1990) and the work of Australian criminologist John Braithwaite, especially his theory of 'reintegrative shaming' (1989), the program directly involves members of the local community and further recognises the importance of victim participation in conflict resolution. In Wagga Wagga, the program is viewed as part of wider police initiatives at the community level, ranging from the introduction of 'beat' policing through to events staged by the Police–Citizens Youth Club.

According to Senior Sergeant Terry O'Connell (1992b), one of the principal organisers of the program, the implementation of this new approach has yielded a significant reduction in local rates of reported crime. According to O'Connell (1992b:11), the Wagga Wagga approach has a number of important strengths:

Its strength is its flexibility, as it only involves people who are directly affected by the offence or are close supporters of the offender and victim. It deals with the unacceptable behaviour whilst encouraging the young offender to play a constructive role within his/her community. It allows offenders to accept responsibility for their behaviour, and parents or others to be more accountable for the young offender. It involves shaming and reintegration into the community, rather than stigmatisation and rejection.

Preliminary statistical results coupled with generally favourable public and academic responses to the program suggest that the Wagga Wagga model may have something to offer as an alternative approach to traditional processing of young people by police. However, in common with all the programs described above, the Wagga Wagga initiative has not been evaluated comprehensively. Two issues particularly require detailed analysis. The levels of resourcing and community support envisaged as vital for the program's full success are acknowledged by O'Connell (1992a:12) to not be in place yet. And the crucial role of police in the program, a role which demands a reorientation of traditional law enforcement philosophies with regard to young people, has yet to be thoroughly examined (see below).

ORGANISATIONAL CONTEXTS OF THE PROGRAMS

The lack of comprehensive evaluation of any of the above programs, acknowledged by each of their proponents, renders it impossible to answer the obvious question of 'what do they achieve?'. While important for a variety of other reasons (as we shall see), the optimistic claims of those proponents for program success in the absence of systematic 'impact assessment' (Polk, 1991:103) do not in fact constitute sufficient evidence of any direct program effects upon youth crime prevention. Of course, comprehensive and persuasive evaluations of programs with aims as broad and as ambitious as the ones enumerated above are extraordinarily difficult and expensive to conduct, and Australian police departments are not alone among government agencies in their lack of commitment to the kinds of sophisticated paradigms that would answer satisfactorily the question of what works (Polk, 1991).

There are some relevant data, however. The recent National Youth Affairs Research Scheme (NYARS) report (Alder, 1992) surveyed 383 young people across Australia, and found that 76 percent had been involved to various extents in some kind of police–youth program. Fifty percent had been visited in school by police, 41 percent had attended Blue Light Discos, and 25 percent had been involved in a Police Youth Club. These figures represent a rather significant exposure of young people to police youth initiatives. Overall, however, 60 percent of those young people who had been involved in programs felt that such involvement had not affected their feelings about police, and only 25 percent were clear about an improved response to police. Attendance at Blue Light Discos or Police Youth Clubs had no significant effect upon attitudes towards police across the sample; however, overall young people who had been visited at school by police were more likely (p<.05) to hold positive attitudes towards police. Interestingly, according to Alder:

> [School] visits did not have a statistically significant impact for young people who are in school or who are now employed full time. However, in the case of marginal young people, if they had experienced a police visit when they were at school, they were more likely (41%) than those who did not experience such a visit (17%) to have more positive attitudes towards police. (Alder, 1992:25)

These data cannot, of course, represent an adequate assessment of program effectiveness; they do, nevertheless, suggest that some degree of caution be exercised before blanket assumptions of program success are made.

While we cannot provide a comprehensive answer to the question of 'do they work?', there are other fruitful questions: what do the programs – with their rationales, their intentions, their activities – tell us about police responses to the issues raised by youth delinquency and crime in the community? And in turn, what do those responses tell us about the police understanding of those issues? To answer these questions, we need to tease out the implications thrown up by the documentation on the programs reviewed above.

Despite their variations, the programs share a number of features which were forecast at the beginning of the chapter. The explicit rationale for program development (or in the case of the Police Youth Clubs, program resurrection and expansion) has been three-fold: an alleged escalation in the lawlessness of the young; concerns about the effectiveness of traditional law enforcement strategies directed at young offenders; and a strongly held belief that police are misunderstood, mistrusted and disliked by young people, and that it is critical to redress these 'dysfunctional' sentiments.

These three features are interrelated, and they need to be understood in terms of broader contexts of contemporary policing developments. The objective realities of youth crime, such as can be accurately determined, are addressed elsewhere, but it is worth noting several points here. Police, for instance, are hardly alone in the present community expressing public concerns about youth crime and their consequences; youth crime-prevention conferences are full of a range of professional and community voices beyond policing describing or calling for urgently needed remedies, (Halstead, 1991; Vernon and McKillop, 1991), buttressed by lurid accounting exercises which cost-out the consequences of contemporary youth crime at $1.5 billion (Potas, Vining and Wilson, 1990). Even voices which are usually raised against the kinds of 'crime wave panic' journalism which typically address youth crime (for example, Warneminde, 1987) are deeply concerned by the economic consequences of the recession upon youth crime (Polk in Milburn, 1991). But police occupy a unique place in the public discourse on crime and crime prevention, because they have traditionally assumed, and let it be assumed about them, that they are the principal crime control institution. That this has always been a rather fatuous assumption is by now well documented (Vernon and Bracey, 1989; Young and Cameron, 1989), and this has required police to face several 'new' realities about their social role. Their response to youth crime and prevention programs is an excellent example of how they have done so.

Police have had to organise themselves in complicated ways so that several 'verities' about their role and capacities are maintained, while they are seen to accommodate to changing circumstances. Traditionally, annually increasing reported crime figures have been a trigger for demands for bigger budgets, more resources, and greater powers, on the grounds that crime increases because police are increasingly insufficiently equipped to do what they have always done: fight crime. While such tactics have by no means been totally abandoned, especially by elements in the police union movement (see Freeman-Greene, 1991), budget contractions have made the automatic annual increase in police allocations a benevolence of the past (Grabosky, 1989). Increases now have to be fought for, and it is difficult to argue persuasively that more resources to traditional law enforcement approaches will pay dividends. Of course, police can (and do) continue to argue that decrements in traditional enforcement resources will be harmful, and that argument remains politically persuasive. But new initiatives which offer some kind of alternative and more effective means of dealing with specific crime problems are needed to satisfy budget decision makers that increased allocations will be something other than throwing money at (increasingly tired) old solutions.

Community-oriented crime prevention very much fits the requirements for new initiatives in tackling crime problems; it has substantial theoretical credentials and popular appeal (see chapter 8). However, several of its principles constitute something of a dilemma for police. For instance, it is axiomatic in the crime-prevention literature that the causes of crime lie in factors beyond the immediate control of any one government agency or institution, including the police (Bottoms, 1990). As a corollary, it calls for concerted crime-prevention action across the community rather than leaving it in the hands of a single agency, such as the police. The traditional pivotal role of crime prevention accorded to police is necessarily abandoned in the broad community crime-prevention model. Police organisations have responded to this assault upon their pre-eminence in crime control by simultaneously embracing (at least rhetorically) the principles of community crime prevention, and making sure that they retain a position of considerable if not hegemonic power in the practice of community prevention. In this regard, it is interesting to note that the Victorian government's recent Vicsafe anti-crime strategy is anchored essentially by the development of Police Community Consultative Committees (PCCCs), which 'will be responsible for co-ordinating and implementing local crime prevention and control strategies' (Justice Branch, 1992:2). The overwhelming majority of the eighty-three PCCCs established to early 1993 are chaired by police officers.

In the youth crime-prevention sphere, consider the rationale for the development of the Police in Schools program. In both of the programs described in detail above, a certain logic is identifiable, although it is more consistently obvious from Shaw's (1991) articulation of the Victorian program. The logic is this:

- youth crime is serious and escalating;
- a prominent cause of this escalation is the absence of the inculcation of appropriate values which would insulate young people from criminality;

- a disrespect for authority and a failure to acknowledge legal and social responsibilities ('good citizenship') are all too evident;
- disrespect for police is both a symptom of this wider malaise and a serious dysfunction because police epitomise legal and social responsibility;
- traditional law enforcement does not serve to redress these problems because it is too reactive;
- both as major recipients of disrespect and as major status-holders in legal and social responsibility, police have a duty to come into the schools in a non-law enforcement manner to inculcate the appropriate values which will engender good citizenship.

The clear implication of this logic that neither the family nor the school is capable of nurturing the appropriate values without police help is somewhat buried under police claims to professional knowledge (of such things as the law and police duties) which cannot be imparted in standard curricula or child-rearing. Thus, simultaneously, police have placed the blame for youth crime within the community, acknowledged the limits of their traditional role (without by any means abandoning it in general), described themselves as misunderstood, re-established a professional and social status, and offered themselves as a remedy to youth crime. This logic is echoed to some extent in the documentation on the NSW police clubs programs: the desire to inculcate citizenship values, the need to improve police–youth relations, and the associated drive to educate young people in the roles and responsibilities of police work, with the implication that these are synonymous with good citizenship.

The simplistic assumptions regarding causation evident in the logic above – particularly the absence of proper moral-value inculcation in the school-based programs, but also the notions of boredom and too much 'spare time' implicit in Carter's descriptions of the police youth clubs schemes – do not require critical attention here; it is sufficient to note that they are rather at odds with current knowledge about the complexities of youthful offending (see particularly White, 1989). The state of police–youth relations can, however, be addressed.

Surveys of public opinion typically indicate that respect for police is positively associated with age; thus younger people tend to have less respect (Swanton, Wilson, Walker and Mukherjee, 1988). However, results are not always highly consistent; the Swanton et al.

survey also found that there was no significant age association with perceptions of police honesty, and indeed under 20s tended to rate police honesty as highly as the group with the most generalised favourable opinions of police – people over 60. In some contrast, the recent NYARS survey found that 78 percent of young respondents felt that police use unfair methods to convict, and 48 percent felt that police should leave young people alone (Alder, 1992). In that same survey, ninety police from three states were interviewed about their interactions with young people, 44 percent felt that very few young people have respect for authority and the police, 32 percent felt that about half of young people have respect, and 24 percent felt that most have respect (White, 1992). These kinds of aggregated results obscure significant variations in both police and young people's attitudes and beliefs, and it is difficult to draw precise conclusions from them about the state of police–youth relations. It is interesting to note, for instance, that despite the numbers of the surveyed police in the NYARS study who indicated that young people did not respect them, some 76 percent of police overall did not find young people in general difficult to deal with. The perception that police are consistently disliked and disrespected by young people may be less a clear statement of fact and more an important organisational premise for program impetus.

A further set of interrelated features which emerges from the program documentation can be examined in light of the observations raised above. These concern the sometimes extravagant claims of program success in the face of little or no systematic assessment of its impact; the strong emphasis by police proponents on the rates of community approval of and demand for their programs; and the acknowledgment of implementation difficulties and resistance followed smartly by claims of success in overcoming those problems. These features, it can be argued, are readily understood within the police organisational context. The optimism of program proponents is undoubtedly heartfelt; many of the proponents quoted above were instrumental in designing and establishing their respective programs, and it is understandable that they want the programs to succeed and believe they have/will.

At the same time, it is clearly necessary for proponents to put a positive face upon the programs, because the initiatives are key strategies in demonstrating the responsiveness of police to complex and changing social and legal circumstances. Having accepted the rhetoric of the need for community-based crime prevention, and wishing to retain a significant institutional role in that prevention, it is incumbent upon police to manage the public impression of their initiatives so that their efforts are seen as legitimate and rewarding. The desire by police to document non-police testimonials can be understood in this context. School-based program documentation makes considerable use of endorsements by school principals, who are often quoted as fully supportive and optimistic about the programs and their gains. In a similar vein, the apparent demand for a police presence is used as an endorsement of program success. Once again, there is no need to doubt the sincerity of school authorities who give their support and co-operation to the programs. But a police presence in schools serves purposes other than those explicitly concerned with nurturing citizenship and improving attitudes to police. At the very least, a police presence provides another body in schools to supervise and interact with students, which frees traditional staff from these duties. If that body has some kind of immediate effect upon routine disciplinary problems, rowdiness and so forth, at no financial cost to the school, it is little wonder that school authorities welcome the police presence. This welcome is likely to be even more pronounced when teachers are relieved of the policing of truancy by the deployment of police as 'truancy patrols' to compel school attendance (as in Western Australia; see White, 1989).

The wider community/school audience is not the only group whose view regarding a program's utility has to be managed. Most proponents of the programs acknowledge resistance from other police to youth and community-based approaches, and eulogistic accounts of program success are oriented as much towards the police audience as they are towards the wider audience. This issue is taken up further in the following concluding sections.

THE BROADER CONTEXTS OF THE PROGRAM

This review and discussion generates a number of broader questions about the engagement of police in youth crime-prevention programs. Perhaps the key one concerns the extent to which such engagement represents a fundamental shift in the policing of young people in Australia. It is important to note, for instance, that few of the program proponents argue for the abandonment of traditional modes of policing young people in favour of the crime-prevention initiatives (for two important exceptions, see Beyer, 1991; and McDonald and Ireland, 1990). Much of the program documentation reveals a distinct impression that the programs are designed as supplements to routine law enforcement rather than as their essential replacement. This is quite evident in the rationales for the school-based programs; among the aims is the desire to improve the understanding of the need for law enforcement and the demands of police work among young people, so that traditional law enforcement is facilitated.

One indication that the programs may be heralding a significant change in the policing of young people would be an articulated commitment that the programs are designed as much to educate police about the need to improve or change their approaches and their attitudes towards policing as they are to educate young people. A comprehensive community-based approach to crime prevention requires that the processes of learning and change are genuinely reciprocal (Bayley, 1991; Kinsey, Lea and Young, 1986). There is no significant evidence within the documentation of such a commitment. On that documentation, it is not possible to counter the allegations by critics such as Cunneen (1991) and Hogg and Findlay (1988) that 'community' policing strategies are barely disguised perpetuations of 'business as usual' with an overlay of efforts to re-enlist understanding and support from those being policed.

A key indication which might illustrate some kind of significant shift in policing approaches to young people would be the extent to which youth crime-prevention efforts are 'mainstreamed' into police organisational culture and work. With their history of marginalisation and the resistance to them by many operational police, prevention programs will remain a policing oddity unless they are integrated fully into routine operational practice. Bayley (1991) and Sparrow (1988) outline the difficulties in general of effecting those changes to police culture which would facilitate the integration of even modest community-based policing into traditional practice. And the open contempt expressed by some influential police for youth crime-prevention initiatives does not give comfort that resistance is moderating (see Freeman-Greene, 1991).

Structurally, it is difficult to argue that schools-based and youth club efforts are integral parts of the policing of young people, despite their expansion and cost. This is a significant handicap to program effectiveness, because it necessarily juxtaposes young people's experiences with police performing avowedly non-law enforcement duties in an avuncular manner with those performing routine law enforcement. In the NYARS study, most of the young people interviewed had encountered routine law enforcement, ranging from street interviews (80%), police station interviews (50%–53% of which in turn were held in police cells), and formal cautions (24%). The impact of these experiences upon attitudes towards police was considerably more consistent than the impact of program involvement; the greater the level of contact, the less positive the attitude towards police (Alder, 1992). As a consequence, while the prevention programs remain supplementary to or marginalised from routine operational policing of young people, it can be expected that their effectiveness with young people and their impact upon traditional modes of policing will remain limited.

The major apparent exception to the outcomes predicted above lies with the NSW GDYO program. Unlike the personnel in the other two major programs, the GDYOs remain in operational work, albeit with a considerably more flexible agenda and range of resources. The program is unashamedly concerned with law enforcement rather than the inculcation of civic responsibility, and thus it does not disguise its purposes behind the rhetoric of a wider social agenda. The target group is explicitly young people involved in trouble rather than the more diffuse groups dealt with by the other programs. The extensive performance-evaluation paradigms designed for the program also set it apart from the other programs. Critically, a key element in the GDYO charter is that participating personnel undertake an advocacy role on behalf of young people, and act to keep them out of the justice system. To this writer, such a role represents a fundamental shift in policing orientation; it requires for its fulfilment that police be reflective of the nature of young people's circumstances, and the (often detrimental) effects upon them of contact with the justice system. It moves beyond the obsession to persuade young people that the law, the justice system and particularly police act inherently in the interests of the young towards the need to demonstrate that police in fact can act in their interests. It allows, in short, the possibility that police themselves transform their work practices with young people.

A considerable amount remains to be learned about the GDYO program. For this writer, two questions stand out. First, to what extent do the work practices of GDYOs in fact reflect the fulfilment of an advocacy role which differs substantially from traditional reactive and simplistic approaches to youth trouble? Second, to what extent has the program received management and rank-and-file support? That is, to what extent has it been 'mainstreamed' into routine law enforcement and forced or encouraged changes in organisational culture? These are critical questions, because practice which does not conform to promise, and continued marginalisation of such programs within that culture perpetuate the very conditions that make initiatives in police–youth interactions so necessary.

In conclusion, and without prejudice, let the writer share a probably apocryphal story told to him by one of the original Victorian police members involved in the Police Community Involvement Program in the early 1980s. Part of the strategy of that program was to place PCIP officers in local schools with very much the same kinds of intentions as the current Police Schools Involvement Program. PCIP personnel were keen to evaluate their endeavours, and it was decided in one school to do a pre-test and post-test of youthful attitudes towards police. In the pre-test, one written response to the question 'What do you think of police?' in a distinctive childish scrawl was this: 'Coppers are mongrels'. Faced with the challenge of converting this child and other like-minded children to a position of respect for police, the deployed officer went all out to be pleasant, resourceful, informative and relaxed in all of the subsequent classroom sessions. Eagerly awaiting the post-test attitudes, the officer identified a familiar childish scrawl, which in response to the question 'What do you think of police now?' answered: *'Coppers are cunning mongrels'.*

REFERENCES

Alder, C. (1991) Victims of Violence: The case of homeless youth, *Australian and New Zealand Journal of Criminology*, 24(1):1–14.

Alder, C. (1992) 'The Young People', in C. Alder, I. O'Connor, K. Warner and R. White, *Perceptions of the Treatment of Juveniles in the Justice System*. Report for the National Youth Affairs Research Scheme. Hobart: National Clearinghouse for Youth Studies.

Bayley, D. (1991) 'The State of the Art in Community Policing: An international perspective', in S. McKillop and J. Vernon (eds), *The Police and the Community*. Canberra: Australian Institute of Criminology.

Beyer, L. (1991) 'The Logic and Possibilities of "Wholistic" Community Policing', in S. McKillop and J. Vernon (eds), *The Police and the Community*. Canberra: Australian Institute of Criminology.

Bottoms, A. (1990) 'Crime Prevention Facing the 90s', *Policing and Society*, 1:3–22.

Boyle, S. (1991) 'Western Australia Position Paper', in B. Halstead (ed.), *Youth Crime Prevention*. Canberra: Australian Institute of Criminology.

Braithwaite, J. (1989) *Crime, Shame and Reintegration*. Cambridge: Cambridge University Press.

Carter, P. (1991) 'The New-Look Police Youth Club', in J. Vernon and S. McKillop (eds), *Preventing Juvenile Crime*. Canberra: Australian Institute of Criminology.

Challinger, D. (1985a) *Detected Young Offenders*. Carlton, Vic.: Victorian Association for the Care and Resettlement of Offenders.

Challinger, D. (1985b) 'Police Action and the Prevention of Juvenile Delinquency', in A. Borowski and J. Murray (eds), *Juvenile Delinquency in Australia*. North Ryde, NSW: Methuen.

Chappell, D. and Wilson, P. (1969) *The Police and the Public in Australia and New Zealand*. St Lucia, Queensland: University of Queensland Press.

Cohen, P. (1979) 'Policing the Working-Class City', in B. Fine, R. Kinsey, J. Lea, N. Picciotta and J. Young (eds), *Capitalism and the Rule of Law: Beyond deviance theory to Marxism*. London: Hutchinson.

Cornish, P. (1991) Police Deputies Club. Paper prepared for the conference National Overview on Crime Prevention, Adelaide, June.

Critchley, T. (1967) *A History of Police in England and Wales, 900–1966*. London: Constable.

Cunneen, C. (1991) 'Problems in the Implementation of Community Policing Strategies', in S. McKillop and J. Vernon (eds), *The Police and the Community*. Canberra: Australian Institute of Criminology.

Federation of Community Legal Services (1991) *Report Into Mistreatment of Young People By Police*. Melbourne: Police Issues Group, Federation of Community Legal Services (Vic.).

Freeman-Greene, S. (1991) 'A Bare-knuckle Approach to the Police Budget Battle', *Age*, 18 June.

Grabosky, P. (1989) 'Efficiency and Effectiveness in Australian Policing', in J. Vernon and D. Bracey (eds), *Police Resources and Effectiveness*. Canberra: Australian Institute of Criminology.

Halstead, B. (ed.) (1991) *Youth Crime Prevention*. Canberra: Australian Institute of Criminology.

Harvey, R.A. (1987) School Based Community Policing Officer. Paper prepared for the seminar Crime in Schools, Canberra.

Hogg, R. and Findlay, M. (1988) 'Police and the Community: Some issues raised by recent overseas research', in I. Freckelton and H. Selby (eds), *Police in Our Society*. Sydney: Butterworths.

James, S. and Polk, K. (1989) 'Policing Youth: Themes and directions', in D. Chappell and P. Wilson (eds), *Australian Policing: Contemporary Issues*. Sydney: Butterworths.

Justice Branch (1992) *Public Safety and Anti-Crime Council*. Melbourne: Justice Branch, Social Development Division, Premier's Department.

Kinsey, R., Lea, J. and Young, J. (1986) *Losing the Fight Against Crime*. Oxford, Blackwell.

Langmair, T. (1991) 'Northern Territory Position Paper', in B. Halstead (ed.), *Youth Crime Prevention*. Canberra: Australian Institute of Criminology.

Lusher, E. (1981) *Report of the Commission to Inquire into New South Wales Police Administration*. Sydney: NSW Government Printer.

Maley, K. (1991) 'School-Based Community Policing', in S. McKillop and J. Vernon (eds), *The Police and the Community*. Canberra: Australian Institute of Criminology.

McDonald, J. (1991a) 'New South Wales Position Paper', in B. Halstead (ed.), *Youth Crime Prevention*. Canberra: Australian Institute of Criminology.

McDonald, J. (1991b) 'The New South Wales Police Service & Youth Crime Prevention', in B. Halstead (ed.), *Youth Crime Prevention*. Canberra: Australian Institute of Criminology.

McDonald, J. and Ireland, S. (1990) *Can It Be Done Another Way?: A New South Wales Police Service proposal for change to the juvenile justice system*. Draft Discussion Paper. Sydney: NSW Police Headquarters, October.

Milburn, C. (1991) 'Criminologist Warns of Rising Youth Crime', *Age*, 13 August.

Muir, W. (1977) *Police: Streetcorner politicians*. Chicago: University of Chicago Press.

O'Connell, T. (1992a) Effective Cautioning: An examination of the Wagga Wagga Police Experience. Paper prepared for the conference on Juvenile Justice, Canberra, May.

O'Connell, T. (1992b) Wagga Wagga Cautioning Programme: It may be the way to go. Paper prepared for the National Conference on Juvenile Justice, Australian Institute of Criminology, Adelaide, September.

O'Doherty, M. (1991) 'Positive Responses to Youthful Graffiti', in J. Vernon and S. McKillop (eds), *Preventing Juvenile Crime*. Canberra: Australian Institute of Criminology.

Pearson, B. (1991) 'Outdoor Adventure Camps: Personal development through challenge', in J. Vernon and S. McKillop (eds), *Preventing Juvenile Crime*. Canberra: Australian Institute of Criminology.

Police Life (Victoria) (1990) September/October.

Polk, K. (1991) 'Evaluation of Programs for Prevention of Youth Crime', in B. Halstead (ed.), *Youth Crime Prevention*. Canberra: Australian Institute of Criminology.

Potas, I., Vining, A. and Wilson, P. (1990) *Young People and Crime: Costs and prevention*. Canberra: Australian Institute of Criminology.

Sanders, W. (1981) *Juvenile Delinquency: Causes, patterns and reactions.* New York: Holt, Rinehart and Winston.

Shaw, B. (1991) 'Encouraging Good Citizenship within Schools', in J. Vernon and S. McKillop (eds), *Preventing Juvenile Crime.* Canberra: Australian Institute of Criminology.

Smith, M. (no date) *Northern Territory School Based Community Policing.* Darwin: Northern Territory Police.

Smith, M. (1991) ' "Project DARE": Drug Abuse Resistance Education', in J. Vernon and S. McKillop (eds), *Preventing Juvenile Crime.* Canberra: Australian Institute of Criminology.

Sobulis, H. (1991) School Watch. Paper prepared for the conference National Overview on Crime Prevention, Adelaide, June.

Sparrow, M. (1988) *Implementing Community Policing,* Perspectives on Policing, No. 9. Cambridge, MA: National Institute of Justice and Kennedy School of Government, Harvard University.

Swanton, B., Wilson, P., Walker, J. and Mukherjee, S. (1988) *How the Public See the Police: An Australian survey – 1,* Trends and Issues No. 11. Canberra: Australian Institute of Criminology.

Tansky, M. (1991) 'Queensland Position Paper', in B. Halstead (ed.), *Youth Crime Prevention.* Canberra: Australian Institute of Criminology.

Vernon J. and Bracey, D. (1989) *Police Resources and Effectiveness.* Canberra: Australian Institute of Criminology.

Vernon, J. and McKillop, S. (eds) (1991) *Preventing Juvenile Crime.* Canberra: Australian Institute of Criminology.

Vicsafe (1992) *A History of Community Based Crime Prevention Projects in Victoria under the Good Neighbourhood Program.* Melbourne: Victorian Ministry of Police and Emergency Services.

Victoria Police (no date) *Police Schools Involvement Program.* Melbourne: Victoria Police.

Vincent, K. (1991) 'Tasmanian Position Paper', in B. Halstead (ed.), *Youth Crime Prevention.* Canberra: Australian Institute of Criminology.

Warneminde, M. (1987) 'Young Predators Behind Bars', *Bulletin,* 14 April:58–61.

Wallace, J. (1988) 'Police in Schools: Teaching the three "Rs" ', *Legal Services Bulletin,* 13:251–2.

West, J. (1991) Problem Oriented Policing: A team approach. Paper given at the conference Future Directions For the Community, Police and Government in Anti-Crime Strategies, August, Melbourne.

White, R. (1989) 'Reading, Writing and Repression: Police in the schools', *Legal Services Bulletin,* 14(2):58–62.

White, R. (1991) 'Taking Custody to the Community: The dynamics of social control and social integration', *Current Issues in Criminal Justice,* 3(2):171–84.

White, R. (1992) 'The Police', in C. Alder, I. O'Connor, K. Warner and R. White, *Perceptions of the Treatment of Juveniles in the Legal System.* Report for the National Youth Affairs Research Scheme. Hobart: National Clearinghouse for Youth Studies.

Williams, D. (1991) 'Yahoos: The Tasmanian response', in J. Vernon and S. McKillop (eds), *Preventing Juvenile Crime.* Canberra: Australian Institute of Criminology.

Young, W. and Cameron, N. (eds) (1989) *Effectiveness and Change in Policing.* Wellington: Institute of Criminology, Victoria University of Wellington.

Youth Justice Coalition (NSW) (1990) *Kids in Justice: A blueprint for the 90s.* Sydney: Youth Justice Coalition.

CHAPTER 10

Reform and Change:
An Agenda for the 1990s

Stephen Hall

Over recent years there has been a significant increase in community awareness and concern with issues surrounding the policing of young people in Australia. It is widely acknowledged that contact between police and young people is fraught with difficulties. There has been, as well, an increased level of contact between young people and police as a result of new programs and new policy initiatives. However, these activities often operate in an ad hoc, isolated and confused way due to a range of contradictory priorities and roles. Inconsistencies associated with these initiatives arise from the inherent friction between 'community policing', which is largely concerned with public relations and conflict mediation, and 'law enforcement', which is central to the normal routines of police work and which relies heavily on the use of coercive powers.

The intention of this chapter is to provide an overview of different measures and strategies that have been, or could be, adopted to ensure that the rights of children are protected and that could lead to an improvement in the relationship between the police and young people. A number of issues have been identified in this book as being at the heart of the problem in the relationship between young people and the police. These have included the extensive use of name-checks, continual harassment, the ignoring of basic legal rights, and antagonisms stemming from different conceptions and uses of public space.

Various reports have made recommendations concerning police practices and policing policies with regard to young people (Alder, O'Connor, Warner and White, 1992; Youth Justice Coalition, 1990; Johnston, 1991; Cunneen, 1990; Moss and Castan, 1991). Rather than attempting to summarise these, this chapter will briefly chart the kinds of suggestions and demands which could and should guide potential strategies for change.

Reform has to be addressed at a number of different levels in society. Fundamentally, if we are to develop a more democratic, responsive, equitable and constructive policing of young people in Australia then a number of interrelated measures will have to be adopted.

POLICE-YOUTH INTERACTION

The nature and scope of the various interactions between young people and the police are crucial areas for substantive change. It is at the level of face-to-face interactions where many of the difficulties discussed in other chapters surface in the first instance. Within specific jurisdictions there can be a variety of police styles in relating the law to young people. The style of policing is especially important in determining relations with young people. An emphasis on a law enforcement approach and an inattention to the basic rights of young people can lead to poor relationships developing between police and young people.

For example, a sergeant who has good judgement about how to develop communication skills with young people and who wants to develop a positive working relationship between young people and police in a particular suburb stands in contrast to a sergeant who does not care very much at all about how police officers work with young people. The sergeant in charge of a station very often sets the overall tone of the station on a day-to-day basis. This is the point at which the practices of a particular station are determined; hence, whether policy or standing orders take effect largely lies at the discretion of senior personnel at a local level. Sergeants in charge of stations therefore hold enormous power and influence over what is and is not acceptable practice in their station. It is easy to see how some sergeants may condone, and possibly encourage certain negative forms of police behaviour towards young people, if the main emphasis in the station is to uphold particular authority relations within the structure of police work itself.

Police are the first point of contact young people have with the criminal justice system. Their role as peace-keepers in communities needs to be encouraged, rather than constantly emphasising the enforcement model of dealing with young people. In Australia we continue to accelerate children into the criminal justice system. This is especially the case with Aboriginal young people. Rather than continuing this practice, there must be an emphasis on developing alternative approaches to dispute resolution. For example, police could be involved in facilitating more informal means of resolving conflict between young people and different sectors within the community. This could lead to police having to step back from some situations in order to enable other participants or organisations in the local community to address specific issues directly with the young people concerned.

Moreover, these kinds of initiatives do not need to come from police alone. Community mediation schemes are emerging in different parts of Australia; some involve parents, others have been started by youth workers or agencies working at a local level. The element common to most of these is that they establish points of liaison and interaction between various local groups; thereby, in some circumstances, diminishing the need for police intervention. These types of initiatives warrant greater levels of support and encouragement from the police and other authorities.

Active monitoring of police activities and dealings with young people is occurring in different parts of the country and this should be encouraged. For example, the Youth Justice Coalition (Western Australia) is compiling data gathered through 'police contact' sheets. These questionnaires have been carefully designed to collect information about police practices in relation to young people and have been circulated to individuals and agencies who work with young people. Initiatives of this type should be seen as a means of gathering information that will be beneficial in attempting to tackle problem areas in police–youth relations. It is unfortunate that organisations with this kind of insight are sometimes dismissed as being troublemakers, because information gathered and collated on this basis can be used advantageously by police authorities as well as by community-based organisations. The information gathered through such ongoing surveys provides a useful barometer of the frictions, and positive elements, of the contact between young people and the police in different locales at any point in time.

The matter of the policing of young people who utilise public space requires urgent attention. Name-checking is an integral part of this process and involves an officer asking for the name of a young person, for whatever reason the officer thinks is necessary. Name-checking occurs regularly and is used as a form of control on young people's movements; it is regularly used around commercial places, such as shopping centres and inner-city areas. This practice occurs in a virtual legislative vacuum, yet it is guided by police assumptions about young people. It is problematic, in that street interactions originating with a name-check often intensify and provoke conflict, resulting in the prosecution of young persons, for street offences. There is, then, a need to reconsider the necessity for the frequent stopping, questioning and moving on of young people. Any current powers police may have to arbitrarily demand a person's name and address should be abolished. Along with an abolition of indiscriminate name-checks, there need to be clear limits established on police 'move on' powers as well.

NATURE OF POLICE WORK

Police management, policy and organisation are areas that provide the framework for the day-to-day operations and ethos of police forces. They are, therefore, spheres that warrant careful scrutiny and consideration when reform is being considered at other levels.

The specific training of police officers needs to include general education in the area of youth studies. There are a number of subject areas specific to young people that warrant attention. For example, an understanding and awareness of factors such as income security, homelessness and familial dysfunction is fundamental when attempting to come to grips with the place of young people in Australian society. This kind of information should be a standard part of pre-service training for police officers. In addition to this, the undertaking of in-service training in youth studies at the tertiary level should be fostered, encouraged and supported – especially given the place young people currently occupy in the Australian criminal justice system.

As well as training and education, it is also necessary that police be kept up to date with broad changes in the lifestyles and life conditions of young people, and with the various government and community programs that are developed in response to particular youth issues. This could be done by way of regular youth-specific bulletins or information sheets that could be designed to be part of an ongoing information kit. Alternatively, well-written articles for police in-house newsletters might be better received and more widely read. Hopefully, this would lead to a positive change in existing police attitudes towards the policing of young people.

A further step in police training, after acknowledging those factors which impact on the lives of young people, would involve the skilling of police officers in areas of how to relate to young people effectively. Police training needs to emphasise the skills which are needed in dealing with young people, as well as provide information about young people. For example, this could involve considering the positive aspects of adolescent peer groups and how to interact with peer groups constructively. The development of systematic pre-service and in-service training on police–youth relations is essential if substantive improvements are to occur.

The role and function of 'community policing' needs to be clarified, developed and enhanced at the level of philosophy and resources. It is unfortunate that many community-policing initiatives seem to be established in a vacuum, often unrelated to mainstream policing and sometimes not connecting up with the community in any real or meaningful way. In many situations, the role of community policing has been built on self-interest within the community, rather than on creating a peaceful community. Neighbourhood Watch is a prime example in that it is a program built on fear, centred around safety and protection of private property. This, in turn, has a negative impact on young people because it projects a skewed perspective of young people as outsiders, thugs and crims; people to be feared, rather than participants in the local community. This generates tension and accelerates alienation between different sectors in the local community rather than enhancing peace at the local level. An alternative model would be for community-policing bodies and associated committees to get into the business of restoring a sense of real community. They could foster and encourage relationships between young people, police and local residents. This would have an educative and informative role, and thereby break down fear, ignorance and prejudice with regard to young people.

Neighbourhood committees could thus achieve a better understanding of young people by getting involved with them and being involved in local youth initiatives. This, in turn, could lead to a better functioning community with police having a more facilitative, peace-keeping role. Links should also be established between various local community-policing committees and other community activities. Groups such as Neighbourhood Watch, Youth Employment agencies, Aboriginal–Police Relations committees, Police and

Citizens Youth Clubs, Youth Drop-in Centres, Blue Light Discos, Youth Accommodation Services and Victim Reparation Committees need to be linked and communicating effectively with each other. People from local communities also need to be involved with youth liaison groups which actually include young people themselves.

This leads into the question of how community-policing initiatives can be made more mainstream within the police force. Community policing needs to overcome the 'police culture' mentality so it can become productive. Police forces need to be encouraged to make the peace-keeping model of policing an absolute priority over the enforcement model, particularly when it comes to the policing of young people. To give an example, over recent years in suburbs and country towns around Australia, a major shift from foot patrols to vehicular vigilance has occurred. The latter works on a model of force and intimidation, rather than a relational approach, and it also leads to far more traffic-related charges for young people.

The peace-keeping role of the police needs to be constantly reinforced. This can be built on an important premise of modern policing, namely that forces should be recognised as serving the communities from which they spring. This philosophy should be enhanced as a part of the police commitment and responsiveness to the needs of the community. For the police to be able to accomplish the ends of maintaining peace and public order, community support and involvement have been recognised as being essential. In practice, this means that a greater portion of the police budget needs to be directed towards the matters currently under discussion. Some sections of the various police forces and some police unions will attempt to counter the peace-keeping role for police with calculated campaigns in favour of the enforcement model of policing. It needs to be recognised that such campaigns are often erroneous, with young people being made scapegoats for other political purposes and agendas.

REGULATION OF POLICE PRACTICES

The state has an important role to play in the regulation of policing matters. Some governments shy away from this responsibility due to a misunderstanding of the concept of 'separation of powers'. It is indeed unfortunate that some police authorities and unions continue to play on this misunderstanding, especially with respect to the issue of police complaints.

The concept of police accountability is fundamental to the force's credibility and to its potential role as peace-keeper in the community. A key component of this is the establishment of a viable, well-resourced and independent police complaints system. It is inadequate for the investigation of complaints to be held internally within police departments and in closed sessions (as is the case in Western Australia). While this remains so, many people who have complaints regarding police practices will not access current systems, for varying reasons.

A recent community survey in Perth found that from a sample of 380 incident reports, over 60 percent of people who consider they had a legitimate complaint about police practices did not make an official complaint. What is even more disturbing are the reasons why: over 50 percent said because it was no use, another 28 percent were too scared (Hall, 1991). This survey demonstrated that existing police complaints processes are problematic due to community experience and perceptions based upon fear of the consequences at a local level and the futility of the exercise. Factors which further disenfranchise young people include problems associated with awareness of and accessibility to complaints procedures and mechanisms. The case for an independent, observable complaints procedure is strong, and such a procedure is long overdue.

A case can also be argued for it to contain a mechanism which encourages and facilitates community feedback generally, rather than only accepting individual complaints. In a similar vein, any future complaints system should have a component that investigates matters pertaining to a particular officer, station or type of incident in terms of its wider temporal and social context. For example, if there are ongoing concerns with the practices of a specific police officer in a local community, or, given the previous discussion on the role of sergeants, within the context of a particular station, how are these to be addressed under the current system of individualised complaints based upon specific incidents? Any single incident, treated in isolation, may not warrant the taking of disciplinary or corrective action.

Similarly, if inappropriate types of police practices emerge as being widespread, as evidenced in research such as that being undertaken by the Youth Justice Coalition (WA), then how is this to be formally raised or tackled? The present situation is unclear and potentially very difficult. It leaves youth workers and other youth advocates in an invidious and, in some cases, vulnerable position. Acts of police violence and harassment against young people, for instance, are difficult areas to address because police authorities and police unions are quick to dismiss anecdotal evidence as simply unsubstantiated allegations. If incidents are proven conclusively to have taken place, they are likely to be treated merely as isolated and exceptional occurrences.

However, reports such as Cunneen's study of police violence against Aboriginal young people cannot be lightly dismissed (Cunneen, 1990). This study was commissioned by the National Inquiry into Racist Violence and involved research in three states. It demonstrated an internal consistency in the type, purpose and extent of the violence. What was disturbing was that many of the young people interviewed viewed police violence as a routine part of their interaction with the police; this point is also acknowledged by many youth workers in the field. Cunneen's research demonstrated that police violence was extensive across the three states, and the consistency of the findings effectively undermined the view that reports of police violence can simply be dismissed as lies, exaggerations or deliberate deceptions. This research, along with that of other researchers (e.g. Alder, 1991; White, Underwood and Omelczuk, 1991), offers compelling evidence of the need for a complaints system that goes beyond the isolated, individual incident.

Given that juvenile offending has become a political football in recent years, young people as a whole have paid the price in terms of accountability. We now need commitments from state governments, cabinets and police ministers that a higher priority and focus be placed on preventive and positive policing methods with respect to young people. Governments should be taking every opportunity to minimise the situation where conflict between young people and police may arise unnecessarily. A logical corollary of this would be to work towards change of overall orientation: giving police forces a much stronger mandate for peace-keeping through community-based policing initiatives rather than a 'law enforcement' and 'get tough' approach.

There also needs to be legislative recognition and support for the *United Nations Convention on the Rights of the Child*, especially with regard to the intervention of the state and its officials in the lives

of young people. This will require each state government to establish
a process whereby all current legislation is reviewed in the light of
the UN convention and amended where necessary. This should be
done in consultation with the wider community, with particular
input from those agencies which have a declared interest in the rights
and well-being of young people and children.

YOUTH RESOURCES

The level of resources available to young people and youth work
agencies needs to be enhanced in a number of areas. This is of crucial
importance in addressing the concerns raised in this volume.

There needs to be better access by young people to legal assistance
and to legal advocates. This may require the establishment of more
youth-specific legal services, as well as secure long-term funding for
existing community legal centres which assist young people. Legal
advocates themselves need to be trained in how to work with young
people, and to be sensitive to young people's experiences of courts,
police and welfare officials.

Young people also require education and information in the
broad area of legal rights and responsibilities. This is not a category
of knowledge that society can assume that young people have
acquired at school or by divine intervention. It will necessitate the
regular production of information kits using a variety of styles and
mediums. The introduction of formal legal studies in the classroom
could be supplemented by regular visits to and by various community
legal agencies, and by widespread circulation of legal resources such
as 'Streetwize' comics.

The introduction of a statutory requirement that a trained
independent adult witness be present during police questioning of
young people, and the active monitoring of such witness schemes,
is long overdue. The role and position of independent persons when
police are interviewing or interrogating young people has been an
area of widespread concern and recommendations focusing on the
issue have been raised in numerous reports. Current structures and
experiences indicate that this is an area of reform that would be
beneficial to police, as well as to young people. There are some
community-based agencies that have done pioneering work in this
area; one is the Balga Detached Youth Work Project's 'Arrest
Express' in the northern suburbs of Perth. 'Arrest Express' works

on a telephone-pager system and uses a network of trained volunteers. It has received much acclaim; however, it suffers in that it remains underfunded and it does not get the support it deserves from some police officers because they perceive it to be a threat rather than an asset.

One of the innovative outcomes of the Royal Commission into Aboriginal Deaths in Custody was the establishment of the Aboriginal Visitors Scheme. This scheme gives trained community members access to prisoners held in police lock-ups. There is good reason for a scheme like this to be established for young people held in police stations and watch-house detention. The matter of parental access to children held in detention is also of concern. It is questionable as to whether there is any time when a parent should be denied access to an incarcerated child.

There needs to be ongoing support for and promotion of the recently established National Children's and Youth Law Centre. The centre's charter includes identifying major legal issues, running test cases, promoting application of the principles in the *UN Convention on the Rights of the Child*, conducting applied research and working with other organisations. It will undoubtedly have many roles and functions as it develops over the next few years. Hopefully, it will also lead to the dismantling of the parochialism of some states when it comes to matters of juvenile justice.

The Australian community needs to be constantly evaluating, and re-evaluating the allocation of community resources. It must take into account broad social justice concerns such as economic wealth, racism, unemployment, gender inequities and so on. Young people are especially vulnerable in today's social landscape. There needs to be real creativity when it comes to the redistribution of resources in society, including that which takes into account matters such as how our police and young people interact.

One way that this could be constructively addressed is to foster the idea of and to actively create 'community spaces', which young people and others could claim and utilise for their own without any commercial incentive or obligation. This would go a long way towards resolving one of our biggest dilemmas. Another would be to allow young people to be responsible for their actions by substantively widening the number of real choices they have in society. In developing choices that would enable them to contribute and develop themselves as individuals and members of a community, clearly major initiatives will have to be taken in the areas of employment and job creation, and in income support and level of wages.

CONCLUSION

This chapter has attempted to give a brief overview of a variety of strategies and measures designed to re-construct the relationship between police and young people in our society. The decisions which are actually made with respect to these issues and questions, however, will in large part be determined by the balance of political forces at any particular moment. The efforts of those who are willing to 'see, judge and act' in the interests of young people are therefore vitally necessary in helping to expose the inequalities, ineffectiveness and injustices of the present economic, welfare and criminal justice systems.

But, ultimately, if significant reform and progressive change is to occur, then change will have to occur at each level identified in this chapter. When all is said and done, there is all too often a lot more said than done. Governments will remain slow to act in this area while 'law and order' issues remain political footballs and are largely dictated by conservative social forces. Some will remain obstinate in the face of sound, well-reasoned criticism. Nevertheless, it is essential that there be a climatic change within the Australian community. For the future well-being of the majority of people, and particularly young people, demands that we do see substantive change in the very near future.

REFERENCES

Alder, C. (1991) 'Victims of Violence: The case of homeless youth', *Australian and New Zealand Journal of Criminology*, 24(1):1–14.

Alder, C., O'Connor, I., Warner, K. and White, R. (1992) *Perceptions of the Treatment of Juveniles in the Legal System*. Report for the National Youth Affairs Research Scheme. Hobart: National Clearinghouse for Youth Studies.

Cunneen, C. (1990) *A Study of Aboriginal Juveniles and Police Violence*. Sydney: Human Rights and Equal Opportunity Commission.

Hall, S. (1991) *Report of the Twenty-four Hour Phone-in on Police Violence and Harassment*, October. Perth: Anglican Social Responsibilities Commission.

Johnston, E. (1991) *National Report* (vols1–5) Royal Commission into Aboriginal Deaths in Custody. Canberra: Australian Government Publishing Service.

Moss, I. and Castan, R. (1991) *Racist Violence*. Report of the National Inquiry into Racist Violence in Australia. Canberra: Australian Government Publishing Service.

White, R., Underwood, R. and Omelczuk, S. (1991) 'Victims of Violence: The view from the youth services', *Australian and New Zealand Journal of Criminology*, 24(1):25–39.

Youth Justice Coalition (NSW) (1990) *Kids in Justice: A blueprint for the 90s*. Sydney: Youth Justice Coalition.

Index

Aboriginal children
  police power of removal 18, 22
  removal from families 129–30, 131–2
Aboriginal criminality, and public order
  legislation, NSW 147–8
Aboriginal descendants, of child removal
  regimes 132
Aboriginal girls
  police treatment of 169–70
  in public places 146
  removal from families 130
Aboriginal males, law and order
  campaigns against 135
Aboriginal offenders, and over-policing 150
Aboriginal offending rates
  and police discretion 150
  and policing 153
Aboriginal overrepresentation, in juvenile
  justice system 134–6
Aboriginal parenting, racist assumptions
  about 131
Aboriginal political organisations 132
Aboriginal Visitors Scheme 241
Aboriginal young people 104, 105
  cautioning of 61–2
  as law and order problem 147–8
  as non-consumers 113
  perceived as criminals 136
  placement and treatment in custody 134–6
  and police, historical background 128–32
  and policing public places 145–7
  referral to children's panels 141–2
Aborigines Protection Board (NSW) 130,
  131
Aborigines Protection Board (Vic.) 130
accessibility to legal services 88–91
accountability to the community, by police
  183–4
acquisition of a criminal record 136–7
admissibility of evidence 21–2, 37
admission of guilt, in cautions 62

adolescent, definition 65
adolescent peer groups, understanding of
  236
adult, definition 64
adult witnesses, presence of during
  interviews 32–6, 240
age groupings, in statistics 64–7
age of persons, impact on arrest rates 163
aggressive police intervention 105
allegations against police 72–3
alternatives, to court prosecution 23
American courts, and wardship 29
anonymous complaints 95
antagonism, between police and youth
  106–7
apprehension statistics, Qld 62–3
arrest
  of Aboriginal youth 137, 138–9
  parental notification of 41
'Arrest Express' 240–1
arrest powers 38–40
arrest rates of children 40–1
Asian immigrants 176, 177
assault, statistics 62–3, 66–7, 68
assaults by police
  on Aboriginal young people 143
  complaints 71–2
  against young people 72–3
  against young women 167–8
assaults by young people, on police 107
authority
  challenge to 106
  respect for 82–3

bail
  for Aboriginal youth 139–41
  release on 43, 44
banishment, as part of bail conditions 140
barriers hindering access to legal services
  88–91
basic rights of citizens 77

244

beat police officers 191
'Beijing Rules' 28, 41
black American women, treatment of 170
black American youth, and recalcitrant demeanour 149
Blue Light Discos 216, 219
"bodgie" cult 20
Bourke, NSW, police–Aborigines confrontation 146-7
breach of bail 140
breaking and entering 80, 81
  statistics 66, 68
'breeding out' Aboriginality 129-31
Brixton riots 176
business proprietors–youth dialogue 124

car offences 22
car theft, statistics 62-3, 66, 68, 80
care applications 164, 167
carnal knowledge 20
Casuarina High School, police in schools program 208-11
cautioning
  of Aboriginal youth 137, 138
  of young offenders 61
cautioning schemes 30, 31
cautions
  absence of in confessions 32
  statistics 61-3
character-building programs 216
chief commissioner, and complaints against police 53, 54
Child Cautioning Program, Victoria, criteria 46-7
child welfare legislation 17-18
children's affairs, police intervention in 17
children's aid panels (SA) 49-50
  Aboriginal referral to 142
children's courts
  Aboriginal referral to 142
  development of 17
  guilty pleas in 92
  historical development 29-30
  jurisdiction 30
children's panels, police referral to 141-2
children's panels (WA) 50
children's rights 76
'cleared' cases 60-1
cleared crime figures 80-1
co-operative behaviour, and arrest rates 162-3
colonial warfare, against Aborigines 128-9
commercial centres, police methods to move young people away from 120-1

commercial space
  function of 111-13
  and public order 110-14
common law riot, Bourke, NSW 146-7
Commonwealth legislation, on juvenile justice 28
communication barriers, with ethnic youth 176-7
communities, policing of 110-11
community, in community policing 185-8
community consultative committees 184
  composition of 186-7, 188
  function of 187
community legal centres 89
community legal education 89
community mediation schemes 234
community-oriented crime prevention 221
community policing 115, 116, 199
  clarification of role and function of 236
  development of 182
  of ethnic communities 181-5
  and ethnic youth 185-8
  initiatives 184
  mainstreaming within police forces 237
  model 182-4
  obstacles to change 192-4
  and police culture 225
  as public-relations exercise 181, 195
  weaknesses 184-5
community service orders, supervised at Police-Citizens Youth Clubs 206
community spaces, development of 241
complaints against police 71-2, 94-5
  by Aborigines 144-5
  mechanisms 52-4
  negative consequences of 94-5
  positive response to 195-6
  survey data 238
  from Vietnamese youth 179-80
compulsory education, and social reforms 16
confessions
  and 'good treatment' 85-6
  voluntariness of 31-2, 33-4
'Constable Care' 217
Constitutional powers of Commonwealth 28
constriction of social space for young people 122
constructive relationship between police and youth, developing 123-4
contact, between police and young people 106
contemporary policing 199-27
corporal punishment 15

cost of lawyers 89
counselling, of young people 22
court appearances, statistics 62–3
court attendance notices 38–9
  of Aboriginal youth 137, 138
court orders, on fingerprinting 42
courts
  failure in monitoring and remedying
    abuses 92
  police influence in sentencing, WA 117–19
  reluctance to enforce the law 116
  as review mechanisms 91–3
  role in sentencing 92, 93
cricket playing, complaints about 10
crime clearance, and non-exercising of
  rights 83, 84
crime fighting 188–9
crime prevention, new initiatives in 221
crime prevention programs, development
  199–200
crime statistics 59–73
  misrepresentation of 98
crime victims, young people as 70
crimes and offences, statistical evidence
  18–22
crimes of youth 67–9
criminal, perception of 116
Criminal Justice Commission 86–7
Criminal Justice Commission (Qld) 53–4,
  72
criminal justice system, basic rights 77
criminal record, acquisition of 136–7
criminal stereotypes 151
criminalisation of Aboriginal juveniles
  133–6
cultural barriers 177
cultural distinctions of young people 113
cultural genocide, of Aborigines 129-32
curfews, as part of bail conditions 140
custody, duration of before first court
  appearance 44–5
custody or release after arrest 42–4

Defence Act offences 19
democratic state, ideology 76
deputy ombudsman, and complaints
  against police 53
detention centres 44
detention in police facilities 43
detention orders, for Aboriginal youth 134
disadvantaged Aboriginal youth 153
discretion
  in admissibility of evidence 34
  use of by police 87
discretionary powers, and legal rights 121

discrimination, by police 105
dispute resolution, alternative approaches
  234
diversion
  and admission of guilt 62
  evaluation of 51–2
  and types of offence 62–3
diversionary system, problems with 49–50
Dog Tag Act 133
dress mode, and police attention 179
driving offences 22
duration of custody before first court
  appearance 44–5
duty lawyer system 91, 93
duty lawyers, failure to lodge complaints
  against police 94

economic recession, and youth consumers
  114
education, and policing of truancy 15, 16
ethnic communities, community policing
  of 181–5
ethnic community liaison officers,
  perception by youth 185
ethnic stereotyping, and police perception
  of respectability 189
ethnic street kids, suspicion of police
  191–2
ethnic youth
  and community policing 185–8
  perception of police 185
  and police 175–7
ethno-specific consultative committees 186
evidence
  admissibility of 31–2, 37
  exclusion of 34
exploitation of women, police response
  to 171

'failed' families 18
fear reduction, in policing 183
federal offences 28
Federation of NSW Police Boys Clubs 204
  programs 206
  purposes and activities 205
  target groups 206
female offenders 68–9
female promiscuity 165
females, in police statistics 19, 20, 21
fighting, police response to 14
fines, for young people 22
fingerprints 41–2
first offenders, treatment of 138
flogging, of children 15
force, use of by police 120–1

formal cautions 46–8, 50
  and admission of guilt 62
  statistics 51–2
formal intervention rates 51–2
frustration, by police 116

gangs 104, 105
  of non-English speaking youth 179
  policing of 11, 14
gender bias, in arrest decisions 160–1
gender stereotyping, of offences 161–2
General Duties Youth Officers (GDYO)
  213–14
  advocacy role 227
  Charter 214
  essence of the program 215
  evaluation techniques 216
  flexibility in working 215
  policing orientation 226
  staff support 227
  training 214
genocide of Aborigines 128–9, 130, 154
girls, in police statistics 19, 20, 21
'good' police 191
'good treatment' by police 85–6
government departments, administration of
  juvenile justice 28
guilty pleas
  in criminal courts 92
  and duty lawyer system 91, 93

'half-caste' Aborigines 18
hanging suggestions, from police 144
harassment
  by young people of police 107
  of Aboriginal young people 105, 142–3,
    153–4
  of Asians 176
  of ethnic groups 178–9
  of potential offenders, official approval
    of 118
  of Vietnamese 179–80
  of young people 105, 106–7
'heavy handed' approach by police 105, 122
historical view, police and young people
  7–23
homeless youth 104, 105
  encounters with police 149
  as non-consumers 113
homicide 80
hoodlums 117
hostile behaviour, and arrest rates 162
human traffic flow, in commercial areas
  109
humanitarian concerns, of police 109

ignorance of rights 89, 97
immigrants 176–7
inadmissibility of evidence 32, 37
incarceration of Aboriginal juveniles 134
indecent assault 20
independent adults, presence of during
  juvenile interviews 32–3, 78, 240
informal cautions 46, 62
informal policing 9
institutional care 17, 18, 22
insulting remarks, to women 11, 12, 13
integrated community-based policing
  strategy, Wagga Wagga 217–18
inter-personal violence, complaints of 14
internal complaints units 52
internal investigation units 54, 71
interpreters, insufficient use of by police
  177
interrogation 31–8
intimidation
  of Asians 176
  in police–youth interactions 85, 86, 120
invocation of rights 190–1

Juvenile Aid Bureau, Brisbane 23, 47–8
juvenile cautioning programs 217
juvenile crime 80
juvenile delinquency 7, 16
  offences 20
juvenile involvement in crime 81
juvenile justice, legal framework of 27–57
juvenile justice system 28
  Aboriginal juveniles in 134–5
  development 29–31
  entering the 136–9
juvenile offences 80
  by state 19–21
  statistics 67–8
juvenile offenders, by age 66–7
juvenile women, police treatment of 160
juvenile–adult distinction, in statistics 65–6
juveniles
  definition 64–5
  treatment of in the legal system 84

knowledge of rights 89, 97

language barriers, with ethnic youth 176–7
larceny, statistics 66, 67
larrikin 'menace', media reports 9–10
larrikinism
  arrests for 9
  Brisbane 9–10, 11–13
  complaints about 8, 9–10
  police rejection of complaints about 10

larrikins 7
  policing of 8–9
law and order campaigns, against
  Aboriginal youth 147–8
law-abiding citizens 117
lawyers
  cost of 89
  presence of during interviews 36
legal advice
  access to 36, 38
  denial of access to 84
legal aid commissions 89
legal assistance, lack of during police
  questioning 90
legal education programs 89
legal framework, of juvenile justice 27–57
legal rights
  abuse of 105
  difficulties of exercising 121
  non-existence of clearly defined 95–6
  of parents and children 78
legal services, for young people 88–91
legal studies, in classroom curricula 240
legislative changes, to assist young people
  239–40
leniency, towards young women 160
'lift under the ear' approach 12, 15
light-skinned children, segregation
  of 131

male offenders 68
male youth, police response to complaints
  about 11
malls 104, 110, 111
maltreatment, by police 105
marginal youth 104, 105, 189–90, 195–6
massacres of Aborigines 129
media campaigns, against offending youth
  81–2
media-generated panics about youth 114
middle-class respectability 189
missionaries, role in removal of Aboriginal
  children 130
mitigation, pleas of 93
monitoring of police activities 234
motor vehicle theft 80
  statistics 62–3, 66, 68

name checking
  abolition of indiscriminate 234–5
  by police 120
  rights over supplying to police 78
National Children's and Youth Law
  Centre, charter 241
negative ethnic stereotyping 178–81

neglected children 15
  of Aboriginal parents 131
  legislation 17, 18
  offences 19, 20, 21
  police role 30
neighbourhood committees, links with
  youth groups 236–7
Neighbourhood Watch 184, 216
  implications for young people 236
neighbourhoods, policing of 110–11
New South Wales, police statistics 21
New South Wales General Duties Youth
  Officers 213–16
non-compliable bail conditions 140
non-compliance by police in obtaining
  confessions, effect of 33
Northern Territory School Based
  Community Policing Scheme
  establishment 208–9
  outcomes 210–11
  position profile 209–10
  resistance to 209
  role in school curricula 210

obscene language 9, 13, 14
offences
  by category 67–9
  definition 60–1, 73
  against morality 20
offenders, age groupings 66–7
official cautions 104
ombudsman 52
oppressed Aboriginal youth 153
oral cautions 46, 50
order maintenance 82, 188–9
'outdoor' programs 216
over-policing, of Aboriginal youth 150

panel system 49–51
parens patriae 29
parental notification of arrest 41
parents
  presence of
    during cautioning 48
    during juvenile interviews 32–3, 34, 37
    during preliminary questioning 34–5
  responsible for bringing their child to the
    attention of police 166
  role during juvenile interviews 38
partnership policing 199, 207
patrol work
  and maintenance of middle-class
    respectability 189
  and pro-active policing 189–90
peace-keeping role, of police 237

petty crime offences 21, 80
physical abuse, by police 121
pleas of mitigation 93
police
  allegations against 71–3
  and citizens views 192–3
  contradictory roles of 123
  and ethnic youth 175–7
  as 'guardians' of Aborigines 131–2
  and juvenile rights, case study 83
  and regard for the due process of the
    law 192–3
  siege mentality of 193, 195
  views on young people 223
  and young people, historical view 7–23
police activities with young people 216–17
Police and Citizen Youth Clubs, activities
  207–8
police annual reports 60
police apprehensions, of Aboriginal youth
  137–8
police approaches to young people 202
police bail *see* bail
police batons, juveniles hit with 143
police behaviour
  and juvenile arrest rates 41
  public perception of 114
police budgets, initiatives to enhance 220–1
Police Careers programs 206
police cautions 14, 46–8, 50
Police-Citizens Boys Clubs 23
  functions of 206
  see also Police Youth Clubs
police collaboration, with parents 15
Police Community Consultative
  Committees (PCCCs) 221
Police Complaints Authority (SA) 71
police complaints system 94–5
  independence of 238
police culture
  and community-based policing 225
  and obstacles to change 194–5
police decisions, in criminal matters 159–63
Police Discipline Board (Vic.) 53
police discretion, and Aboriginal offending
  rates 150
police forces, cultural changes in 184
police harassment *see* harassment
police help, young women seeking 170–1
police in schools program 208–13
  endorsements of 224
  rationale 221–2
police intervention
  in Aboriginal life 130, 131
  with Aboriginal young people 134–6

in children's affairs 17
methods 120–1
in removing Aboriginal children from
  parents 18
in truancy clauses 16–17
and welfare objectives 107–8
police officers
  authorised to give formal cautions 47
  characteristics of 121
police organisations
  response to criticisms from marginal
    youth 195–6
  structural changes in 184
police perceptions, of young people 69–70
police policy, on arrest 39–40
police powers
  and common sense 149–50
  exercising of 119
  and police culture 114–21
  to 'do their job' 117
  WA 117–18
  and welfare policing 15–18
  and young offenders 30–1
police practices, regulation of 237–40
police prediction of trouble 148, 149–50
police presence, impact of 23
police programs with young people 203–18
  evaluation of 202–3
police rank structure, and problems of
  change 193–4
police referral, to children's panels 141–2
police reforms, in treatment of ethnic
  groups 180
police resources
  allocation of 119
  to combat crime 97–8
police responses, to complaints of
  larrikinism 9
Police/Schools Involvement Program
  (PSIP) 211, 227
  aims and objectives 212
  outcomes 212–13
police station, and exercising of rights
  86–7
police statistics 59–73
police success, measured by statistics 60–3
police training
  on how to relate to young people 236
  in youth studies 235
police use of media 82, 97
police values, change in 193–4
police views, on gender offending 161–2
police violence
  as recognition of their authority 149
  as routine 239

police work
  functions of 115
  reforms associated with 235-7
Police Youth Clubs 199, 200, 204-8
  activities 204
    for wider youth population 206-7
  attendees, attitudes to police 219
  marginalisation of police allocated to 205
  rationale behind 222
  work with young offenders 206
police-youth interactions
  experiences 70-1, 84-5
  location of 103-10
  reforms and changes in 233-5
  solutions 98-9
police-youth policies, rate of change in 202
policing
  in Aboriginal communities 145-6
  aims of 116
  sex-based dimension of 10-11
policing Aboriginal youth
  Aboriginal views 153-4
  dynamics of 148-51
  historical foundations 151-2
  pro-active role in containment 152
  racist doctrine in 152
policing functions 79-84
policing of juveniles, by state 19-21
policing of young women 159-72
policing styles, and relations with young
  people 233
policing the community 116
policing young women's welfare 163-7
power, abuses of by police 86
powers of arrest 38-40
preliminary questioning, presence of
  parents during 34-5
presence of adult witnesses
  during preliminary questioning 34-5
  at juvenile interviews 32-3
  observation of rules 35-6
  requirements evaluation 36-8
pressures on police, to do their job 122-3
prison population, modal age of 66
private sector 'coalitions', to counter
  juvenile crime 207
pro-active policing 183, 199, 210
  and marginal young people 189-90
probation system 22, 29, 30
Problem Oriented Policing (SA) 199, 216
process of punishment 137
property offences
  clear-up rates 151
  by young women 161
prostitution of young girls 16

psychological abuse, of young women 106,
  168
psychological effects, of racist and sexist
  abuse 144
psychological intervention, in management
  of problem children 22
public complaints, and police response
  8-15
public confrontations, between police and
  Aboriginal youth 146-7
public disorder offences 19, 21
public order legislation, NSW 147
public perception
  of juvenile crime 80, 81-2
  of police 222-3
public spaces
  function of 111-13
  as locality of police-youth interaction
    104
  and perceived risk from youth 81, 82
  police attention to young people in 190
  policing of 110-14
    Aboriginal young people in 145-7
  use by Aboriginal young women 169
punishment
  of children 15
  process of 137
'pushes', policing of 11, 13, 14

Queensland, police statistics 19
questioning
  time limits for 45
  of young people 32-3
questionnaires, for monitoring police
  activities 234

racism
  and Aboriginal human rights 132-3
  in police-Aboriginal relations 105
  in policing Aboriginal youth 153-4
  towards Aboriginal young women 169
racist abuse, by police officers 144
racist views, about Aboriginal parenting
  131
rape victims, disbelieved by police 171
recognisance, release on 44, 45
recording of formal cautions 46, 47
reformatory schools 17, 18
  establishment 29
reintegrative shaming theory 217
remand centres 43
repeat offenders
  in the court system 93
  WA 117-18
resisting arrest 119